The Labyrinth We Walked

The Labyrinth We Walked

The Cold War Deconstructed

MARK C. JENSEN

RESOURCE *Publications* • Eugene, Oregon

THE LABYRINTH WE WALKED
The Cold War Deconstructed

Copyright © 2024 Mark C. Jensen. All rights reserved. Except for brief quotations in critical publications or reviews, no part of this book may be reproduced in any manner without prior written permission from the publisher. Write: Permissions, Wipf and Stock Publishers, 199 W. 8th Ave., Suite 3, Eugene, OR 97401.

Resource Publications
An Imprint of Wipf and Stock Publishers
199 W. 8th Ave., Suite 3
Eugene, OR 97401

www.wipfandstock.com

PAPERBACK ISBN: 979-8-3852-1507-2
HARDCOVER ISBN: 979-8-3852-1508-9
EBOOK ISBN: 979-8-3852-1509-6

05/29/24

For Marjorie

Why have I been standing here for the last twenty years?
—HELMUT STÖSS, EAST GERMAN BORDER OFFICER, AFTER OPENING OF BERLIN WALL, NOVEMBER 1989. QUOTED IN *THE COLLAPSE*, BY MARY ELISE SAROTTE

Contents

List of Photographs   ix
Acknowledgments   xi
Introduction   xiii

1. The Cold War: A Deconstruction   1
2. Vietnam: A Half-Remembered Tragedy   26
3. Nuclear Counterintuition: Risk Reduction during the Cold War   51
4. An Evanescent Coalition: How Civil Rights Became a Priority (Briefly) in the 1960s   67
5. Decade of Reckoning: Two Takes on the US Experience of the 1970s   88
6. The Long Memories . . . of Others: US Intelligence "Projects" in the Cold War   110
7. The Paradox of China's Rise and the Veneration of Mao   131
8. Marx's Crafty Nemesis: The Evolutions of Capitalism   148

    Ghazal of a Mathematician's Lament   174

Bibliography   175
Index   181

List of Photographs

Georges Bidault, French Foreign Minister, 1945	xvi
Ho Chi Minh, 1920	25
Operation Cue, 1955	50
A. Philip Randolph, 1964	66
Richard Nixon, Spiro Agnew, and the Shah of Iran, 1969	87
Richard Nixon and William Ruckelshaus, 1970	87
General Smedley Butler, 1922	109
Shanghai Bund, 2012	130
Shanghai Pudong District, 2015	130
Harry Truman and FDIC Officials, 1946	147

Acknowledgments

I FIRST WANT TO thank and acknowledge Tony Tsonchev, editor of *The Montréal Review*, for reading and originally publishing most of these essays, and for his advice and encouragement in turning them into this book. With the demise of so many print outlets for work of this type, the *Review* provides an invaluable outlet for professional scholars and other writers to publish longer form commentary about history, philosophy, and world events, to a general audience. Likewise, the editors at Wipf and Stock have patiently supported and guided me through the process of turning these essays into a book.

Six of the eight essays first appeared in *The Montréal Review*:

1. The Cold War: A Deconstruction (November 2017)
2. Vietnam: A Half-Remembered Tragedy (February 2019)
3. Nuclear Counterintuition: Risk Reduction during the Cold War (July 2021)
4. The Paradox of China's Rise and the Veneration of Mao (December 2021)
5. An Evanescent Coalition: How Civil Rights Became a Priority (Briefly) in the 1960s (June 2022)
6. The Long Memories . . . of Others: US Intelligence "Projects" in the Cold War (April 2023)

The book's title is from a phrase in the poem "Ghazal of a Mathematician's Lament," which appeared in *The Ghazal Page* in 2019, which was sadly the last edition of that poetry journal.

ACKNOWLEDGMENTS

I want to thank the ongoing work of the generation of historians that inspired me and provided the basis for this work of interpretation. Probably the first book that fascinated me about this seemingly vanished era was Anne Applebaum's award-winning *GULAG: A History*.

Though the Cold War was a contentious and sometimes frightening period, I recognize that I am fortunate simply to have been a US citizen while it was going on. I could list many influences of the period, but I'll mention just a few of the most important. My parents Val and Mary Ellen Jensen were always extraordinarily supportive of my education as well as experience in securities and investment analysis of specific importance to writing about economic issues in the Cold War. My late wife, Lisa Martin, and our children Claire and Skye got me out of my armchair with their passion for travel and cultural exchange and inspired me with their sense of social justice.

Finally, I've dedicated this book to my wife Marjorie Thomsen. We met through a mutual interest in poetry, and we support each other through the challenges of writing. But it is through sharing our lives, work, friends, and families that she has dissolved loneliness and forever enriched my life.

Introduction

MY HOPE IN WRITING this collection of essays has been to reflect on the Cold War era in a different way, as a set of issues or questions rather than a chronological narrative.

I came to this project to resolve one mystery—and found others. Like all post-World War II kids, I grew up knowing only a world split in two, in which my country had an implacable enemy firmly in control of the other side of the globe. In 1977, I had traveled with a group of highly nonpolitical college classmates to West Berlin; East German soldiers searched our train compartment at midnight on the trip from Frankfurt, and police shouted to keep us within the lines of the crosswalks in the four-block section of East Berlin that Western tourists were allowed to visit. In 1979 the US, already weary from Vietnam and Watergate, experienced a second oil shortage, the taking of hostages in Iran and, just in time for Christmas, the Soviet intervention in Afghanistan. Incredibly, just ten years later, ordinary Berliners opened the wall between east and west, while we watched on NBC. The fall of Soviet Communism was as much a surprise to US intelligence as to the general public. Had the Communists simply surrendered to Reagan-era rhetoric, or was there something else we had missed?

Almost every issue I explored—Vietnam, race relations, weapons development, CIA interventions—had some version of the same problem. Most of us in the US had at best a partial view of the issues, exacerbated by a lack of curiosity and some willful ignorance. This is why it's so important to do this kind of revisiting: not to condemn people who got things "wrong" or to valorize those whose views line up with ours today, but to see events as dynamic and unpredictable, and to pay better attention to our own incomplete information, inattention, and biases.

INTRODUCTION

In researching and writing, I found that each essay needed to address at least one broad question:

1. Why did the Soviet Union and its Eastern European allies fall so suddenly and surprisingly?
2. Was the Vietnam War avoidable?
3. How did Cold War leaders manage not to use nuclear weapons systems that they had built at such great expense?
4. Was the Cold War a spur or a hindrance to the US civil rights movement?
5. Just how depressing was it to live in the US in the 1970s?
6. How can we assess the benefits and blowbacks from the CIA's covert projects?
7. Mao's rule was a disaster. Why does the Chinese government still venerate him?
8. How did "capitalism" survive its critics and enemies?

These essays involve my interpretation and personal judgment of verifiable and widely accepted facts, rather than novel archival research. While I am not a professional historian, my work as a business litigation attorney has given me several decades of experience addressing questions in a similar way, providing advice to clients based on analysis of facts and application of historical precedent, as well as a solid grounding in the adjacent fields of business and economics. Of course, as a novice in this field, I am not only indebted to but am a great fan and almost compulsive reader of the writings of dozens of professional historians. We are all incredibly fortunate to live in a society that has fostered their careers and published their work. I hope that this inspires you to pick up many of the works recognized in the bibliography, including these especially insightful and well-written histories: *The Collapse*, by Mary Elise Sarotte; *Postwar*, Tony Judt; *Vietnam: A New History*, Christopher Goscha; *The Warmth of Other Suns*, Isabel Wilkerson; *Cuba: An American History*, Ada Ferrer; *The Search for Modern China*, Jonathan Spence; and *The Free World*, Louis Menand. For context I also rely whenever possible on movies that came out during the Cold War, from major productions like *Apocalypse Now* to less widely seen films like Gordon Parks's *The Learning Tree*, because these can serve as markers of what the public watched and understood at the time.

INTRODUCTION

As you can tell from the weight of this book, I can make no claim to have covered every issue or important event of the Cold War period. Full histories often run five hundred pages or more, and I have necessarily left out many significant episodes and events. The Cold War itself is a framework for world history but not a comprehensive or necessarily a descriptive one. There was nothing cold about the history of East Asia, for example, where real wars with millions of casualties raged almost continuously from 1945 to 1979 in China, Korea, Vietnam, Cambodia, and Laos. Civil wars and violent government oppression plagued Latin America (Argentina, Brazil, Chile, Cuba, El Salvador, Guatemala, and Nicaragua), Africa (notably in Kenya, Nigeria, Congo, Angola, and South Africa), and Indonesia. In other conflicts, the Cold War was secondary to regional disputes, for example in the Middle East and India. Finally, the demise of European colonialism was at least as important and dangerous as the main Cold War rivalry between the US and USSR—probably more important to more people in the long run. The essays on Vietnam, China, and the CIA do discuss colonialism and some of these conflicts but can at most spark interest in the wider history.

At the same time, I hope that these essays provide a new and different focus on major Cold War events and serve as something of a corrective to subjective memories and simple lessons. This is not to say that our memories and learnings are wrong, though they often are. It's that they are momentary and selective. We remember vivid events and how they affected us, but often very little about their context or the reasons they came about.

French Foreign Minister Georges Bidault (center) with Acting US Secretary of State Joseph C. Grew and French Ambassador Henri Bonnet, 1945. Bidault led the French government's effort to win a very difficult 1948 parliamentary vote to join an Anglo-American postwar economic plan that included rebuilding western Germany.

Credit: Harris and Ewing, Harry S. Truman Library.

1

The Cold War
A Deconstruction

VASTNESS PRESENTS THE REAL challenge in writing about the Cold War. It's as if *Game of Thrones* went on for forty-five years. Our strong memories of the Cold War's intense episodes, especially the bitter tragedy of Vietnam, don't provide much insight on the conflict as a whole. The real hostilities and near-misses make it especially easy to discount the disquieting early episodes that, I believe, had an outsized impact on the surprising conclusion.

My own effort to better understand this sprawling epic became this essay about the importance of initial conditions, the outsized rewards of self-interested generosity, and some courageous French legislators. And while I am reluctant to draw analogies to any specific current foreign policy issue, these stories do illustrate the risks of a hard and brittle isolation.

1. THE MOST IMPORTANT PROBLEM

I recently watched *The Last Man on the Moon*, a biographical documentary about the astronaut Gene Cernan. It is a great adventure story—the risks they faced!—and a lasting testament to the engineering, manufacturing, and operational achievements of hundreds of thousands of people on the ground. The rockets, the spacecraft, and even the astronauts' equipment struck me as more impressive and eerily beautiful than I remembered as a grade schooler, when the space program seemed like a cool but totally normal thing.

Apollo's sublimity is captured in the famous images of and from the moon, a sunlit desert in a sky forever black. The gorgeous blue and white-sworled Earth looked familiar, but stunningly small and isolated in the depthless universe. Cernan himself made a poignant remote clip of his own lunar craft taking off from the moon with the Earth in the background, the tiny capsule carrying the last two human visitors on the long journey home.

The Cernan documentary also made me think the space program was kind of crazy. Put aside the danger, the loss of two astronauts in a capsule fire in 1967, the astronomical cost (sorry), the comparatively modest scientific results (far cheaper unmanned projects, like the Hubble telescope and probes of almost every planet, have yielded much more information), the moon's very inutility for, say, a manned base or mining operation. Put all that aside. What was the rush? It would have been just as exciting in 1979 or 1989. It would be riveting news today.

Every American then knew the answer. We wanted to get there before the Soviets. The country had been repeatedly shocked by Soviet achievements in space: Sputnik, the first unmanned space orbiter, and Yuri Gagarin, the first human in space. They had sent up a space dog, too. These served as barely coded demonstrations of Soviet weapons delivery capabilities, like North Korea's ongoing missile demonstrations. The Cernan documentary replayed part of the American response: one set of cameras set up to display the power of the five rockets arrayed beneath the first stage of the thirty-story Saturn V, all having to fire in perfect symmetry to reach the moon. That crotch-shot was for a very specific audience.

Don't get me wrong. The Apollo program was just what it looked like. It was peaceful, it was exciting, it expanded the boundaries of science and technology, it was more than cool—it was quite intentionally awesome. It just wouldn't have made any sense outside the strange logic of the Cold War.

Apollo was also a proxy for what was truly crazy: the manufacture of thousands—thousands!—of thermonuclear warheads and their delivery mechanisms, airplanes, submarines, and missiles. The reason for these numbers was redundancy, which, if you think about it, is only ever a reason to make too much. The US military felt it needed to have enough weapons in enough places to be able to counter, and to counter overwhelmingly, a successful Soviet first strike. Redundancy would in theory deter the Soviets from striking first. Of course, once we had that many weapons, the Soviets would become that much more concerned about their own ability to counter a US first strike. Each side meant to show that it would *always* be able to commit genocide.

The cost of the US nuclear program was estimated at 5.5 trillion dollars in 1998, shortly after the Cold War's end. This is something like fifty to one hundred times the cost of the entire Apollo lunar exploration program, which was widely (though not universally) criticized as an excessive expense at the time. That made the nuclear arms race, as Tom Vanderbilt put it, "the most expensive war that was never fought."[1] And, it goes without saying, not fighting a war with these weapons was the best possible outcome. The US spent over five trillion dollars on weapons that it *intended* never to use. Unlike the Vietnam War, another project that could only be justified in Cold War terms, this dangerous and almost intentionally wasteful military spending prompted only bipartisan budget approval votes.

My point is that people treated the Cold War as the most important problem in the world. That's why it was so astonishing when one superpower seemed simply to give up.

2. THE QUOTA OF INTERVENTIONS

The gates at Bornholmer Bridge were opened and crowds poured through, as the overwhelmed East Berlin border guards looked on. Like millions of Americans, I watched the story unfold on NBC nightly news, Thursday, November 9, 1989. The conflict that had overshadowed everything the postwar generation had known about politics, domestic as well as international, seemed to evaporate before our eyes. One of the East German border guards, overcome with emotion, could not stop asking himself, "Why have I been standing here for the past twenty years?"[2]

The story of that night is far more contingent and exciting than it appeared on NBC. The remarkable story of the East German protest movement and the miscommunication and bungling of the Soviet and East

---

1. Vanderbilt, *Survival City*, 14. The cost of Apollo has been estimated at 28 billion dollars in then-current dollars, which would have been the equivalent of 100–130 billion dollars in 1998. Planetary Society, "How Much Did the Apollo," para. 1. Precise comparisons are difficult because each program covered different time periods and differences in inflation measurement assumptions. See also Schwartz, *Atomic Audit*, preface.

2. Sarotte, *Collapse*, 147.

German governments is brilliantly told in *The Collapse* by Mary Elise Sarotte.[3] But all the Warsaw Pact regimes were fated for dramatic change for one simple reason: the Soviet leadership had decided not to intervene to protect them. In 1988 and early 1989, Mikhail Gorbachev had even made speeches effectively abandoning the Brezhnev doctrine, which declared that the Soviet Union would use its army to protect socialism—as they defined it—in countries where it existed. To Western observers, history counseled against taking Soviet pronouncements too literally.

It turned out, however, that the policy of nonintervention had been quite a long time in the making. During the mass demonstrations of the Solidarity movement in Poland in late 1980 and 1981, Leonid Brezhnev and his advisers firmly decided not to intervene, but kept this decision to themselves.[4] As historian and former Soviet official Vladislav Zubok has explained, Soviet leaders at the time actually did not view their military actions in Hungary (1956) or Czechoslovakia (1968) as unmitigated successes; rather, the actions had been expensive and morale-sapping internally, and nothing short of disastrous in international relations. The decision to invade Afghanistan, on Christmas Day 1979, had already brought the same combination of expense, disappointment, and international outrage. Even KGB head Yuri Andropov, a hard-liner who had supported all of the prior military actions, opposed direct action in Poland: "The quota of interventions abroad has been exhausted."[5] At that point, however, Brezhnev was still able to bluff Polish leaders into thinking that the Red Army might "go in," which was enough to embolden the Polish government to declare martial law.

The Kremlin's inaction in Poland foreshadowed its policy in 1989. The historian Matthew Ouimet even concluded that "though still unaware of their accomplishment, the Polish people had forced the Soviet colossus into a retreat from which it would never recover."[6] And the factors driving the Kremlin's Poland policy only got worse during the 1980s. The Soviet

---

3. Sarotte, *Collapse*, xvii–xx, 127–53. Sarotte's book covers the months-long protest movement in East Germany and elsewhere in the Soviet-dominated bloc and illuminates the confusion and miscommunications within the East German government and between Moscow and Berlin.

4. The Soviet decision not to intervene against the Solidarity movement in Poland, unknown at the time in the West, is confirmed by many historians. Zubok, *Failed Empire*, 266–67; Brown, *Rise and Fall of Communism*, 430–32; Stone, *Atlantic*, 532; Gaddis, *Cold War*, 259.

5. Zubok, *Failed Empire*, 265.

6. Ouimet, *Rise and Fall*, 243.

economy's expenses and revenues both went the wrong direction. Defense-related expenditures remained around an astonishing 40 percent of the government's budget, due in part to the Afghanistan action, and policymakers unquestionably felt pressured by the (somewhat speculative) plans of Reagan's Strategic Defense Initiative. The cost of the arms race, together with the Chernobyl nuclear accident, accounted for much of Gorbachev's eagerness to negotiate disarmament treaties. The cost of more distant Soviet alliances, with billions of dollars annually going to Vietnam, Cuba, and Syria, also became much harder to justify.[7]

Worse, the Soviets had no way to replace, much less raise, foreign exchange revenue from the sale of oil. Prompted in part by President Reagan's pressure on Saudi Arabia and other friendly OPEC states to reopen the spigots, oil prices plunged from thirty-eight dollars per barrel in 1979 (about 170 dollars in today's dollars) to under fifteen dollars in 1986 (about forty-two dollars today).[8] This left Gorbachev's government with two principal sources of revenue, raising consumer prices or raising taxes, which amounted to much the same thing in the planned economy.

As he was retreating from the Brezhnev doctrine, Gorbachev finally went to a third option, cutting military expenses. Citing a severe financial crisis, in January 1989 Gorbachev announced a 14 percent reduction in forces in Eastern Europe and a 19 percent cut in arms production. The last Soviet troops marched out of Afghanistan in February 1989. With this in mind, it no longer seems surprising that the Soviet Union stood by as Polish citizens voted for Solidarity that June; as Hungary, influenced by a billion West German marks, opened its border with Austria to a stream of East German "vacationers" in August; and as East German officials bungled their way into opening the Berlin border crossings in November.

Zubok concluded that "the Soviet leaders did not have the money to influence the events in Central and Eastern Europe."[9] Gorbachev seems to have had a long-term goal of integrating Russia and the former Soviet dominions into a common European home; he even asked the first President Bush to consider a new Marshall Plan, a request that was promptly declined.

---

7. For economic pressures on the Soviet Union in the 1980s, see Zubok, *Failed Empire*, 267–68, 298–99; Stone, *Atlantic*, 544–46; Brown, *Rise and Fall*, 499, 522–25, 582.

8. For oil price decline, see Stone, *Atlantic*, 546; Gaddis, *Cold War*, 261. For inflation adjustments, see McMahon, "Historical US Inflation Rates."

9. Zubok, *Failed Empire*, 322.

This is not to say that the Soviet Union's retreat and collapse was economically ordained. Gorbachev plainly wanted to reform the country under his political leadership, not abandon it. But in making the political and economic decision not to use force to retain Eastern Europe, Gorbachev and his many political allies underestimated the dissatisfaction in the Soviet republics and the extent to which the threat of force held the structure together. Everyone noticed that the emperor had doffed his clothes. Independence movements first popped up in the Baltic states and then across the empire, leading finally to the emergence of Russia itself behind the charismatic (but deeply flawed) Boris Yeltsin. When Yeltsin almost personally stopped the attempted coup aimed at Gorbachev in August 1991, it was clear that there was nothing left of the Soviet Union.

The West breathed a sigh of relief as the Soviet enemy and—with China's very different reform—virtually all traces of Communism as an economic system disappeared. But I felt as though I must have missed something. Like everyone born after about 1940, I had grown up hearing very effective, consistent, bipartisan warnings about the existential threat posed by the Soviet Union. And by the late 1970s, after the loss of the Vietnam War, the shock of the 1979 Iranian revolution (belated blowback from the covert CIA-sponsored 1953 coup) and the first wave of industrial decline, the US hardly looked like a sure winner. With the economy beset with persistent inflation, high unemployment, and dependency on increasingly hostile oil exporters, US stock indices reached new lows in the summer of 1982.

After the Soviet Union's fall, many commentators tried to assign political credit for winning the Cold War, if winning is what happened. The more I read about it, however, the more I wondered how Gorbachev found himself in such a poor strategic position that he felt compelled to abandon it. That situation was inherited over generations.

3. A LONG SIEGE

In trying to understand how the Soviet Union got boxed in to its hermetically sealed Eurasian fortress, I found it very easy to get sidetracked; with eight US presidents, at least six Soviet Central Committee general secretaries (a bit harder to count), and Cold War–related governmental violence in dozens of countries and on every continent except (to my knowledge) Australia, there were a lot of subplots. But the net result of these machinations and eruptions was a stalemate. A stripped-down summary might go something like this:

> After the two most destructive wars in world history, the exhausted victors desperately wanted to avoid a World War III, though they judged it unwise to say so. Instead, each focused on consolidating their hegemony in the European and East Asian territories under their respective occupations: the Americans using money whenever possible, the impoverished Soviets preferring soldiers. In one hot spot, Germany, neither side rose to the other's provocations, resulting in a mutually tolerable division on wartime borders by 1949 (though each side officially objected to it). The Korean War did result from Communist aggression and involved direct fighting between American and Soviet-allied Chinese armies, but by 1953 the conflict bogged down on the original border; neither the territory nor the principles were important enough for either party to push further. An exodus of young and energetic people from East Germany forced the Soviet Union and its "allies" to close their western borders, walling their own people in. The struggle became a long political and economic siege of the Soviet bloc. China gradually permitted private ownership and trade after Mao's death in 1974, abandoning collectivist principles in favor of a more worldly and much richer empire. When the Soviet Union, overburdened by its foreign commitments, did not object to the opening of Eastern European borders in 1989, its satellite governments fell, soon followed by the USSR itself.

I don't mean this to diminish the importance of the arms race, famous superpower confrontations, or proxy wars. If these had turned out differently, the Cold War might have ended far more dramatically, and not in a good way. I have also cheated, by referencing a "long political and economic siege," which encompasses war or insurrection in Vietnam, Hungary, Cuba, Czechoslovakia, and Afghanistan, as well as the massive buildup of increasingly dusty nuclear weapons. Each of these subjects is of major importance in its own right; the mere side effects of the bipolar rivalry killed millions. But none turned out to be decisive.

"An end has been put to the Cold War and to the arms race," declared Mikhail Gorbachev in his farewell address. "The threat of nuclear war has been removed."[10] He might have added that the principals' casualties were

---

10. Clines, "Gorbachev," 1.

surprisingly light. The US and USSR had learned fairly quickly to keep their own armies apart.

4. ANOTHER SEPARATE PEACE

At the Yalta and Potsdam summit conferences in February and July 1945, as World War II ground to an end, the weary Big Three leaders of the US, Britain, and the Soviet Union found many issues on which they could only agree not to disagree, for the moment. As Tony Judt has explained, the parties still had self-interested reasons to work together. Specifically, at Yalta in early 1945, each side was most concerned about keeping the other engaged against Germany,[11] about preventing the other from making what was perceived as a separate peace with Germany—*another* separate peace, each would have said, in reference to the Allies' pre-war concession of Czech territory to Hitler at Munich in 1938, and to the 1939 Soviet-Nazi nonaggression pact. No one wanted to face the undivided attention of the Wehrmacht. Germany's unconditional surrender was reaffirmed as the Allies' central commitment. The US, moreover, still insisted on gaining Stalin's commitment to open a second (really a third, counting China) front against Japan within ninety days of Germany's surrender.[12] US military plans in February 1945 still anticipated that an invasion of Japan's home islands could at best be completed in six months to a year. But there was no agreement about postwar plans for Germany.[13]

Most of the European territorial settlements were simply consistent with the location of the armies. The borders of Bulgaria, Hungary, Romania, Finland, and Italy were settled in official treaties, and the parties would in time respect the informal, not quite secret, territorial understanding Churchill made with Stalin, the last piece of which meant that Stalin would not intervene in Greece. Given the size and proven effectiveness of those armies, formalizing borders was still a clear step toward de-escalation.[14] The Big Three also signed the Declaration on Liberated Europe, "to foster the conditions in which the liberated peoples may exercise those [democratic]

---

11. Zubok, *Failed Empire*, 17–18; Judt, *Postwar*, 100–101.
12. Goodwin, *No Ordinary Time*, 582; Kennedy, *Freedom from Fear*, 805.
13. Kennedy, *Freedom from Fear*, 804; Judt, *Postwar*, 102.
14. Judt, *Postwar*, 134.

rights, all three governments will jointly assist the people in any European liberated state or former Axis satellite state in Europe."[15]

As to Germany, too, an official consensus emerged. The Nazis should be tried and punished for their war crimes as expeditiously as possible. Eventually all occupying forces would be withdrawn, and Germany should become a single state, disarmed, neutral, and democratic. For the present, the three powers would divide both the country and the city of Berlin into zones of administrative responsibility.[16]

These points did not suit either side's strategic concerns, however. Given that Russia had been invaded from the west three times in the past 150 years, Stalin would never give up armed control of an Eastern European buffer zone. But even that was not as important as preventing Germany from rising again; in the era of mechanized transport, Germany was still right next door. The Red Army would not be leaving Eastern Germany anytime soon.[17] The root-and-branch elimination of fascism was an equally immediate national security priority.

The US and its allies most feared another "Munich."[18] The key error, they thought, had been the failure of Britain and France to stand up to Hitler's designs on Czechoslovakia (and never mind the self-disabling American neutrality laws). They worried, accordingly, about the Red Army divisions that Stalin had kept in the Soviet sector of Germany and every Eastern European state except, at first, Czechoslovakia. The Western European states were now poor, weak, and barely armed. The US badly wanted to reduce its military commitment, but without American forces as a deterrent, the Red Army could march straight through to the coast of France. Western Germany might represent a sort of buffer against that outcome, and if that meant ignoring the wartime activities of a few capable German administrators, well, the alternative might be worse.[19]

Thus, as Judt observed, the de facto solution to the problem of Germany would be just about the opposite of the official consensus: a divided

---

15. Judt, *Postwar*, 101.

16. Judge and Langdon, *Cold War*, 8–9 (excerpting Potsdam Conference Report); Judt, *Postwar*, 122.

17. Zubok, *Failed Empire*, 21–22, 62–63; Figes, *Revolutionary Russia*, 230–31; Goodwin, *No Ordinary Time*, 581.

18. Judt, *Reappraisals*, 322, 358.

19. Western Allies' "lip service" regarding German unification; Judt, *Postwar*, 147.

state; each side aligned with and supporting a different foreign military power; a long, militarized border. One side left, the other right.[20]

5. AN INVITATION DECLINED

In early 1946, barely six months after Hiroshima and the Japanese surrender, Treasury officials were stunned by the Soviet Union's announcement that it would not participate in long-planned postwar financial arrangements. Though the plans had been initiated by the legendary British economist John Maynard Keynes, and dominated by the US and British delegations, the Soviet Union had participated and the resulting objectives were not considered controversial. They were even, in a way, altruistic.

The key to Keynes's vision was facilitating international trade, aimed at preventing the breakdown that had occurred in the early 1930s. German reparations payments under the Versailles treaty had been Hitler's political stalking horse. The US had done its share of damage by insisting on loan repayments from its Great War allies, and by passing the trade-inhibiting Smoot-Hawley Tariff Act at the outset of the Great Depression in early 1930. These actions as a whole were sharply deflationary; they had reduced trade and taken currency out of circulation. Deflation both reflected and engendered a lack of trust. By acting as though economics is a zero-sum game aimed at accumulating the most currency, economic actors both domestic and international managed to send growth well below zero. In a sharp turnaround, American leaders had since discovered their own interest in helping European countries become self-sufficient again as soon as possible. To put it more bluntly, the US wanted to end its military and economic aid to its allies as soon as it could.

Beginning at the famous 1944 conference at the Bretton Woods resort in New Hampshire, delegates followed Keynes's roadmap, using American capital. The key components included a General Agreement on Tariffs and Trade (GATT, later the World Trade Organization) to reduce tariffs in an orderly way, and a specialized central bank, the International Monetary Fund, which would facilitate—stand as trusted intermediary in—foreign exchange transactions under an agreed dollar-based currency exchange system.[21]

---

20. Judt, *Postwar*, 126–28.
21. Judt, *Postwar*, 107–8; Stone, *Atlantic*, 56.

The elements of Bretton Woods all sounded duly technical and unobtrusive—no one would force governments or private companies to trade—and even generous: the US put up most of the capital! It nevertheless proved to be an arduous journey. Yes, trade was voluntary, and most Western governments, impoverished by the war, saw little choice but to participate. But proud governments in the West took their time adjusting to the fixed exchange rates; an even larger problem was the creation of an extra-national system of trade outside of government control.

That was where Stalin got off the train. The Soviet refusal seemed inexplicable to US Treasury officials when it occurred, in February 1946.[22] From their perspective, it was like offering free membership in a club, with no strings attached. They asked the State Department's top Soviet expert for an explanation.

6. THE STRUGGLE STALIN WANTED

George Kennan was, almost uniquely among US diplomats, a very experienced observer of Soviet leadership. With barely concealed condescension over his colleagues' ignorance, he took Treasury's inquiry about Bretton Woods as an excuse to send the nineteen-page Long Telegram on February 22, 1946.

In compelling, often quite beautiful language, sometimes clipped with telegram shorthand, Kennan explained Soviet thinking: "USSR still lives in antagonistic 'capitalist encirclement' with which in the long run there can be no permanent peaceful coexistence." He quoted a Stalin speech—from 1927!

> In course of further development of international revolution there will emerge two centers of world significance: a socialist center . . . and a capitalist center . . . Battle between these two centers for command of world economy will decide fate of capitalism and of communism in entire world.[23]

It is more than a little depressing to think that for forty-five years most of the world would be caught up in the very struggle Stalin had so long wanted to fight.

---

22. Judt, *Postwar*, 108.
23. Kennan, "February 22, 1946," 1–2.

Kennan went on to explain that Stalin needed an eternal struggle with a hostile outside world, no matter how fictional. It was a story ordinary Russians remembered from the tsarist years, and still critical to domestic politics. In Stalin's modern retelling, the capitalist countries were corrupt and riddled with internal conflicts that would inevitably lead to war between them. That would be good for the USSR. A capitalist intervention against the USSR "would be disastrous to those who undertook it, [but] would cause renewed delay in progress of Soviet socialism and must therefore be forestalled at all costs."[24] In short, Kennan felt the Soviet Union would play capitalist countries against each other, but would back down when confronted directly. Stalin's mythical worldview arose from an almost poignant need to hide insecurity:

> Nevertheless, all these theses, however baseless and disproven, are being boldly put forward again today. What does this indicate? It indicates that Soviet party line is not based on any objective analysis of situation beyond Russia's borders; that it has, indeed, little to do with conditions outside of Russia; that it arises mainly from basic inner-Russian necessities which existed before the war and exist today...
> They have always feared foreign penetration, feared direct contact between western world and their own, feared what would happen if Russians learned truth about world without or if foreigners learned truth about world within...
> Only in this land which had never known a friendly neighbor... could a doctrine thrive which viewed economic conflicts of interest as insoluble by peaceful means... In this dogma, with its basic altruism of purpose, they found justification for their instinctive fear of outside world, for the dictatorship without which they did not know how to rule, for cruelties they did not dare not to inflict, for sacrifices they felt bound to demand. In the name of Marxism they sacrificed every single ethical value in their methods and tactics. Today they cannot dispense with it. It is fig leaf of their moral and intellectual respectability.[25]

So, what did Kennan recommend in response to this implacable foe? Although he was an early advocate of the policy of containment, his initial analysis suggests that the Soviets would mostly contain themselves. Rather, he advocated a five-part approach that reads, as much as anything, like

---

24. Kennan, "February 22, 1946," 2.
25. Kennan, "February 22, 1946," 5–6.

a program of self-improvement: (i) study the enemy; (ii) educate the US public about the problems and dangers; (iii) "solve internal problems of our own society"; (iv) advocate "a much more positive and constructive picture of the world we would like to see"; and (v) "have courage and self confidence to cling to our own methods and conceptions of human society. After all, the greatest danger that can befall us . . . is that we shall allow ourselves to become like those with whom we are coping."[26]

Stalin got ahold of the Long Telegram quickly—and was extremely irritated by it.[27] He nevertheless continued to behave just as Kennan described.

7. MARX'S BLUEPRINT

Stalin's decision to drop out of the Bretton Woods system didn't doom the economies of the Soviet bloc. The region is easily large and diverse enough to have recovered and developed on its own. But he did not intend to let it develop on its own.

Vladimir Putin, speaking from deep personal experience, has said that a planned economy "is less efficient than a market economy. History has staged two experiments that are very well known in the world: East Germany and West Germany, North Korea and South Korea."[28]

Putin stated his conclusion carefully. Communism was never an economic system; Marx left such details to be sorted out after the revolution. Lenin, the Communists' other accredited theorist, had been in practice somewhat flexible on the question of private enterprise. It was Stalin's government that implemented the planned economy, to fill in the yawning gap in Marxist theory and, more to his point, to secure its own political control, a goal the founders would have appreciated.

Stalin had absorbed both the economic and political lessons of his predecessors. And Marx did make important insights about the excesses of the Industrial Revolution in England and Germany. The need for capital to acquire machinery and raw materials for the large-scale manufacturing and transportation that dominated that era gave the few who had capital an extraordinary, self-perpetuating advantage over all other economic participants. Therefore, he continued, the low pay, terrible conditions, and near-servitude of the workers were inherent in capitalism. These criticisms

26. Kennan, "February 22, 1946," 18–19.
27. Gaddis, *Cold War*, 41.
28. Dawisha, *Putin's Kleptocracy*, 34.

helped to inform many later reforms in capitalist countries, such as antitrust and labor laws. But they don't necessarily lead to Communism.

Marx then proceeded to jump the shark. He read the contemporary philosopher G. W. F. Hegel to conclude that (a) human progress *must inevitably* occur and (b) when it does occur, it *can only* do so through a pendulum-like process of thesis, antithesis, and synthesis. Applying this so-called rationalist view, Marx speculated that industrial capitalism *must progress* in its then-current manner until it (i) reached a level of efficiency that everyone's needs could easily be met and (ii) became so harsh that it provoked its antithesis, a workers' revolution; the revolution would in turn be followed by (and we can hardly blame Hegel for this) (iii) a synthesis, some kind of unmediated equality in which each person's voluntary contributions would suffice to provide a decent living for everyone. Since no other path was even theoretically possible, mere reform would actually hinder or delay the day of revolution. Perhaps in fear of appearing to endorse any such counterproductive efforts at consensus-building, Marx gave no guidance on how to achieve and administer their mythical end state.[29]

Thus, Marx provided a successful *political* game plan for Lenin. Lenin's genius was to act out Marx's disdain for merely liberal reformers, whom he had viewed as apologists for the status quo. On his famous return to the Finland Station in wartime Petrograd in 1917, Lenin rejected coalition efforts and ruthlessly eliminated or discredited those he deemed false friends on the left. In the peculiar vacuum left by Tsar Nicholas's forced abdication, the failure of Russia's war effort, and the long-standing unhappiness of soldiers, farmers, and urban laborers, Lenin's Bolsheviks made themselves the only viable alternative to the failed republican coalition.[30]

After Lenin's death in 1924, Stalin demonstrated his mastery of these political principles, periodically eliminating almost everyone who might have an independent power base. The long game, according to theory, was to wait for revolutions to break out in the rest of the developed nations; in

---

29. On Marxist and Leninist theory, see generally Brown, *Rise and Fall*, 18–25, 49–52, 57; Menand, *Free World*, 336–39 (interpreting Isaiah Berlin's 1939 intellectual biography of Marx, *Karl Marx, His Life and Environment*).

30. Figes explains that, in Lenin's speech upon arriving at Petrograd's Finland Station in April 1917, "the message was simple: no support for the Provisional Government [of Alexander Kerensky]; a clean break with the Mensheviks and Defensists of the Second International; the arming of the workers; the transfer of all power to the Soviets; and the conclusion of an immediate peace [with Germany]." Figes, *Revolutionary Russia*, 81. He continued to oppose compromise after the October Revolution, even with potential allies on the left. Figes, *Revolutionary Russia*, 97.

the meantime, the Five-Year plans would assure that the Communist Party retained control.

Stalin, however, ignored one of Marx's key points: workers were cogs in the mills of the Industrial Revolution. By setting prices and production quotas, and assigning employment, the Soviet planners would waste workers' lives as efficiently as any nineteenth-century industrialists.

Stalin also ignored the capacity of developed countries to evolve; under Marxist theory, they were doomed anyway. But in the century after the Industrial Revolution, advanced economies did evolve dramatically and in unexpected ways. The changes have to do with the creativity of market forces, of course, but also the negotiated balance between the freedoms of citizens and the functions performed by the government to foster safety and fair play. The earliest of these government functions are as familiar as wallpaper: national defense, public safety, issuance of widely accepted currency, judicial enforcement of private contracts, and—a nineteenth-century innovation—corporation laws limiting shareholder liability. Then in the late nineteenth and early twentieth centuries, suffrage was granted to historically excluded groups, i.e., women and minorities; courts evolved the common law doctrine of negligence to assign responsibility for the inevitable accidents of modern technology; responding in part to the challenge of socialism, legislatures enacted laws to protect workers, consumers and, much later, the environment from externalities—harms to third parties from the activities of private business. Imperfect as our society is, it does have a high level of group trust: a large population of consumers, workers, business owners, and investors who deal with each other without undue fear that they will be treated unfairly. Those millions of decision-makers enable market forces to work.

The thought of millions of decision-makers would have sent Stalin into a cold sweat. Marx had seen the future, and the duty of Communist leaders was to make sure nobody got in its way.

8. FOMO

The superpower rivalry broke out into the open in March 1946, when Winston Churchill delivered his Iron Curtain speech in Fulton, Missouri. Churchill was a private citizen at the time—better to say, a representative of the British loyal opposition—but President Truman's attendance signaled the intended importance of the message.[31] "From Stettin in the Baltic to Tri-

---

31. Brown, *Rise and Fall*, 176–77.

este in the Adriatic, an iron curtain has descended across the Continent."[32] Referring to a fire safety mechanism used in theaters, he railed against Moscow's efforts to shut down political debate, travel, and communications in what became the Soviet bloc.

In truth, this was only the first step in a long debate, in which each side strenuously argued that the other was to blame for breaking up the shared vision of world peace. The finger pointing was nonsense. The long-term aims of the superpowers were irreconcilable, and both parties well knew it.

Churchill was right that the Soviet Union cared little about the democratic principles in the Declaration on Liberated Europe. Polish elections resulted in an uncanny 80 percent vote for Moscow's local affiliates.[33] But the ever-sensitive Soviets kept their story alive. "It's got to look democratic," (East) German Communist leader Walter Ulbricht instructed his comrades in 1945, "but we must have everything in control."[34] Thus Communists appeared to accept poor electoral results in Germany, Hungary, and Austria, settling for minority roles in coalition governments with center-left parties, so long as they got a few key ministries. Control over Interior or Justice ministries, coupled with the presence of the Red Army, proved more than enough to arrest, intimidate, and expel opponents and rivals.

On the other hand, the US and Britain dreaded the prospect of a unified Germany, also specified by treaty, if Red Army divisions would forever remain. In the meantime, humanitarian concerns made western Germany an economic dependent. After poor harvests in 1945 and 1946, and a near-record freeze in 1947, food shortages swept across Europe. The equally desperate need to repair war-damaged transportation and manufacturing capacity made it even harder to address shortages of food and consumer goods.[35]

These responsibilities fell to the occupiers. The British borrowed money from the US to import wheat and potatoes to northwestern Germany; the costs of occupation far exceeded the reparations to which the British were entitled. The US was also unhappy: "the unconditional surrender of Germany . . . has left us with the sole responsibility for a section of Germany which has never been economically self-supporting in modern times and the capacity of which for self-support has been catastrophically reduced,"

32. Judge and Langdon, *Cold War*, 15.
33. Judt, *Postwar*, 136.
34. Judt, *Postwar*, 131.
35. On French and European postwar economic malaise, see Judt, *Postwar*, 86–93.

observed Kennan.³⁶ In an effort to alleviate this absurd situation—to enable the Germans to come closer to supporting themselves—the US and British broke their Yalta obligations by suspending reparations from their zones of Germany (to the Soviet Union and everywhere else), and combining their zones into an economic Bizone in 1946. But the Soviet Union and France, Hitler's direct victims, still wanted their reparations.

Shortages contributed to a mood of depression—a potentially dangerous indicator of a return of political extremism. After another bad winter, working class living standards in Paris had actually declined since liberation, to about 50 percent of prewar levels in the spring of 1947. Janet Flanner wrote in the *New Yorker* of "a climate of indubitable and growing malaise in Paris, and perhaps all over Europe, as if the French people, or all European people, expected something to happen, or, worse, expected nothing to happen."³⁷ Kennan, too, commented on Europe's "profound exhaustion of physical plant and spiritual vigor."³⁸

To avert this looming crisis, US Secretary of State George Marshall put forward his game-changing proposal. In a commencement speech at Harvard in June 1947 he proposed to replace the failing program of emergency loans with a program of American *grants*, which war-damaged countries could use for longer-term investments of their own design. The Marshall Plan would provide its intended benefits, and a few more.³⁹

First, the use of grants intentionally deviated from the crippling debt financing used in the 1920s, which had the effect of deflating Western European economies. Second, the plan required the recipients to coordinate their large-scale economic planning, since it would have made little sense for each country to use the funds to rebuild their steel industries all at once. Cleverly, the aid was delivered in goods, which the recipients could then sell to generate cash: it stimulated the US economy and made recipients more creditworthy trading partners. Third, Marshall Plan aid proved to be large enough to restore economic confidence.

I have never liked using the word *confidence* in this way, as it implies that economic problems can be solved with a change of attitude, a punch in the shoulder, or little bit of Prozac. What actually changes is the direction of fear: a critical mass of economic actors becomes more worried

36. Judt, *Postwar*, 123.
37. Judt, *Postwar*, 89.
38. Judt, *Postwar*, 89.
39. Stone, *Atlantic*, 57–59; Judt, *Postwar*, 96–98.

about missing future opportunities than about a future recession. A store manager, long burdened by bad checks or excess inventory, might suddenly face the prospect of running out of the latest appliances and losing customers to rivals. American millennials gave this attitude an acronym, FOMO, fear of missing out. FOMO doesn't even require that most of the pessimists change their minds, only that there be a meaningful increase in the number of boom-expecting actors and in the amounts those actors are willing to put at risk. If enough of those early adopters succeed (to use another phrase that came along much later), the change in behavior will ripple through the economy.

As it turned out, the Marshall Plan worked, and just as important, was seen to have worked. In early 1949, French Finance Minister Maurice Petsche celebrated the influx of fuel, wheat, and cotton, "a great lifting of the heart goes from us toward the generous American people and toward its leaders."[40] Those were the Marshall Plan's intended and foreseeable consequences. The unintended consequences included creation of the precursors to the European Union and the further isolation of the Soviet bloc.

9. A UNANIMOUS DECISION

Long before a dollar of aid emerged, the Marshall Plan also turned the Soviet Union down the road to disaster. Despite Stalin's refusal to join Bretton Woods, Marshall proposed to include Eastern European countries (not quite yet a bloc) and the Soviet Union in his aid plan.[41] This was certainly a calculated risk on Marshall's part—how it would have flown in Congress is anyone's guess—but a shrewd one. If the offer had only been extended to Western European countries, Stalin would have accused the US of seeking to buy alliances and to undermine Communism: he could have painted the US as the party dropping the Iron Curtain. And there was a low risk of complications. Marshall had to believe that Stalin wasn't any more likely to accept Western aid than he was to change his mind about Bretton Woods.

Yet the offer was not entirely insincere. Things weren't going well diplomatically by 1947, it is true, but further conferences about Germany were still scheduled. Moreover, the Soviet Union and Eastern Europe could very much have used the aid. The nationalist Uncle Joe of World War II would gladly have accepted additional aid to restore his weakened and besieged

---

40. Flanner, *Paris Journal*, 98.
41. Stone, *Atlantic*, 40; Patterson, *Grand Expectations*, 129–31.

homeland. So, the offer can also be seen as an invitation to restart or reframe the relationship and a second chance for Stalin to participate in the European trade relations.

Stalin was not amused. His response to Marshall's olive branch set a precedent that no later leader dared violate. When invited to Paris to discuss Marshall Plan implementation in June 1947, most Communist-dominated governments of Eastern Europe correctly saw Soviet disinterest as a signal to decline. But Jan Masaryk, the non-communist foreign minister of Czechoslovakia's coalition government, promptly accepted the Franco-British invitation. This response had to be immediately walked back. Although the Red Army did not occupy Czechoslovakia at the time, Czech leaders were summoned to a meeting with Stalin himself and then issued a statement: "Czechoslovak participation would be construed as an act directed against friendship with the Soviet Union and the rest of our allies. That is why the government unanimously decided it will not take part in this conference."[42] That "unanimously" was an especially nice touch.

Now Stalin had twice sharply rejected Western, specifically Anglo-American, economic programs. He had forced his Czech "allies" to very publicly reverse their position on American aid, explicitly attributing their change of attitude to the demands of Moscow's friendship.[43] (The unfortunate Masaryk would fall out of a window in Prague's foreign ministry the next year.[44]) Stalin well knew that his country lagged far behind the United States in industrial capability and sheer wealth and but for the war would have lagged Britain, Germany, and France as well. Yet he had refused aid and trading relations and now plainly intended to isolate Eastern Europe as well. It appeared to be nothing more than a perverse assertion of his political supremacy.

Stalin was certainly a tyrant, but there was more to his strategy than mere opposition. A true believer and a serious scholar of Marxism, he seems to have believed that capitalism would either advance toward revolution or degenerate into another war between greedy imperialists.[45] Thus Bretton Woods and the Marshall Plan were especially insidious, apparently generous efforts to undermine socialism in its secure homeland. As we have seen, wiping out mere liberals, mere apologists for capitalism, was a central tenet

42. Judt, *Postwar*, 92.
43. Brown, *Rise and Fall*, 156–57; Zubok, *Failed Empire*, 72.
44. Stone, *Atlantic*, 53–54.
45. Zubok, *Failed Empire*, 17–18, 20; Gaddis, *Cold War*, 38.

of Marxist doctrine and Leninist political tactics; in fact, Stalin would soon redouble his efforts in that direction. (One imagines him in a soliloquy: "It's my own fault, really, for being too nice.")

Stalin both misunderstood and miscalculated. He misunderstood the economics. Isolating his bloc was profoundly demotivating. A shopkeeper in Budapest would never have to worry about losing customers to a rival who stocked Belgian chocolate; an East German electronics manufacturer would likewise never be concerned about gaining market share in Cleveland. Participation in Europe's postwar economy would have greatly reduced incentives for East German emigration as well, the very public embarrassment that eventually required a prison wall. Accepting Marshall aid would not have been completely consistent with Marxist philosophy, but Lenin had shown significant flexibility when the country had been in dire economic straights. "It doesn't matter if the cat is black or white," the Chinese Communist reformer Deng Xiaoping would later say, "if it catches mice, it is a good cat." This was not to be Stalin's path.

He also miscalculated, in that the western countries proved willing and able to work together in a common cause, motivated in no small part by his own actions. Having been caught off guard by Marshall's calculated offer of generosity, Stalin promptly convened European Communist Party leaders, western and eastern, in Szklarska Poreba, Poland, in September 1947, to get everyone on the same page via the new Cominform.[46] No longer would the party tolerate "rightist" deviations, like that of Masaryk, or "Titoist" deviations—Yugoslav leader Marshall Tito's independent effort to set up a personality cult. The hard line straightjacketed the western Communist parties, which lost both their independence and their credibility as advocates for their own nations' interests. It also provided George Orwell with further inspiration for Newspeak—a language constructed to allow for no negative sentiments about the fictional totalitarian regime—when he wrote his most famous novel the next year, its title inverting the last two digits of 1948.

10. JUDGMENT AT PARIS

It was a considerable political accomplishment to catch Stalin out.[47] This achievement would not have had long-lasting consequences, however, if

---

46. Judt, *Postwar*, 143–44.
47. Gaddis, *Cold War*, 44.

Anglo-American plans for European self-sufficiency had not worked. For American allies to regain their economic independence, the goal of punishing Germany would be subordinated to a restoration of trade, of the intra-European division of labor that had preceded the world wars. Specifically, the French would have to work with the Germans. And that was a problem.

In the postwar condominium over Germany, France's position had been closer to Russia's. French leaders sought to extract additional reparations from Germany, while restricting its re-industrialization and forbidding rearmament; recognizing a new and independent state was a nonstarter. This was not an unreasonable position, as France had been even more thoroughly abused than Russia. Three German invasions in the past seventy-five years had resulted in crushing military defeats in 1870 and 1940; near-defeat turned into a Pyrrhic victory in 1918, and only with the help of powerful allies; four years of terror under Marshall Petain's puppet government, ended only by the Allies' liberation in 1944.

French hostility to German restoration went deeper than merely logical security concerns. An American army psychologist wrote in his diary in 1945 that, to the French, Belgians, and Russians, "the only good Germans are dead Germans."[48] After liberation, French vigilante groups, often composed of *résistantialistes* whose support for the resistance had often been recent in origin, had taken revenge on suspected German collaborators.[49] And there was acute sensitivity to France's sudden dependence on the US and Britain for economic and military security, as well as its new status as a second-tier power. Nowhere was this sensitivity made clearer than in General DeGaulle's speech to liberated Paris in August 1944:

> Paris! Paris humiliated! Paris broken! Paris martyrized! But Paris liberated! Liberated by itself, by its own people with the help of the armies of France, with the support and aid of France as a whole, of fighting France, of the only France, of the true France, of eternal France.[50]

For DeGaulle, who had spent much of the war in England, this was more than just slipping free from dependency on the much-resented US and British; he needed to proclaim that the French people could still stand—were already standing—on their own.

---

48. Judt, *Postwar*, 100.
49. Rousso, *Vichy Syndrome*, 28.
50. Rousso, *Vichy Syndrome*, 16.

As we have seen, however, the reality was that France had fallen into a near-depression by 1947 and was temporarily rejuvenated by the announcement of the Marshall Plan. But the political situation remained extremely tense. As Rosemary Wakeman has written, French Communists, a major political force in the Paris region, protested vehemently against American anti-communism. When they were kicked out of the French cabinet in May 1947, after the breakdown in negotiations with the Soviet Union over Germany, the Communists staged major strikes throughout the rest of the year, culminating in a violent march led by Renault factory workers at Vel d'Hiv on November 22. They derided the Marshall Plan as "Coca-colonisation."[51]

By March 1948, the British and Americans had given up on dealing with Stalin and wanted to move quickly to put their European recovery plans into effect. In London, they pushed through a Six-Party Agreement to establish a unified West German state, which would be able to participate in the Marshall Plan.

Inevitably, French Communists and Gaullist nationalists adamantly opposed the London accord from opposite sides of the political spectrum. Janet Flanner reported that the Communists had "plastered the boulevards with a Party poster, which, for once, was generally popular: 'L'Allemagne d'Abord? Non!'" This sentiment was hardly confined to the political extremes. Flanner observed that the Six-Power plan left many French feeling that "France figures not as one-sixth but as one-twelfth." "Most frightening of all," she continued, "any plan for unifying western Germany instead of isolating each of its provinces, reminds them of Germany's organizing genius, which Parisians can see at work again, as it was during the Occupation, simply by shutting their eyes, and can hear, like an echo of the rhythm of Nazi feet along the Champs-Élysées."[52]

These sentiments were so strong that the cabinet instructed Foreign Minister Georges Bidault to withdraw from the London agreement in May 1948, throwing the entire recovery plan into jeopardy. Even with additional security guarantees from the US and UK, Bidault's politically exposed French government felt they needed to seek approval of the National Assembly.

With obvious reluctance, Bidault rebuffed criticisms from the Socialist Party within his governing coalition. "There is not the slightest chance of combining the benefits of Marshall Aid and the rejection of Germany which would all the same conform to fifty percent of our desires. There are

---

51. Wakeman, *Heroic City*, 108–9, 119–22.
52. Flanner, *Paris Journal*, 88.

moments when it is necessary to know how to act to bring things to an end. If we want to act alone, we will lose everything."[53]

Having narrowly held the cabinet together and holding little hope of success, Bidault then took his case to the Assembly. "His three years of peace as France's leading diplomat of the younger generation," observed Janet Flanner, "seemed to have cost him more than the long years of war, during which he functioned as . . . the bold and successful chief of the underground forces in France." He argued that France would gain some benefit from the London accords, despite serious shortcomings; again, he put the real issue more starkly: that the Assembly must choose between cooperation with close friends and international isolation. Flanner gave American readers a timeless description of the proceedings, which it seemed could only have taken place in Paris. "As the talk grew more tense, the daytime hours did not suffice for it, and Deputies took to arguing all night and voting at dawn; in all Paris, for those hours, only Parliament and the Montmartre night clubs were up and hard at it, with some of the city's few taxis working both stands, carrying the dissimilar, tired stragglers home."[54]

In the end, the Socialists within the governing coalition held the deciding votes. On June 17, 1948, they swung the vote in favor of the London agreement (citing their objections as future negotiating points), simultaneously choosing to keep the coalition government together and to keep France allied with the western bloc.[55] The final vote was 297–289.

Tony Judt later characterized French leaders as having accepted a "'European' solution to France's German problem," in effect neutralizing Germany by harnessing it to a collective project. "In those three years France had, in effect, to come to terms with the abrupt negation of three hundred years of history. In the circumstances this was no small achievement."[56] Norman Stone went even further, calling the vote "one of the deciding moments of French history, in that the main danger was now recognized as Soviet, and the way forward, the elaboration of a pan-European system which the French would have a hand in managing."[57]

53. Eisenberg, *Drawing the Line*, 403.
54. Flanner, *Paris Journal*, 89–90.
55. Eisenberg, *Drawing the Line*, 169–70, 208, 395–403.
56. Judt, *Postwar*, 117.
57. Stone, *Atlantic*, 64.

11. THE BORDERS HARDEN

Within a week of the French vote, West Germany was formed and introduced its own currency. Stalin again overreacted, cutting off entry into West Berlin (which was surrounded by overwhelming Red Army forces). The US and Britain responded with the famous Berlin Airlift, flying in supplies for almost a year before Stalin, fearful of starting a war over the issue, backed down.[58] Still, he'd drawn his borders and boxed himself in with his allies.

These decisions did not preordain the collapse of the Soviet empire in 1989. Stalin's successor, Nikita Khrushchev, who disavowed much of Stalin's legacy, and Khrushchev's successors could have made different decisions in their own rights. Instead, they doubled down on Stalin's view of empire and economics. They used the Red Army to quell uprisings in Budapest in 1956 and Prague in 1968; they solved the crisis of emigration out of East Germany by building fortified border walls not only in Berlin (1961) but around the entire country. And despite the evident futility of Khrushchev's promise to catch up to the US GDP per capita by 1970,[59] they never gave up on central planning. In 1964, the economist Abel Aganbegyan made a wry counterprediction that the entire population would need to work full time on rebalancing the ever more complex annual economic plan by 1980.[60] By then, the plan itself had become the subjects of widespread jokes: "The plan is fulfilled, but there is nothing in the shops."[61]

It was no sure thing, either, that the Western alliance, reflected in organizations like NATO and the precursors of the European Union and World Trade Organization, would stay together. The US in particular made a number of strategic errors, the worst of which was Vietnam. But those mistakes did not make the Soviet system any more palatable. Left and right would always agree on that, if not always for the same reasons. The Soviets lost their bet that the capitalist countries would fragment or collapse.

Stalin emphatically decided to isolate his new empire, physically and economically. He chose the losing strategy that his successors continued for decades, and that Gorbachev attempted, unsuccessfully, to escape.

---

58. Zubok, *Failed Empire*, 76; Stone, *Atlantic*, 66–67; Gaddis, *Cold War*, 46.
59. Brown, *Rise and Fall*, 256.
60. Spufford, *Red Plenty*, 219, 398.
61. Figes, *Revolutionary Russia*, 267.

Nguyen Ai Quoc (Ho Chi Minh), French Communist Party Congress, Tours, France, 1920. After US President Wilson and the other World War I victors ignored pleas for self-determination from both China and Vietnam, Ho turned to Communism as a way to oppose French colonialism.

Credit: U.S. National Archives, "Remembering Vietnam" exhibition, November 10, 2017—February 28, 2019. Photographer unknown.

2

Vietnam
A Half-Remembered Tragedy

By 1995, the liveliest bar in Saigon was Apocalypse Now.[1]

With admirable economy, the bar's owners managed a gentle dig at America's infamous military defeat by giving a nod to its ongoing cultural dominance, trivializing both by using the iconic movie name to sell alcohol. If anyone could fully appreciate the wicked ironies of war, even those of victory, he or she would be southern Vietnamese.

Great, ostentatious—even its making-of documentary, *Hearts of Darkness*, makes best movie lists—Francis Ford Coppola's *Apocalypse Now* was only the first among equals.[2] By my authoritative count, at least six other outstanding Vietnam War movies came out of Hollywood within a dozen years of war's end. Almost all are stories about anti-heroes: men placed in morally difficult situations by a distant or misguided higher authority, men who sometimes behave badly for reasons that we (the audience) nevertheless understand. Their alternatives look worse. Parallels with the larger American experience in Vietnam were not hard to see.

The big-screen images, though fictional, also resonated with audiences by reviving wartime feelings of anger and frustration, a sort of gallows nostalgia. We remember how it was for us. That's fine; no one wants to repeat the experience.

1. Karnow, *Vietnam*, 47.
2. Schneider, *1001 Movies*, 652–53, 808–9.

But neither the movies nor the still-echoing political recriminations of the 1960s and 1970s tell us much about how the tragedy arose, or how it might have been avoided.

1. VIETNAM IN HOLLYWOOD

The movies really were great, though.

First, and in some ways the most influential, was Robert Altman's *M*A*S*H* (1970). Nominally set in the Korean War but shot in a tropical setting and released at the peak of domestic unhappiness with Vietnam, *M*A*S*H* is less a story than a series of episodes in which capable, smart-ass Ivy League surgeons get laid and break rules made by their slow-witted bureaucratic superiors. (Its theme and tone echo earlier antiwar satires, Joseph Heller's *Catch-22* and Berthold Brecht's *Mother Courage and Her Children*.) The only thing resembling a plot involves a suicidal surgeon who recovers after a night in the sack with an empathetic but rather easily manipulated nurse. Altman lets us in on the joke: the acting credits—for the likes of Donald Sutherland, Eliot Gould, and Sally Kellerman—are announced over the army camp loudspeaker. The film's cynicism is salvaged only by its sense of humor and by our identification with the wise guys who know the whole game is pointless.

One might have thought that this edgy, arty film would have a narrow audience. To the contrary. Its TV sequel, a half-hour sitcom complete with the movie's intentionally cloying theme song, "Suicide Is Painless," ranked among the most popular series over its eleven year run, from 1972 to 1983. The era of the popular anti-hero had begun.

The first major Vietnam movie released after war's end was *Coming Home* (1978). In this formally conventional love triangle, a gung-ho military officer, his stateside wife, and a paraplegic war veteran (Bruce Dern, Jane Fonda, and Jon Voight) each wrestle with the moral and ethical issues of *this* war, reflected in personal damage (physical disability, infidelity, alcoholism). Because the characters do begin to come to terms with their trauma and anger, *Coming Home* has a redemptive quality absent in the other films—and absent in America itself.

That same year, *The Deer Hunter* told a much larger and more troubling story. The film begins with a long establishing sequence about the lives and aspirations of young, blue-collar guys of Slavic descent in mountainous western Pennsylvania. It then abruptly jumps to the boys "in country," fighting heroically, being injured and captured by the enemy. Eventually the survivors return to Pennsylvania, their lives' possibilities much reduced. Although criticized for its factual liberties (the crucial scenes of Russian roulette in NVA prison camps were metaphors at best), the film was the first to portray the war's effects on individuals without political predispositions. It is nevertheless clear by the end that the strongest survivor (Robert DeNiro) started out as the deadliest hunter.

Famously late, overbudget, and even further from historical reality, *Apocalypse Now* (1979) follows a hardened young officer (Martin Sheen) on a secret mission far upriver, beyond where the Army is authorized to go. His imperious superiors have ordered him to relieve Colonel Kurtz (Marlon Brando), who has gone rogue and set himself up as absolute ruler of the local *montagnard* population, with extreme prejudice. During this violent odyssey, loosely paralleling Joseph Conrad's *Heart of Darkness*, the younger officer realizes that the Army's mission itself has corrupted Kurtz and will corrupt him as well. "The horror, the horror," whispers the dying Kurtz. It's an accusation as well as a warning.

The last films backgrounded character and plot for hyper-realism. Oliver Stone's *Platoon* (1986) put the audience on the ground, slogging through the jungle right behind the unlucky soldier walking point that day. There is a storyline, left unresolved, in which a fresh private (Charlie Sheen, of all people) must choose between the methods of the platoon's two charismatic leaders; one (Willem Dafoe) tries to do war the right way, following the rules he thinks govern the fighting and agonizing over life and death decisions, while the other (Tom Berenger) does whatever he thinks necessary to survive. But the film's biggest star was its cinematography: I remember emerging from the theater shaken from the primitive mines exploding at close range and tracer bullets whizzing past me. There was no time for judicious reflection on those trails.

In *Full Metal Jacket* (1987), Stanley Kubrick juxtaposed two stories connected by one character, Joker (Matthew Modine), and implicitly by cause-and-effect. The first features R. Lee Ermey as a Marine training instructor, a Shakespeare of verbal abuse, who succeeds in making his recruits into killing machines but drives the weakest of them to a murder-suicide. The second finds Joker, a *Stars and Stripes* reporter, assigned to write a feel-good piece about a mission to retake an ancient capital city, building by building; it, too, ends with lives pointlessly wasted. The audience gets breathtakingly little with which to identify, much less empathize.

The hoodlums of Kubrick's *A Clockwork Orange* have shaved and joined the US Army.

What can we conclude from this remarkable string of movies? Vietnam, certainly, was a potent setting for American tragedy and satire. It drew some of the most important director/auteurs of the era, their careers well established, to take great formal and financial risks on stories that substantially overlapped and competed for the same audience. They cast established stars like Sutherland, Gould, Fonda, DeNiro, and Brando, and launched many careers: Meryl Streep, Christopher Walken, Charlie Sheen, Dafoe, Berenger, and Modine. (To say nothing of TV's Alan Alda, who may not even have been acting.) They won Oscars. *The Deer Hunter* and *Platoon* were Best Pictures; Fonda, Voigt, and Walken won acting awards. *Apocalypse Now*, largely passed over by a Vietnam-weary Academy, appears on almost everyone's GOAT list. Even with their grim stories and unlikable characters, they were commercially successful. Much of the American public wanted or needed to see these films.

We had a lot to work through. During the period of direct US military intervention, 1965–73, Vietnam was by far the biggest domestic political issue. Unlike the Cold War, of which it was a peripheral part, Vietnam was domestically divisive and not susceptible to consensus solutions. Yet the films don't seek to answer the question of where things went off the rails. The official decisions that put the characters in difficult situations take place offscreen; audience familiarity is largely assumed.

Instead, the films succeed by personalizing the tragedy and the hubris and by acknowledging the impossibility of the situation the soldiers found themselves in. In *Apocalypse Now*, for example, the protagonist can either follow his orders to murder the mutinous, corrupted Kurtz (thereby following in Kurtz's footsteps) or acquiesce in Kurtz's brutal regime. The young soldier of *Platoon* sees his paths as those of brutality or of unreasonable, unknowable risk. The surgeons of *M*A*S*H* may act like frat boys, but only after sewing up unspeakable wounds. Even the gung-ho officer in *Coming Home* is in the end a victim of circumstances beyond his control.

This is a crucial point of all of these films: it was not the ordinary soldiers' fault. Whether due to enemy brutality or incompetent leadership, no one could have succeeded in those situations and no one could come out undamaged. By extension, the war itself was, for America, an ugly, wasteful exercise with no redeeming value. The films instead valorize their charismatic anti-heroes. But these characters may make it a little too easy to break rules: not every situation poses a choice between behaving badly and behaving worse. From there, it's a short path to Rambo—and to My Lai and Abu Ghraib. Anti-heroes don't relieve us of the duty to agonize over life and death decisions.

Then there is a seventh great movie: *The Killing Fields* (1984). An American reporter and his translator decide not to evacuate when the Khmers Rouges take control of Cambodia. Armed teenaged soldiers rule the streets of Phnom Penh while Maoist leaders proclaim the Year Zero. The sobered journalists get the hell out. The movie, based on a true story, follows the capture, "re-education," and escape of the Cambodian translator, including his unforgettable passage through a rice paddy littered with hundreds of skulls. The horror, indeed. But it doesn't fit the model of the other films. There's a hero, for one thing. And he is a fully realized Asian character, played by Hiang Ngor, in an Oscar winning role.[3]

2. QUESTIONS OF PERSPECTIVE

Movies may especially color the memories of Americans too young to have served in or debated Vietnam, that is, anyone born after about 1955. I turned eighteen in 1975, fortunate not to have faced the agonizing choices of young men just a few years older, who could be drafted, much less the traumatic experiences of those who did serve. At the time, one could hardly find a middle ground between those who believed the US should persevere and support the troops on the official mission and those who turned against this particular war as impracticable or immoral.

These debates continue as history, and turn on unanswerable questions:

- Was Vietnam of strategic importance in the Cold War?
- Were the South Vietnamese governments of President Diem and his successors effective and worthy allies?
- Should the US have declared and fought an unlimited war against North Vietnam?
- Could a more intelligent counterinsurgency strategy, similar to that practiced by General Abrams after 1968 (as troop levels declined), have led to a different result?

3. I saw each of these movies in original theatrical release, except *Full Metal Jacket*, and have seen some several times. I did, however, refresh my recollection of cast and plot points with online sources and confirmed Oscar details on the Academy website.

These issues, important as they are, focus on the US portion of a multinational humanitarian disaster. The names of over 58,000 American dead are inscribed in polished black granite on the hauntingly beautiful Vietnam Memorial in Washington. The long wall gradually descends from street level and reemerges some four hundred feet later, the names and distance at once personalizing and demonstrating the magnitude of the losses.[4]

In addition, on the order of 3.5 million Vietnamese, soldiers and civilians, died on both sides of the conflicts of 1945–79.[5] We will never know the exact number, much less the names, of these casualties, about 10 percent of the entire Vietnamese population of the time. In raw numbers, this is roughly fifty times the US figure, ten times the American losses in World War II, five times those of the US Civil War. The Khmers Rouges also killed perhaps two million of their fellow Cambodians. All these lives, and many others, were sacrificed in conflicts that everyone, somehow, lost: the French, Americans, Cambodians, Vietnamese non-communists and, eventually, Vietnamese Communists as well.

Of course, no one wanted this to happen. Discussing his very dark and very funny novel, *The Sympathizer*, Viet Thanh Nguyen remembered that he was tempted to focus blame on the Americans—and he does include a wicked send-up of Coppola—but he wrote a more interesting story instead.

> Everybody in this book, especially our [Vietnamese] protagonist, is guilty of some kind of terrible behavior. For me, the ability to acknowledge that we are all both human and inhuman at the same time is really critical because that acknowledgement characterizes dominant culture. For example, in American movies about the Vietnam war, Americans want to be on screen regardless of whether they have to be villains or antiheroes. It's much better to be able to do that than to be the virtuous human extra in the margins. . . . Being able to present a narrator who's both human and inhuman was my way of challenging our subordination in dominant culture.[6]

But if all sides behaved badly, the historical problem is less about who is to blame than how such circumstances arose. Could this tragedy have been averted? To address that question, we must acknowledge that people

---

4. Vietnam Veterans Memorial Fund, "About the Wall."
5. Karnow, *Vietnam*, 59; Goscha, *Vietnam*, 372.
6. Nguyen, *Sympathizer*, 398–99 (author interview).

believed they had good reasons for acting as they did at the time. We might have done no better.

3. ARMS AND RACE

"Political power grows out of the barrel of a gun."[7] Mao's epigram is unprincipled, brutal, and pragmatic. And, possibly, his takeaway from the prior century of European involvement in East Asia. Colonialism did not just trigger the Vietnam conflicts; it was a living memory in every Vietnamese family. The more educated knew it as a bitter lesson repeated over and over in East Asia.

It was the repetition of external force that mattered, not which nations were doing it. Americans thought of themselves as reformers, but by the mid-twentieth century it didn't matter which flag flew over one's battleship.

The British had led the way. In response to Lord Macartney's 1793 trade mission to Beijing, the Qing dynasty Emperor Qianlong had written: "We have never valued ingenious articles, nor do we have the slightest need of your country's manufactures."[8] This was not a farsighted policy, to be sure, but in the short run it greatly advantaged China, which could demand silver in exchange for Chinese silks and porcelain. The need to pay in silver created a huge balance of payments problem for European importers.

Opium was Britain's substitute. Imported from colonial India, deliveries of opium skyrocketed from four thousand chests per year in 1800 to forty thousand in the late 1830s (at about 150 pounds/chest). When the Chinese government took serious countermeasures, destroying half a year's trade at Canton, British Foreign Secretary Lord Palmerston responded decisively with modern warships. The 1842 Treaty of Nanjing gave the British five treaty ports, the then-barren island of Hong Kong, monetary reparations, and a most-favored-nation entitlement to any favors later granted to others, of whom there would be many, including the US.[9] This and later humiliations ended only after World War II. The next leader of a unified, sovereign China would be Mao Zedong in 1949.

With this example in mind, US Admiral Matthew Perry sailed a black battleship into Edo (Tokyo) harbor in 1854, which persuaded the astute Japanese to open their ports to trade. The British used superior firepower

---

7. Karnow, *Vietnam*, 416.
8. Spence, *Search*, 122–23.
9. Spence, *Search*, 128–29 (opium trade), 148–49 (Treaty of Nanjing).

to suppress the 1857 rebellion in India. The Dutch colonized Indonesia; the Spanish and then the US controlled the Philippines. Japanese elites replaced the isolationist shogunate with the Meiji emperor in 1868, in order to industrialize on a European model. Japan's modernized military soon defeated its much larger neighbors China (1894–95) and Russia (1904–05), and annexed Korea as a virtual colony (1910).

Meanwhile, the French government first officially entered Indochina in 1858, to protect Christian missionaries and settlers. Like other outnumbered colonizers, they did not hesitate to use superior firepower. After French forces defeated Nguyen defenders in a one-sided battle at Thuan An in 1883, the diplomat Jules Harmand minced no words in proposing the Treaty of Hue, making Tonkin (northern Vietnam) a French protectorate:

> Now, here is a fact which is quite certain; you are at our mercy. We have the power to seize and destroy your capital and to cause you all to die of starvation. You have to choose between war and peace. We do not wish to conquer you, but you must accept our protectorate. For your people it is a guarantee of peace and prosperity; it is also the only chance of survival for your government and your Court. We give you forty-eight hours to accept or reject, in their entirety and without discussion, the terms which in our magnanimity we offer you. We are convinced there is nothing in them dishonorable to you, and, if carried out with sincerity on both sides, they will bring happiness to the people of Vietnam. If you reject them, you must expect the greatest evils. Imagine the most frightful things conceivable, and you will still fall short of the truth. The Dynasty, its Princes and its Court will have pronounced sentence on themselves. The name of Vietnam will no longer exist in history.[10]

As in British-controlled India, French governance left important positive legacies, especially in industry, infrastructure, and education. Both Ho Chi Minh and Diem Ngo Dinh benefited from education in French-founded schools. But such benefits came with a price. The tiny French population, just thirty-five thousand in the early 1940s,[11] could hardly have ruled this region alone. They relied heavily on local allies, including a powerful minority of converted Catholics who were resented by many others. A British India hand, circa 1907, recognized similarities. "Like ourselves . . . the

---

10. Goscha, *Vietnam*, 69–70.
11. Goscha, *Vietnam*, 161.

French have gone forward with the Bible in one hand and the Gatling gun in the other, and if the native did not accept one he got the other."[12]

Americans behaved differently, somewhat. Perry had "opened" Japan without actually firing his cannons; US Secretary of State John Hay helped to end the anti-foreigner Boxer Rebellion in China in 1901, and Teddy Roosevelt had mediated the end of the Russo-Japanese war (1906). The US had also kicked the Spanish out of the Philippines in 1898 but, deciding that Filipinos were unable to govern themselves, used brutal counterinsurgency methods to suppress their independence movement.

Real disappointment with America started after World War I. Hoping to prevent future conflict, President Wilson had advanced his Fourteen Points, including the principle of self-determination. Citing this principle, would-be regional leaders from around the globe came to Paris in 1919 to plead their cases for independence (and favorable border-drawing).

In one of their most consequential mistakes, the ill-prepared Big Four (the US, Britain, France, and Italy) awarded Germany's treaty possessions in the Shandong peninsula to Japan, despite China's eloquent and well-grounded appeal for restoration of its historic province. The decision reflected the triumph of power over principle on at least two levels. First, the Japanese had aided the Allies, in a manner of speaking, by occupying Germany's undefended Asian holdings early in the war, and they had forced the Chinese government into a secret treaty acknowledging Japanese rights in Shandong. The Big Four thus effectively ratified Japan's military power play. Second, Japan had proposed a racial equality clause that seemed entirely consistent with the Fourteen Points. Britain vetoed it, to placate immigration-fearing Australia and New Zealand, which had contributed vitally to Britain's war effort. (US leaders breathed a silent sigh of relief.) That veto gave Japan leverage to threaten to walk out if it had been denied Shandong as well.[13] These decisions revealed European and American priorities hidden behind the Fourteen Points: color first, followed by military might.

Demonstrations erupted after this news reached China, on May 4, 1919. The nationalist Guomindang Party and the nascent Chinese Communist Party rallied together under the flag of the May 4 Movement until their split in 1927.

A second mistake was of omission. A young Indochinese leader in Paris wrote Wilson several times, in English, to ask for a meeting to discuss

---

12. Sidel, *Old Hanoi*, 15.
13. MacMillan, *Peacemakers*, 331–53.

independence. Wilson ignored his letters. Only the Communists, Ho Chi Minh would decide, could help him do away with imperialism.[14]

Ho was wrong, but only about the Communists.

4. CREATING VIETNAM

In his recent history, Christopher Goscha emphasizes that the country we now know as Vietnam had existed in its present form for just forty-four years before 1975, all but six months of which were in the early 1800s.[15] For almost two thousand years, the region was split among rival principalities. The northern region was often a tributary of China; the south loosely connected with Thailand or even India by ships plying the Spice Route. This history reminds me of the Balkans, where small independent states were so often overwhelmed in the back and forth among the Habsburgs, Ottomans, and Russians.[16]

The French colonial administration divided the region as well, into five colonies: Cochinchina (southern Vietnam, including Saigon), Annam (central Vietnam, including Hue), Tonkin (northern Vietnam, the Red River region including Hanoi and Haiphong), Laos, and Cambodia.[17] In addition, the ethnically diverse groups, whom the French called *montagnards*, continued to maintain separate identities in mountainous border region of north and central Vietnam, Laos, and Cambodia.[18] This configuration even continued through World War II, because Japan allowed the Nazi-allied French Vichy government to remain in Indochina. Only after France's liberation did the Japanese army occupy Indochina in March 1945. In the vacuum created by Japan's surrender that August, Ho Chi Minh proclaimed the Democratic Republic of Vietnam (DRV) in Hanoi on September 2, 1945.[19]

It was an audacious move. Ho was practically inventing a new country. And we have to give him credit: Though Communism would be discredited, Ho's vision of the country motivated millions to make great sacrifices, and it is that country that abides today. Ho was a giant figure of the twentieth

14. Karnow, *Vietnam*, 133–34.
15. Goscha, *Vietnam*, 3–4.
16. Goscha, *Vietnam*, 12–44.
17. Goscha, *Vietnam*, 87.
18. Goscha, *Vietnam*, 87.
19. Goscha, *Vietnam*, 182.

century. Much more cosmopolitan than Stalin or Mao, Ho (a nom de guerre) was educated in a French lycée in Hanoi; spoke at least Vietnamese, French, English, Chinese (Mandarin and Cantonese), and Russian; traveled to Paris, London, New York, Moscow, Bangkok, and much of China; founded Communist parties in several countries; and, finally, inspired his followers to complete the country's unification.[20] As perhaps the only Communist leader ever to publicly walk back his own policies—the ill-fated land reforms of the 1950s—he might even have approved his successors' eventual abandonment of failed Soviet-style economic planning.

But it would be a mistake to romanticize Ho's movement, as some Westerners later did, largely in frustration over US policies. Ho had always expected to use force to expel the French and unite Vietnam's historically distinct regions. Ho's Viet Minh party also knew they would face resistance from Vietnamese Catholics and others who had thrived under the French. There would have been a civil war in any circumstances.

Besides, Ho was a real Communist. He likely chose Communism for pragmatic reasons—it offered a critique of colonialism that he needed—but he had assembled the regional Indochinese Communist Party in 1931 and had deep connections in the Soviet Union and with Chinese Communists from long before their triumph of 1949. Like Lenin and Mao, he leveraged the political potential of Communism to greater effect than its economic principles: its insistence on orthodoxy and conformity, its requirement of mass organization and group action. These counted as powerful weapons for a movement that often made do with purloined French muskets.

At the outset, the impoverished new country had to be concerned with both France and republican China (the Guomindang), which asserted traditional proprietary interests. Since Ho, like the pope, commanded no divisions, he made a provisional deal with the French in late 1945, simply because he thought they would be easier to defeat. He famously (perhaps apocryphally) explained: "I prefer to sniff French shit for five years than eat Chinese shit for the rest of my life."[21]

For all these reasons, war was inevitable in 1945. But the war that actually ensued, with the loss of three and half million lives, would have been unimaginable.

---

20. Lawrence, *Vietnam War*, 18–23; Karnow, *Vietnam*, 130–38.
21. Karnow, *Vietnam*, 169; Goscha, *Vietnam*, 205.

5. THIRTY YEARS OF BAD DECISIONS

The tragedies told in American films, set at the peak of US involvement but late in the longer war, raise this question above all others: Could the horror have been averted?

I don't think so. I mean that the people of the time, knowing what they knew and under the pressures they faced, followed a logic from which almost no one dissented in a timely way.

Tragedy was inevitable for two broad reasons. First, as noted, war on some scale was expected in Vietnam. Ho planned for an anti-colonial war from the outset, and that certainly included fighting with the French and French-allied Vietnamese. The DRV would in time become a garrison state, a modern Sparta whose principal purpose was war. The South, while more open, was highly factionalized and could only be held together by a military dictatorship and Cold War–inspired financing. The great powers' weapons made the conflagration much more deadly, but the building was already on fire.

Second, US policy—decisive in establishing and maintaining South Vietnam—was always driven by events outside of Vietnam. This would be true of many superpower relationships in the Third World. Vietnam just happened to be the place where the outcome was in play. And it was there that American leaders made an unerring string of bad decisions over thirty years.

Decision A: Supporting the French (1945–54)

At the end of World War II, as throughout its history, the US officially disfavored outright colonialism. Often enough the US had pursued its own quasi-colonial projects, in Central America and Hawaii, for example. But it had never participated in the scramble for Africa and, as we have seen, acted to moderate colonial practices in Asia. Most recently, it had recognized Philippine independence after World War II, giving up its only substantial holding outside the Caribbean. (It wasn't a partisan issue, either. Republican icon Douglas MacArthur was a firm supporter of Philippine independence; Eisenhower would thoroughly humiliate the French and British in their plot to retake control of the Suez Canal in 1956.)

Vietnam did not get that treatment. The reasons for this are complex and objectively understandable, but they had nothing at all to do with

Vietnam. France was a crucial but shaky ally in holding off Soviet expansion in Europe. The French government had barely, and with understandable reluctance, joined in Anglo-American plans to reopen trade with their recent enemies in western Germany. Dignity required all French parties—even the French Communists—to insist upon maintaining France's overseas empire and its *mission civilisatrice*.

That would explain US neutrality but would hardly have justified financing that reached 80 percent of French war expenses by 1954.[22] Mao's victory in 1949, however, and North Korea's invasion of South Korea nine months later, suddenly brought the Cold War to Asia. These events also gave US Republicans a rhetorical cudgel for years to come: "Who lost China?"

We can only speculate about opportunities that may have been lost during the French war in Vietnam, if the US had not financed the French. Non-communist, anti-colonialist Vietnamese leaders might have had a better chance to organize in the South. If Ho had needed less Soviet and Chinese aid, he might have followed a neutralist path like Marshall Tito in Yugoslavia. (Tito could take an independent line, to Stalin's everlasting irritation, because he'd achieved wartime victories and political leadership without Soviet assistance.) Moreover, neutrality became a desirable policy for many Third World leaders in the fifties.

These scenarios are hypothetical; my point is that US policy never gave them a chance. Given the political fallout over China and a hot war in Korea, paying French war expenses was a relatively low-cost, low-profile decision. A no-brainer, if you will.

Decision B: Forgoing Diplomacy (1954–59)

Having just concluded a painful and expensive stalemate in Korea, the Cold War powers pressured the Vietnam combatants to negotiate a truce at Geneva in 1954. French forces had just suffered an embarrassing defeat in the highlands at Dien Bien Phu, leaving them in a poor bargaining position. Ho, under pressure from his allies, reluctantly accepted partition of Vietnam at the seventeenth parallel, coupled with an international promise to hold nationwide elections within two years.

For the next several years, the two weak Vietnamese half-states focused on consolidating their internal political support, often violently. During this period, before the mass casualties, population displacements, and

---

22. Lawrence, *Vietnam War*, 42.

environmental destruction, serious opportunities may have been missed. Not so much because South Vietnam's Ngo Dinh Diem, to the Eisenhower administration's great relief, rejected the national elections called for in Geneva. Diem was simply concerned that the far better-known Ho would have won. But it's hard to imagine that any election held in that split country would have been free, fair, or widely acknowledged.

The international situation, however, offered possibilities. Soon after Stalin's death, the US, China, and Soviet Union worked out a truce in Korea, and the Soviet Union and China pressured Ho to accept partition. The two Vietnams looked inward, rather than on projecting power across the border. Most important, Soviet leader Khrushchev announced a reformist path in 1956. As late as 1957, the Soviets proposed that *both* Vietnamese states be admitted to the United Nations, that is, to give global recognition to the split-country compromise as in Germany and Korea.[23] This could only mean that Khrushchev would have pressured Ho to accept the legitimacy of the Republic of Vietnam—a deal that President Nixon and Secretary of State Kissinger would not come close to achieving in the much different circumstances of 1972. Ho would have had a hard time resisting Soviet persuasion; he needed modern Soviet weapons with a US-supplied enemy on his southern border.

Although we can see Khrushchev's offer as a missed opportunity, recognition was never remotely likely to be US policy at the time. Again, this had little to do with Vietnam. The US had not recognized Communist China, so the implications of recognizing North Vietnam would have been profound. And the Eisenhower administration presumably felt that US support for South Vietnam would make a diplomatic solution unnecessary.

Decision C: Deposing Diem; No Backup Plan (1959–63)

Ngo Dinh Diem returned from exile in 1954, with the symbolically important blessing of hereditary emperor (and European dilettante) Bao Dai, to lead the Republic of Vietnam. Catholic, well-educated, and free of Communist association, Diem proved willing to act decisively, and often harshly, to impose order on a diverse and fragmented population. Americans raved. Diem was a "tough miracle man" with a "deep religious heart" (*Life* magazine, 1957), and "the Winston Churchill of Asia" (Vice President

---

23. Lawrence, *Vietnam War*, 62; Karnow, *Vietnam*, 240.

Johnson, 1961).[24] Many observers came to disagree, regarding Diem as an isolated ruler who expected Confucian devotion from his subjects. He ignored constitutional principles and ruled through his brothers and his fashionable, outspoken sister-in-law (inevitably dubbed the Dragon Lady in the Western press).

The miracle did not last. When surviving southern Vietnamese Communists reorganized as the National Liberation Front ("Vietcong" to Americans), war flared up in the South after 1959. Over several years, the South Vietnamese army increasingly disappointed US military advisers. In 1963, Buddhists across the country mounted dramatic protests against his rule.[25] The US ambassador Henry Cabot Lodge and other officials hinted, winked, and nudged some of his generals toward the November 1, 1963, coup.[26]

While Diem's removal is generally seen as a mistake due to the ensuing chaos it caused, I had not thought of Diem himself as a major loss until I read *Triumph Forsaken*. The historian Mark Moyar contends that Diem's single-party approach to internal security was both appropriate for wartime and critical to retaining political support among a population that prized strength. He calls Diem's removal "one of the worst debacles in the history of American foreign relations."[27]

I wouldn't go quite that far. If Diem's *political* support required enforced loyalty, and if some Buddhist protesters were Communists, Americans were entitled to question his leadership methods and popular support. And the Pentagon Papers would later reveal that the US military and diplomatic corps always doubted South Vietnam's prospects. But I take Moyar's points that: with US aid, Diem retained significant support in the army and the population at large; much of the beleaguered population was likely to accept any leader who could provide some genuine security; and it was unrealistic (if not hypocritical) for Americans to expect Diem to behave like a liberal parliamentarian in the midst of a civil war.[28] In the circumstances, authorizing a military coup against Diem was at once the least democratic and most destabilizing course imaginable.

Moyar blames the American reversal mainly on Lodge, a prominent Republican whom Kennedy sent to Vietnam for the cynical purposes of

24. FitzGerald, *Fire in the Lake*, 72.
25. FitzGerald, *Fire in the Lake*, 129–34.
26. Moyar, *Triumph Forsaken*, 248–50, 256.
27. Moyar, *Triumph Forsaken*, 275.
28 Moyar, *Triumph Forsaken*, 275, 279–80.

sidelining his presidential candidacy in 1964 and neutralizing Vietnam as a campaign issue. By all accounts, Lodge was the crucial advocate for regime change but, as Moyar also points out, Kennedy and his advisers botched several chances to derail the operation, if that was what they meant to do.[29] "Never do business on a weekend," Kennedy advisor McGeorge Bundy remarked at one point,[30] in a postscript for the administration's clumsy management of the entire situation. Kennedy privately expressed shock over Diem's gangland-style murder the night of the coup, but it was a little late.[31]

As in *Macbeth*, the murder of a flawed ruler only led to worse. Diem may have failed to develop popular support—he seems to have found such activities beside the point—but no one else had any plausible claim to legitimacy. Worse, neither the plotters nor the Kennedy foreign policy team planned for the day after. The vacuum then pulled the military—the only institution with the power and resources to govern—into a two-year scramble for domestic power. Battlefield results did not improve. Eventually, two younger officers, Nguyen Van Thieu and Nguyen Cao Ky, assumed the presidency and vice presidency. Thieu and Ky held together a fragile coalition within the military at the cost of tolerating widespread corruption.

No South Vietnamese government ever escaped its lack of popular support or its resulting dependency on US arms and money.

Decision D: Stunted Development (1955–73)

While the US leadership spoke of winning the "hearts and minds" of Vietnamese civilians, it was military spending that changed South Vietnamese society. It was like the casinos arriving in tiny Las Vegas. Michigan State researcher Robert Scigliano reported that the US paid for all of South Vietnam's military spending and about 60 percent of its government budget over the period 1954–61—well before the Johnson-era escalation. The prioritization of this aid was stark: 78 percent went into the military budget; of the remaining 22 percent, 40 percent was spent on transportation. A twenty-mile highway from Saigon to Bien Hoa, "to take care of heavy military traffic," cost more than US aid for all development programs for the entire seven-year period. He concluded that "the greatest beneficiaries have been the urban dwellers, especially the small middle and upper classes . . .

---

29. Moyar, *Triumph Forsaken*, 254–56; Karnow, *Vietnam*, 302–11.
30. Karnow, *Vietnam*, 303.
31. Moyar, *Triumph Forsaken*, 275–76.

American aid . . . has also led the Vietnamese government to depend on a foreign power instead of its own people for support."[32]

Like "Dutch disease," named after the puzzling side effects of the discovery of oil in the Netherlands, this sudden source of wealth distorted incentives. In her 1971 book *Fire in the Lake*, Frances FitzGerald observed:

> The effect is a curious one. The United States has no direct economic interest in Vietnam. Over the years of the war it has not taken money out of Vietnam, but has put large amounts in. And yet it has produced much the same effects as the most exploitative of colonial regimes. The reason is that the overwhelming proportion of American funds has gone not into agricultural or industrial development but into the creation of services for the Americans.[33]

Neil Sheehan, the former *New York Times* correspondent, gave this example: To provide non-combat personnel with a reminder of home, the Army built some 40 ice cream factories in South Vietnam, a formerly self-sufficient rice-producing region. Needless to say, the cream had to be imported.[34]

The lure of dollars and the perils of the countryside led to what Samuel Huntington labeled "forced draft urbanization," decimating village life and increasing the population of Saigon from 500,000 in 1939 to 1.7 million at the end of the French war in 1954 to 4 million in 1975.[35] "The American war only completed the process the Diem regime had begun, moving peasants out of the villages and into the refugee camps and the cities, the real strategic hamlets of the war," wrote FitzGerald.[36]

It also resulted in massive corruption in the South Vietnamese government and military. Sheehan observed that "corruption guaranteed incompetence in office, high or low."

> Inflation had undermined salaries during the Diem years, and corruption negated any incentive to increase them to realistic levels. . . . Even if [an officer] took only what he needed and kept his wife under control, he still had to permit corruption to go on around him, and he often had to embezzle money for payoff demands by his superiors. If he insisted on honesty to the point of

32. Scigliano, *South Vietnam* 111–16, 126; FitzGerald, *Fire in the Lake*, 102.
33. FitzGerald, *Fire in the Lake*, 433.
34. Sheehan, *Bright Shining Lie*, 623.
35. Goscha, *Vietnam*, 227, 383.
36. FitzGerald, *Fire in the Lake*, 430.

refusing others access to corruption, he became an outsider and was pushed from office.³⁷

Traditional work could not compete. Young women, in particular, could make far more money as hostesses and/or as prostitutes in the cities than their families could in growing rice. Many American servicemen, other than the unfortunate minority of grunts in active combat, found their status suddenly inflated in what Sheehan called the "sexual cornucopia of an American's Vietnam." FitzGerald captured this scene:

> Before entering Saigon, the military traffic from Tan Son Nhut airfield slows in a choking blanket of its own exhaust. Where it crawls along to the narrow bridge in a frenzy of bicycles, pedicabs and tri-Lambrettas, two piles of garbage mark the entrance to a new quarter of the city. Every evening a girl on spindle heels picks her way over the barrier of rotting fruit and onto the sidewalk. Triumphant, she smiles at the boys who lounge at the soft-drink stand, and with a toss of her long earrings, climbs into a waiting Buick.³⁸

This was perhaps the truly unavoidable error. For those who gave it any thought, the displacement of Vietnam's social and economic structure was likely viewed as a mildly unpleasant side effect of the far more important war against Communism. And it's hard to imagine any effective US intervention that would not have had at least a similar impact. Would a Cold War US president take the chance that an under-financed mission might fail?

Decision E: Entry (1964–65)

Lyndon Johnson deserves just about every bit of the criticism he has received over Vietnam. Except for this one, possibly decisive thing: his August 1964 decision to enter the war officially, under the Tonkin Gulf Resolution. That, any contemporary American politician would have done.

Why? Because of China and Korea. Because of Cold War machismo, often referred to as maintaining credibility in the eyes of the Soviets. Because of Barry Goldwater.

Everybody understood the dynamics. If Vietnam went down on a Democratic president's watch, the Republicans would roll out another

---

37. Sheehan, *Bright Shining Lie*, 514.
38. FitzGerald, *Fire in the Lake*, 425.

"who lost China?" campaign. Jack Kennedy had had to run to the right of Richard Nixon in 1960. Goldwater was *already* going even further right as he accepted the 1964 GOP nomination. To be sure, containment of Communism was a genuine bipartisan priority, and for good reason, but it could be used to justify almost any expense or program.

Lest this sound too theoretical, remember, the Senate vote on Tonkin was 88–2. The House was unanimous.[39] Johnson won the 1964 election in a landslide. The most prominent Tonkin dissenter, the famed parliamentarian Senator Wayne Morse of Oregon, was defeated in his reelection bid in 1968, even as many voters had come around to opposing the war. Too preoccupied with Vietnam, his Republican opponent, Bob Packwood, argued.

Americans never truly agreed among themselves about goals and priorities. There was broad support for halting the spread of Communism in the region, which President Eisenhower had belittlingly described as "the falling domino principle."[40] But the public was not asked, and did not agree, to "bear any burden," in Kennedy's words, to do so in Vietnam, and felt little affection for what became a highly corrupt military dictatorship in the South.

This is not to absolve Johnson of his many errors. The shooting in the Tonkin Gulf incident was hyped—arguably provoked—and used as an excuse for a previously drafted congressional resolution; Johnson used the resolution as though it was a declaration of war, which it plainly was not. Rather than brace American voters for a long slog, Johnson, like his predecessors, disguised as much of the cost in men and material as possible. If Johnson had asked for a massive commitment up front, objections would surely have emerged long before half a million US troops were stationed there. His failure to do so only raised the emotional stakes as the bad news dripped out. In truth, both political sides were right to feel betrayed, just not by each other. Little wonder that the great American films would later show their protagonists trying to follow a mission they scarcely understood.

Johnson's mistakes brought down his presidency. But the decision to enter? Johnson shares responsibility with the vast majority of Americans, circa 1964.

---

39. Karnow, *Vietnam*, 391–92.
40. Lawrence, *Vietnam War*, 48

Decision F: War of Attrition; War of Press Releases (1965–68)

As protests against the war mounted, Senator George Aiken of Vermont famously proposed that the US simply declare victory—that it had achieved its objectives—and bring the troops home. What makes this comment especially painful, in retrospect, is that General William Westmoreland had been so busy declaring victory every week in the form of body counts and in press conferences describing progress in phases, right up until the Tet offensive in January 1968.

Given massive advantages in resources and technology, Westmoreland pursued a strategy of attrition, seeking large battles with the enemy and reducing their numbers. Unfortunately, this frequently put his soldiers in very dangerous and unfavorable situations; it also resulted in highly inflated enemy body counts as US troops could not reliably distinguish dead Vietcong guerillas from dead civilians. In 1967, Westmoreland nearly admitted to futility. Requesting another troop increase, he explained to President Johnson that the current 470,000 would result in "a 'meatgrinder' where we would kill large numbers of the enemy but in the end do little better than hold our own, with the shortage of troops still restricting [US forces] to a fire brigade technique—chasing after enemy main force units when and where it could find them."[41] But in November 1967, Westmoreland nevertheless told home audiences that "the ranks of the Vietcong are thinning steadily," and that "we have reached an important point when the end begins to come into view."[42]

Westmoreland's strategy of attrition—to kill so many enemy soldiers that they run out of replacements—made little sense in a defensive civil war. Rather than security for the South Vietnamese people, he sought out set-piece battles in which he could use overwhelming force, and frequently retreated once the battle ended. These tactics also undermined American efforts to seek local support. He strove for large numbers of casualties, with little regard for which Vietnamese were killed or displaced.

Some military strategists argued for a more targeted, civilian-sensitive approach, most famously John Paul Vann, the charismatic—and deeply flawed—veteran officer profiled by Sheehan in *A Bright Shining Lie*. Later historians argue that better execution (much, much better) might have changed the outcome of the war, meaning (I think) that South Vietnam

---

41. Greenfield et al., *Pentagon Papers*, 580.
42. Karnow, *Vietnam*, 527.

could have been saved. In *Triumph Forsaken*, Mark Moyar contends that the Diem regime was having success and could have persevered with its approach to securing safe havens. In *A Better War*, Lewis Sorley argues that the post-Tet (1968) anti-insurgency strategy of Westmoreland's successor Creighton Abrams—"clear-and-hold" rather than search-and-destroy—*did* succeed for several years and was undermined by collapsing political support at home.[43] These revisionist theories are necessarily speculative and leave some vital issues unaddressed. Still, much of what they say is persuasive: this disaster had many fathers. The voices advocating different strategies simply did not prevail in the American establishment of the time.

As Britain learned after World War I, a war of attrition should only ever be a last resort for a democracy. The arithmetic of X enemy soldiers for every Y Americans guaranteed a lot of American casualties, even if the ratio was ten to one, and voters (much less draft-aged young men) could never have supported this indefinitely. Westy built his own short window for success.

Tet closed the window. The allegedly thinning Vietcong, supported by North Vietnamese regular divisions, launched attacks throughout South Vietnam in January 1968. Even the US embassy in Saigon was seized for several hours. The attacks eventually failed, with crippling losses to the Vietcong—indeed, observers on both sides consider it to have been a military loss for the North—but the damage to the credibility of US leadership was even greater.[44]

Decision G: Strategic Bombing (1965–73)

In a memorable outburst, Air Force General Curtis LeMay threatened to "bomb them back into the Stone Age."[45] The genial Ronald Reagan backed him up with a homey metaphor: "We could pave the whole country and put parking strips on it, and still be home by Christmas."[46]

The US began the strategic bombing of North Vietnam (as distinguished from battlefield air support) in early 1965, even before the first Marines landed on the beach at Pleiku. A Pentagon historian summarized

---

43. For General Abrams's strategy, see Sorley, *Better War*, xiv–xv (comparative success), 28–30 (sharp change in tactics), 172–74 (confusion in Washington).

44. Sorley, *Better War*, 12–14; Karnow, *Vietnam*, 536–38, 558.

45. Karnow, *Vietnam*, 415.

46. Geyelin, "When Reagan," 1.

the discussion of the initial bombing strategy: "There was no dearth of reasons for striking the North. Indeed, one almost has the impression that there were more reasons than were required. But in the end, the decision to go ahead with the strikes seems to have resulted as much from the lack of alternative proposals as from any compelling logic in their favor."[47]

The US never gave up trying to use bombing as leverage for a favorable political settlement. Though the strikes did aim to disable industrial and military resources, they were never effective in cutting off supplies or in discouraging the DRV. The nonprofit Institute for Defense Analyses reported to the Pentagon that "as of July 1966 the U.S. bombing of North Vietnam (NVN) has had no measurable impact on Hanoi's ability to mount and support military operations in the South."[48] Even Walt Rostow, a notable hawk in the Johnson administration, was left to backpedal in a May 1967 memo:

> We have never held the view that bombing could stop infiltration [of South Vietnam]. We have never held the view that bombing of the Hanoi-Haiphong area alone would lead them to abandon the effort in the South. We have never held the view that bombing Hanoi-Haiphong would directly cut back infiltration. We have held the view that the degree of military and civilian cost felt in the North and the diversion of resources to deal with our bombing could contribute marginally—and perhaps significantly—to the timing of a decision to end the war.[49]

Without smart bombs or GPS targeting, more tons of bombs were dropped on North Vietnam than during the entirety of World War II.[50] Napalm and agent orange, chemical weapons by any reasonable definition, were freely used as defoliants and against jungle-based enemy units. It didn't work; the North Vietnamese worked around supply interruptions and dug an extraordinary number of tunnels and bunkers. Worse, civilian casualties—estimated by the CIA at 80 percent of all North Vietnam bombing casualties in January 1967[51]—reinforced North Vietnam's anti-American agenda. This is no surprise to us today, as we see from the reaction to incidents of merely negligent mistargeting of drone strikes in Afghanistan

47. Greenfield et al., *Pentagon Papers*, 353.
48. Greenfield et al., *Pentagon Papers*, 513.
49. Greenfield et al., *Pentagon Papers*, 586.
50. Goscha, *Vietnam*, 326–27.
51. Greenfield et al., *Pentagon Papers*, 535.

and elsewhere. The Nixon administration doubled down on the tactic, apparently feeling that it had few other options after having committed to massive and politically popular troop withdrawals.

The bombing campaigns, conceived without defined goals, continued long past knowledge of their military ineffectiveness and were frankly justified on the grounds of terror (especially at the end): little more than a politically cheap way of inflicting misery. Once their ineffectiveness had become clear, the targeting of urban areas certainly violated international conventions.

When he announced the first atomic bombing in August 1945, President Truman issued a statement that called Hiroshima "an important Japanese army base." This was wildly inaccurate; Hiroshima was a city of 350,000. Later defenders of the action pointed instead to the strategic impact of the A-bomb, arguing that it shortened World War II, which was a declared war against a nation that had directly attacked the US. The strategic bombers of Vietnam had no such rationalizations.

6. REGENERATION

The American war in Vietnam ended not with a bang. Pursuing his 1968 promise to achieve peace with honor, Nixon drew down troop levels and finally ended American involvement with the 1973 peace treaty—one that the South Vietnamese government swallowed with bitterness because it didn't obligate the DRV troops to withdraw to the north. In the wake of Nixon's 1974 resignation, North Vietnamese troops stormed southward and took Saigon on April 30, 1975. Weeks before, the Khmers Rouges had taken Phnom Penh.

Perhaps Ho Chi Minh and his partisans were lucky in drawing such myopic opponents. For the war's final irony is that the Democratic Republic of Vietnam, having turned itself into a garrison state and evicted the French and Americans, could not govern effectively.

Following the early Soviet model, the unified Vietnamese government conducted reprisals, killing many and enrolling large numbers of southerners in so-called re-education programs.[52] It expropriated private land and businesses and implemented a planned economy, with disastrous effect.[53] Per capita annual income remained very low, around two hundred to three

---

52. Goscha, *Vietnam*, 374.
53. Goscha, *Vietnam*, 384–85.

hundred dollars as late as 1984.⁵⁴ In a final twist, Vietnam invaded Cambodia to depose the Chinese-allied Khmers Rouges in 1978–79, then fought a successful rearguard action against a hapless Chinese invasion, insistently isolating itself when it desperately needed economic development and international alliances.⁵⁵

In the mid 1980s, a former American soldier described the streets of Hanoi at night:

> There were few streetlights and they were very dim. The city was dark, and in the middle of the block where the lights did not reach, it was black. This made walking difficult because of the disrepair of the streets... But even so, the bicycles streamed by in multitudes. They had no lights; like phantoms they glided out of the darkness to silently brush by and disappear back into the darkness.⁵⁶

By 1986, like China and Gorbachev's Soviet Union, Vietnam had to switch course, allowing private ownership and profit-making, and forming diplomatic alliances. The economic reforms, known as *doi moi* ("renovation"), led to a period of rapid expansion from a very low base. The US recognized Vietnam in 1995. In the 2000s, at least until the US's recent withdrawal from Trans Pacific Partnership negotiations, Vietnam began to see the US as its best hope of avoiding domination by China. And per capita income has continued to rise, to over 2,500 dollars per year in 2018.⁵⁷

Within a year after the volcanic explosion blew two thousand feet off the top of Mount St. Helens, plants were found growing in the ash and pumice-covered landscape. For its inheritors, the war's lesson may simply be that somebody opened a bar in Ho Chi Minh City and named it after an American war movie.

---

54. Cima, *Vietnam*, 143.
55. Goscha, *Vietnam*, 394–96.
56. Sidel, *Old Hanoi*, 37.
57. Bevins, *Jakarta Method*, 262 (citing World Bank figures).

Operation Cue atomic bomb test, May 5, 1955. Prompted in part by concerns about downwind fallout from nuclear bomb testing, the 1963 Limited Test Ban Treaty would become one of the first international nuclear arms control agreements.

Credit: Office of Civil and Defense Mobilization, U.S. National Archives.

3

Nuclear Counterintuition
Risk Reduction during the Cold War

PRESIDENT OBAMA HAD MADE it clear in advance that he would not apologize, when he became the first sitting US president to visit Hiroshima in May 2016. His position followed that of eleven prior administrations and was vocally supported by China and Korea—Japan's principal war victims—and many US veterans' groups.

But Hiroshima is complicated. Apology or no, Japan was officially happy to host the president, and many expressed gratitude that he could acknowledge the pain and horror experienced by civilian casualties of the 1945 bombings. Obama concluded with a prayer for "a future we can choose, a future in which Hiroshima and Nagasaki are known not as the dawn of atomic warfare but as the start of our own moral awakening."[1]

The long delay and great delicacy of this visit speaks volumes. American presidents have never hesitated to visit other major battlefields of World War II, especially sites of Allied triumph. Nuclear weapons are different, in the scale of their destruction, the health and environmental effects of radiation, and the risk of reprisals. And Hiroshima was not a site of great American courage. Though committed in wartime for the purpose of defeating an aggressive and brutal Japanese empire, the atomic bombings of Hiroshima and Nagasaki were massive, poisonous attacks on very soft civilian targets.

---

1. Harris, "In Hiroshima," 1.

After Hiroshima, the Cold War rivals somehow both built and refrained from using nuclear arsenals that really could have destroyed large parts of humanity. The superpowers' leaders feared reprisals, it is true, but their abstinence was not just due to the balance of power or isolated cases of restraint. A long series of leaders came to realize, in the manner of Clausewitz, that there would be no political point to victory if nuclear weapons were used: even the "victors" would lose and become pariahs to the rest of the world. So the US and USSR, and their allies, made a series of agreements to reduce the risk that *anyone* would use the weapons. Even Ronald Reagan, who'd once suggested that "we could pave the whole country [of North Vietnam] and put parking strips on it," became a nuclear abolitionist in the words of the historian John Lewis Gaddis.[2] As president, Reagan negotiated some of the most sweeping arms reductions of the Cold War.

These were acts of self-interested self-restraint, made between parties that continued to disagree about much else, in service of larger goals. Perhaps more important, these actions signaled that nuclear weapons were undesirable—ruinously expensive, difficult to manage, unusable—at least to countries that aspired to participate in the global economy. And that may be the Cold War's most important lesson for the future.

1. FOUR MONTHS

The story of President Truman's decision to drop atomic bombs is as necessary and irresistible as Pandora's Box. We are riveted by its ethical questions: whether it was right or wrong; whether it was necessary or proportionate to US war aims; how many US lives were saved by the sacrifice of two or three hundred thousand Japanese people; whether it violated international treaties against the targeting of civilians and the use of chemical weapons (reading chemical to include radiation); whether the US should have demonstrated the bomb first, provided a clearer warning, made its surrender demand clearer with respect to the status of the Japanese emperor (who was ultimately allowed to remain as head of state, subject to US occupying authority). Unfortunately, as with the Smithsonian's ill-fated fiftieth anniversary exhibition, the public discussion in the US often gets reduced to two groups talking past each other, as though respect for military service and avoiding unnecessary civilian casualties were mutually incompatible.

---

2. Gaddis, *Cold War*, 264.

NUCLEAR COUNTERINTUITION

But Hiroshima's most pertinent lesson is actually this: no future leader will face a situation like Truman's. The unprecedented decision about whether to drop atomic bombs on Japanese cities was made in wartime by an intelligent and humble but completely unprepared man who had known about the weapon for less time than it takes to teach the first semester of college physics, during which time he also happened to be employed as president of the United States. No future leader will write on such a blank slate.

When he became president in April 1945, Truman was not even well-prepared to follow the course he publicly promised and intended: to follow Roosevelt's own policies and plans as closely as possible. Indeed, he had barely been part of the administration. He had only become vice president that January; he had met with President Roosevelt just a couple of times after the 1944 election; FDR hadn't even invited him to the Yalta summit with British Prime Minister Churchill and Soviet Chairman Stalin in February 1945.[3] (Truman's lack of preparation is a scandal of its own. Roosevelt's inner circle, including the sainted Eleanor, was well aware that the president had been forced to take a six-week "vacation" in the spring of 1944 due to serious heart disease and kept his condition from public scrutiny through the 1944 election.[4] Even if electoral considerations were a sufficient justification for this non-disclosure—a highly debatable proposition—they would provide no excuse for failing to prepare a new vice president *of the same party* to take on his most important responsibilities.)

Among other things, Truman had not lived through the history of the Manhattan Project. As Albert Einstein's famous 1941 letter to President Roosevelt had advocated, this vast initiative had always been motivated by the fear that Nazi Germany, which had the expertise and resources, would build a bomb first. An American weapon might deter the Germans from using theirs. But Germany fell in May 1945, before either side's atomic program had succeeded. Regarding Japan, which was understood to have no nuclear program, the best indication of FDR's thinking was a rather inscrutable summary of a private discussion with Churchill in September 1944, to the effect that the bomb "might perhaps, after mature consideration, be used against the Japanese, who should be warned that this bombardment

---

3. For Truman's exclusion from Roosevelt policy discussions, see Lifton and Mitchell, *Hiroshima in America*, 124–25; Gaddis, *Cold War*, 19.

4. Goodwin, *No Ordinary Time*, 493–501.

will be repeated until they surrender."[5] We don't, of course, know what Truman or his advisors would have made of this statement if they had seen it. In hindsight, however, it is hard to miss Roosevelt's hedging—"might" "perhaps" "after mature consideration" and, most notably, that the Japanese "should be warned."

The Manhattan Project was cloaked in great secrecy, improbably so, with its massive tasks divided among three very remote major sites (Los Alamos, New Mexico; Hanford, Washington; and Oak Ridge, Tennessee) and dozens of others. Only a few top-level scientists and military officers knew with certainty that the project was to build an atomic bomb. Truman wasn't among them. (Ironically, Stalin had high level spies inside the project, so that when Truman finally revealed the bomb's existence to Stalin at Potsdam in July 1945, it only served to reinforce Stalin's lack of trust.[6])

In the event, Truman first learned of the project in a forty-five-minute briefing from Secretary of War Henry Stimson and the Manhattan Project's military leader General Leslie Groves on April 25, 1945, almost two weeks after he'd been sworn in.[7] Coming in as late as he did, Truman chose to defer to the process then in place, postponing political or foreign policy implications. His direct advisors were defense leaders. Stimson convened a panel of eight civilian officials and a separate four-person scientific advisory panel, which met for about a month in May 1945.[8] These groups featured no voices of caution. Churchill likewise recalled there was "unanimous, unquestioned agreement" about using the bomb to compel Japanese surrender.[9]

The White House announcement of the bombing, delivered while Truman was still steaming back from the Potsdam conference, reflected this military focus.

> Sixteen hours ago an American airplane dropped one bomb on Hiroshima, an important Japanese Army base. That bomb had more power than 20,000 tons of TNT. It had more than two thousand times the blast power of the British "Grand Slam" which is the largest bomb ever yet used in the history of warfare.

---

5. Kennedy, *Freedom from Fear*, 839.
6. Patterson, *Grand Expectations*, 108; Gaddis, *Cold War*, 37.
7. Kennedy, *Freedom from Fear*, 838.
8. Kelly, *Manhattan Project*, 290–91.
9. Kennedy, *Freedom from Fear*, 838–41.

> The Japanese began the war from the air at Pearl Harbor. They have been repaid many fold. And the end is not yet. With this bomb we have now added a new and revolutionary increase in destruction to supplement the growing power of our armed forces. In their present form these bombs are now in production and even more powerful forms are in development.
> It is an atomic bomb. It is a harnessing of the basic power of the universe. The force from which the sun draws its powers has been unloosed against those who brought war to the Far East.[10]

This was a remarkable statement for many reasons, including its righteous and threatening language, its factual inaccuracies, its low-key delivery. But: talk about burying the lede! The technology that will forever hang over civilization merits no mention before the third paragraph.

The statement focused instead on winning the current war, intimidating the enemy, and reiterating the enemy's aggression and the justifications for violence. The inaccuracies crept in, apparently for these very purposes. The bomb actually targeted and hit the center of a major city, not a nearby army base.[11] The US had no actual production capability for atomic bombs; just two were then available, each with a different experimental design.[12] The Hiroshima device also didn't employ nuclear fusion like the sun, although fusion weapons were on the drawing board.

Truman and his team did have legitimate strategic objectives: to end the Japanese war; to do so before the Russians' anticipated entry entitled them to demand influence or territorial advantage. And, as Truman's bombing announcement repeatedly emphasized, the US had a clear *casus belli*. But the leadership punted on the really difficult question of what the decision might mean for the world's future safety. His statement went no further than to say that he would make some proposals to the US Congress on that subject, as though the rest of the world might have nothing to say about it.

---

10. Kelly, *Manhattan Project*, 339–42.

11. The "Little Boy" bomb detonated 1,900 feet above and 550 feet southeast of the Aioi bridge target. Kelly, *Manhattan Project*, 333. The bridge, since rebuilt, is in central Hiroshima.

12. The US had a single-digit arsenal for at least a year after the war. Stone, *Atlantic*, 121; Schweber, *Einstein and Oppenheimer*, 178.

2. ALL THOUGHTS ARE SPLIT

Americans naturally celebrated Japan's sudden surrender. About the bombs, however, there were a few voices of concern from the first. "All thoughts and things are split," wrote James Agee in *Time* magazine.[13] Conservative commentator David Lawrence condemned the bombing of thousands of civilians in *US News*.

> We shall not soon purge ourselves of the feeling of guilt which prevails among us. Military necessity will be our consistent cry in answer to criticism, but it will never erase from our minds the simple truth that we, of all civilized nations, though hesitating to use poison gas, did not hesitate to employ the most destructive weapon of all times indiscriminately against men, women and children. What a precedent for the future we have furnished to other nations.[14]

A year later, *The New Yorker* devoted an entire issue to John Hersey's "Hiroshima." A classic of what would later be called New Journalism, Hersey's piece followed six residents of the city through the day of the bombing and afterward. Beyond personalizing the attack on specific civilians, Hersey spotlighted the effects of radiation which, as Lawrence had perhaps intuited, bore a stark resemblance to the chemical weapons that had been condemned by treaty since World War I.[15] In the wake of the strong public response to the *New Yorker* article, the retired Stimson was drafted to write a semi-official response for *Harper's*, soberly walking through the decision-making process that led to the bomb's use against Japan. Stimson's article was also well-received and, though somewhat self-serving, performed a public service by opening the door on what had been a top-secret decision of monumental public importance.[16] However, Stimson offered no comfort for the future; after Hersey's article, no one could claim ignorance of the consequences.

The culture soon reflected these technological fears. Apocalyptic tales have been a religious and literary staple from the beginning of time, but now these fears could be made specific. Uncontrollable technology, driven by witless and/or power-hungry scientists, became an enduring plot device

---

13. Lifton and Mitchell, *Hiroshima in America*, 36.
14. Lifton and Mitchell, *Hiroshima in America*, 37.
15. Lifton and Mitchell, *Hiroshima in America*, 86–90.
16. Lifton and Mitchell, *Hiroshima in America*, 103–6.

for drama and satire. Among the first was the Japanese movie *Godzilla* (1957), in which the monster's power came from nuclear fallout. This was practically a current event: radiation from a 1953 US thermonuclear test in the South Pacific killed the sailors on a downwind Japanese fishing boat.[17] Later: *The Blob* (1958), a cult classic with Steve McQueen and some comically bad special effects involving carnivorous goo; the dark comedy *Dr. Strangelove* (1964), with Peter Sellers playing three roles including the title's mad-bomber physicist; *2001: A Space Odyssey* (1968), featuring HAL, a mutinous spaceship computer, as a major character; *The China Syndrome* (1979) with Jack Lemmon and Jane Fonda, an almost too realistic foreshadowing of the Three Mile Island nuclear power plant accident; *Blade Runner* (1982), in which no one can tell the humans from the artificial replicants; *Jurassic Park* (1993) with aggressive dinosaurs recreated genetically rather than from nuclear waste.

But nuclear weapons and other exotic quasi-scientific speculation weren't necessary to promote mass fear. The famous air raids upon London and Pearl Harbor at the outset of World War II had been answered, on a much larger scale: US and British air forces had dropped incendiary bombs in carefully designed circular patterns to create unearthly firestorms in Dresden and Tokyo, which left tens of thousands of civilians dead. These and other "conventional" attacks inspired their own line of antiwar literature, like Kurt Vonnegut's *Slaughterhouse Five* and Isao Takahata's animated film *Grave of the Fireflies*.

The French New Wave film *Hiroshima, Mon Amour* (1959) perhaps best combines these themes of fear, guilt, and individual powerlessness in the nuclear age. The film opens with images of the atomic bomb's radiation victims, rarely shown in the US, and bright scenes of peace demonstrations, part of the real worldwide movement for a nuclear test ban in the late 1950s. Two lovers—a French actress, in Hiroshima to film a peace movie, and a Japanese businessman—recount their World War II experiences in simple repetitive phrases, stories they have never told their spouses because war no longer makes sense in the new "normal" world. While he was serving elsewhere in the Japanese army, the man's family and hometown were obliterated by a horrifying, humiliating, and unimaginable event. In the war's aftermath, the actress was ostracized by ugly crowds in her pretty little French town because of her teenage relationship with a German soldier during the occupation. In the film's last scenes, the lovers name each other

---

17. Stone, *Atlantic*, 121.

after their hometowns, Nevers and Hiroshima, tying together the fates of now powerless peoples.

The comparison of the conflicted war histories of France and Japan shows that an ordinary person's life (simply living in the Japan or France of the time) may tempt fate in extraordinary ways. When the man asks the woman about her reaction to the bombing of Hiroshima, she says that she was amazed that they, the Americans, built it, *and* that she was amazed that they used it. Amazed, in other words, at what the US had proved capable of, both in invention and in destruction. And if that was the reaction of a liberated ally, how might a potential enemy respond?

3. THE DECISION-MAKERS' LEARNING CURVE

The reduction of nuclear risk has two general components: reducing the number of opportunities in which anyone might consider using the weapons, and reducing the likelihood that, in each case, the actor will decide to use them. It's vitally important to do both for a rudimentary statistical reason: even events with a low likelihood in each case become likely to occur with enough chances. For example, if we (arbitrarily) assume there is a 10 percent probability that a nuclear state will use nuclear weapons in any given confrontation (90 percent chance of non-use), and if each such decision is independent of all others, after just the seventh standoff, it would be more likely than not that someone would have dropped a bomb on at least one occasion. By the fifteenth, the likelihood of at least one bombing would approach 80 percent.

To be sure, the conditions I've assumed here are wrong. I presume that the likelihood of non-use in any given situation is much higher than 90 percent. Moreover, each decision is far from independent of the others, because national leaders have been well aware of history and precedent. But the principle remains: Even if a nuclear attack is quite unlikely in any one situation, it does not take many such situations to make it likely that at least one will be used. And the wider the number of nations with nuclear capacity, the greater the number of potential confrontations.

In the shadow of Hiroshima, the nuclear strategies of successive Cold War leaders all evolved in a consistent way. The more they learned, the more reluctant they became to engage in brinksmanship, and the more willing they were to look for other solutions to conflict, often against the advice of their own more hawkish advisors.

By 1949, when deciding whether to fund the vastly more powerful hydrogen fusion bomb known as the Super, President Truman's attitude had shifted. "We had got to do it—make the bomb—though no one wants to use it. But . . . we have got to have it if only for bargaining power with the Soviets."[18] While this was quite the opposite of what peace advocates wanted, it was also a far cry from the Truman who often claimed that he'd never lost a moment of sleep over the decision to bomb Japan. The Super was now part of the strategy of containing the Soviet Union, an effort to prevail without starting World War III. Winston Churchill, who had known about the Manhattan Project from the beginning and voiced no objections to the atomic bombing of Japan, came to agree that the thermonuclear devices were unusable. But he felt that the "element of equality" with the Soviet Union offered reason for hope.[19]

At the outset of the Korean War, Truman initially fell back upon a reflexive answer to a reporter's question about nuclear weapons, deferring to military leadership by saying that everything was on the table. He promptly backtracked from that stance, not wishing to expand that particular war.[20] (As would be the case in Vietnam, there was fierce disagreement between those who didn't want to risk open war with the Soviet Union and China and those who felt victory was worth that risk.) Months later, US General Douglas MacArthur, field commander in Korea, proposed dropping a couple of *dozen* atomic bombs along the Chinese-North Korean border, to leave a toxic wasteland that would isolate and prevent reinforcement of the Chinese and North Korean troops.[21] MacArthur *may* have been posturing. His horrifying escalation proposal, along with numerous public disagreements with the Truman cabinet that bordered on insubordination, essentially forced Truman to relieve him. (MacArthur's public didn't care, showering him with praise and tickertape parades on his return. Truman, more unpopular than ever, dropped out of the 1952 presidential race.)

Dwight Eisenhower, probably the most experienced general ever to occupy the White House, underwent a similar transformation. In the words of Jim Newton, a sympathetic biographer: "Faced with the awesome implications of the Soviet Union's ability to wage nuclear war, Eisenhower

18. Gaddis, *Cold War*, 79.
19. Gaddis, *Cold War*, 82.
20. Lifton and Mitchell, *Hiroshima in America*, 186.
21. Lifton and Mitchell, *Hiroshima in America*, 186; Herman, *Douglas MacArthur*, 799.

changed. The nuclear enthusiast of 1953 had become a more sober leader by 1956."[22] Eisenhower had once said that the military could use nuclear weapons "exactly as you would use a bullet or anything else."[23] Later he rejected multiple staff policy proposals that would condone the limited use of nuclear weapons, seeing such decisions as having unique international political risks as well as the risk of annihilating escalation. "We must now plan to fight peripheral wars on the same basis as we would fight a general war."[24] The historian John Lewis Gaddis interprets this as a reflection of Clausewitz's dictum that war must serve political ends: there could be no political end in the end of civilization. By making every decision all or nothing, guaranteeing "maximum massive retaliation," Eisenhower believed that both sides would refrain from nuclear war.[25]

This policy seemed crazy to many (see *Dr. Strangelove*), but it took the twin Kennedy-Khrushchev crises of Berlin in 1961 and Cuba in 1962 to show that limited nuclear war might have been even riskier.

When the Berlin Wall went up overnight in 1961, the US conventional forces then stationed in Germany had no realistic hope of holding back the Red Army should it seek to take over the entire city. President Kennedy sought alternatives to Eisenhower's massive first strike policy. A September 1961 report by Carl Kaysen, a Harvard economics professor then working for the Defense Department, laid out a plan that, if executed without mistakes, gave the US "a fair probability of achieving a substantial measure of success" in degrading Soviet nuclear capabilities, at a cost of between half a million and a million Soviet casualties. Allowing that the Soviets might not see this as a show of US restraint, Kaysen estimated that Soviet retaliation on American cities might produce losses of *five to ten million people.*[26] Although some administration officials were appalled, Kennedy approved back-up plans that included, in its final stage, the use of tactical nuclear arms.

That crisis receded, but just months later, Khrushchev approved the secret installation of short and medium range missiles in Cuba, weapons that could easily reach New York and Washington.

---

22. Newton, *Eisenhower*, 261.
23. Gaddis, *Cold War*, 81.
24. Newton, *Eisenhower*, 263.
25. Gaddis, *Cold War*, 83; Newton, *Eisenhower*, 267.
26. Kempe, *Berlin 1961*, 431–33.

NUCLEAR COUNTERINTUITION

When US surveillance discovered the missile installations in the fall of 1962, Kennedy did not object through back channels as Khrushchev had expected. Instead he took to the airwaves to make a public demand for withdrawal of the missiles, intentionally leaving himself little room to back down, and therefore raising the stakes for Khrushchev.[27] Against the advice of his more hawkish advisors, who advocated immediate bombing of the installations, Kennedy imposed a quarantine of Cuba—a clever relabeling of what amounted to a blockade, which would have been an official act of war. Even with delicate phrasing, the parties remained a step away from the brink.

Fortunately, Soviet resupply ships turned back. But four Soviet submarines, carrying nuclear-tipped torpedoes, were ordered to evade the quarantine and supplement forces already deployed in Cuba. The subs' commanders did not have clear instructions about what to do in the event of a confrontation, so it is also extremely fortunate that they did not fire when the US Navy forced them to surface. Later, Kennedy displayed similar restraint when a US U-2 plane was shot down. In these extremely tense two weeks, a deal was struck: removal of the missiles from Cuba, a US pledge not to invade Cuba, and a secret US pledge to later remove intermediate-term missiles from Turkey (which submarine-based missiles would effectively replace).

This terrifying episode convinced Robert McNamara, Defense Secretary to Presidents Kennedy and Johnson, of the futility of even limited use. McNamara had initially believed that the US and USSR might abide by rules of war without nuclear weapons, but after Cuba he saw there was no controlling what might happen in a crisis. He converted to an explicit proponent of "mutually assured destruction," effectively Eisenhower's policy.[28]

A similar evolution took place on the Soviet side. After the Cuban crisis, Khrushchev came to the view that a nuclear war, once started, could not be limited. He sharply rebuked Castro for suggesting a preemptive strike: "There will always be a counterstrike.... Only a person who has no idea what nuclear war means... can talk like this."[29]

---

27. The Cuban Missile Crisis is recounted by many historians. Gaddis, *Cold War*, 95–98; Stone, *Atlantic* 204–6; Tye, *Bobby Kennedy*, 262–68; Patterson, *Grand Expectations*, 499–509; Zubok, *Failed Empire*, 146–50.

28. Gaddis, *Cold War*, 99.

29. Zubok, *Failed Empire*, 148.

This did not make Khrushchev's comrades any happier about his improvised saber-rattling. While on a Black Sea vacation in 1964, "crazy Nikita" was summoned back to Moscow by his well-organized deputies.[30] It was to his credit, Khrushchev thought, that he could be peacefully removed. "Could anyone have dreamed of telling Stalin that he didn't suit us and suggesting he retire? Not even a wet spot would have remained where we had been standing."[31] The new leadership under Leonid Brezhnev prized order and discipline; they would be more careful to avoid high-stakes conflicts with the West.[32]

4. IN SEARCH OF A GENERAL SOLUTION

The physicist Leo Szilard, who had urged Einstein to write his 1941 letter to President Roosevelt, also wrote a letter to President Truman in July 1945. Now that Germany had surrendered, Szilard asked Truman not to use the bomb in Japan unless Japan had refused detailed public terms of surrender, and only after considering that "a nation which sets the precedent of using these newly liberated forces of nature for purposes of destruction may have to bear the responsibility of opening the door to an era of devastation on an unimaginable scale."[33]

Truman probably did not see Szilard's letter. If he had, he probably would have handed it off to the advisory committee, led by the Secretary of War. And the truth is that the funding and resources needed for scientific and development work would always put the government in control of the projects. Exactly this had happened with the Manhattan Project itself; General Groves effectively decided when and how the bomb would be used.

After the war, several prominent groups advocated for international bodies to regulate nuclear technology. The most prominent was a report by US Secretary of State Dean Acheson and David Lilienthal, chair of the Tennessee Valley Authority, one of the largest electricity producers in the country. Their report called for, among other things, sharing scientific knowledge about nuclear energy and establishing a system of inspections by a United Nations agency to ensure that the technology would be used peacefully. The American financier Bernard Baruch, whom President

---

30. Brown, *Rise and Fall of Communism*, 266; Zubok, *Failed Empire*, 150.
31. Gaddis, *Cold War*, 144.
32. Zubok, *Failed Empire*, 151.
33. Kelly, *Manhattan Project*, 292.

Truman had appointed to represent the US at the UN, modified the plan in its last stages, leading to its rejection by the Soviet Union. But Stalin, though without his own nuclear weapons at the time, might have declined to participate in any such plan, just as he declined to join postwar international economic recovery programs.

The idea did not die. In a 1950 letter to the United Nations, Niels Bohr, a Nobel Laureate in quantum physics, advocated for international transparency to reduce the chance of nuclear war. "The ideal of an open world, with common knowledge about social conditions and technical enterprises, including military preparations . . . will . . . obviously be required for genuine co-operation on progress of civilization."[34]

A few years later, after both the US and USSR had detonated fusion bombs thousands of times more powerful than the Hiroshima device, Albert Einstein and the philosopher and mathematician Bertrand Russell—each an international celebrity in his own right—issued a manifesto calling for nothing less than the abolition of war. Short of that, "the abolition of thermo-nuclear weapons, if each side believed the other had carried it out sincerely, would lessen the fear of a sudden attack in the style of Pearl Harbour."[35]

The internationalists, scientists and others, were accused of being naïve, or worse, in matters of foreign policy, especially during the frosty 1950s. There was reason for skepticism, too. After World War I, the victors had tried to put arms controls in place. The Versailles Treaty forbade Germany from re-arming, chemical weapons were banned, and the major powers entered into the Washington Naval Treaty limiting major warship construction (freezing advantages then enjoyed by the US and Britain). But by the mid-1930s, Germany had renounced Versailles and Japan had pulled out of the Washington Naval Treaty.

The imposition of terms by the World War I victors was not a completely fair comparison to a multi-lateral treaty. In any case, regarding nuclear weapons, the internationalists understood the risk-reduction problem exactly right; they were just ahead of their time. By preventing the spread of arms, reducing stockpiles, and requiring inspections, their proposals would have limited the number of opportunities for the use of nuclear weapons. And the logic first seen by these scientists in the 1940s and 1950s would

---

34. Kelly, *Manhattan Project*, 432.
35. Kelly, *Manhattan Project*, 446.

gradually, and with other labels, be adopted by alarmed Cold War leaders after the Cuban crisis.

Beginning with the Limited Test Ban Treaty (1963), long a goal of peace groups, the nuclear club agreed to some mutual rules.[36] The nuclear nonproliferation accord (1968) forbade its signatories from assisting new countries in acquiring weapons, obviously a critical step toward reducing the number of opportunities for escalation.[37] It also guaranteed its participants nuclear exclusivity, but that did not make it a bad idea for the rest of the world. In 1972, the US and Soviet Union signed two treaties: the Strategic Arms Limitation Treaty (SALT), which placed limits (rather high limits) on the parties' long-range land- and sea-based missiles; and the anti-ballistic missile (ABM) treaty, which banned certain defensive weapons which could, if successfully deployed, remove one side's fear of counterattack, the kind of one-sided situation that Truman enjoyed in 1945.[38]

It is important to remember that much of this difficult diplomatic work took place while war raged between the superpowers' respective client states in Vietnam. Negotiations were at all times very difficult and often broke down. A collapse of trust in the late 1970s, due in part to Soviet adventurism in a period of America's post-Vietnam hangover (and in part to high oil prices), sidelined and threatened to reverse progress on arms reduction. Indeed, President Reagan's announcement of the practically nonexistent "Star Wars" missile defense initiative in the early 1980s went against the spirit of the ABM treaty. But the anti-communist crusader was also an extreme skeptic—a nuclear abolitionist by some accounts—of nuclear weapons.[39] In the end the US and USSR, and later Russia, cooperated for many years to reduce their arsenals. The danger and cost of practically unusable weapons was ultimately a subject about which the enemies could agree, and they found that they needed each other in order to reduce their arsenals.

Eisenhower came up with a valid solution to the problem of nuclear game theory, in the two-power setting, in seeing that mutual destruction deterred any use. But the "naïve" scientists had seen the more general solution.

---

36. Judt, *Postwar*, 255.
37. Gaddis, *Cold War*, 101; Stone, *Atlantic*, 237.
38. Gaddis, *Cold War*, 101.
39. Gaddis, *Cold War*, 265.

5. ABANDONING A TREATY

President Trump dramatically rejected this approach in 2018 by withdrawing the US from the 2016 six-country treaty, under which Iran agreed to discontinue its nuclear arms program for an extended period in exchange for a lifting of economic sanctions. He hoped this harder line would result in a more favorable political outcome in the region (presumably regime change in Iran). His flamboyant unilateralism, often dismissive of allies, was very widely criticized in other contexts, but a significant number of more conventional analysts also agreed with his abandonment of the Iran deal. These observers generally argued that the treaty would reward Iran's political and military interventions on behalf of its regional allies, while merely delaying Iranian nuclear capabilities.

In the context of the consistent evolution of the views of Cold War leaders, this position strikes me (and many others) as short sighted: it elevates a regional foreign policy goal regarding Iran above the decades-long multinational effort to reduce nuclear weapons risk. For one thing, a hard-line position is not the only path to positive change in the region: peace may also come in a series of small steps that build trust on issues of consensus. The US had not needed to settle every score with the USSR in order to find areas of agreements about nuclear weapons. Of much greater concern is the American willingness to step back from the global consensus toward nuclear risk-reduction. Now any autocrat can cite US inconsistency as a reason to ignore international norms.

The concern is not simply about this particular bet, or the next one. It's the number of bets, the number of bettors, and their understanding of the Cold War leaders' experience with nuclear weapons. Winning nine out of ten is a losing proposition.

Still, to use Truman's words, the end is not yet. The war in Ukraine and the renewed hostilities in the Middle East may remind people that there are still conflicts that raise some the possibility, hopefully remote, of nuclear weapons use. Perhaps, like the Cold War leaders before them, the parties may find mutual benefit in dialing that risk down.

A. Philip Randolph, 1964. By the time of his leadership of the 1963 March on Washington, Randolph had worked for decades to improve the economic and political status of Black Americans. He was a longtime president of the Brotherhood of Sleeping Car Porters and, among other things, played a key role in President Truman's 1948 decision to desegregate the armed services.

Credit: Ed Ford, New York World Telegram & Sun, U.S. Library of Congress.

4

An Evanescent Coalition
How Civil Rights Became a Priority (Briefly) in the 1960s

ONE OCTOBER DAY IN sixth grade, I stayed home sick from school but summoned the energy to watch the Detroit Tigers host the St. Louis Cardinals in game five of the 1968 World Series. (Back then, World Series games were only played during the day.) A singer I had not heard of, José Feliciano, sang a very unusual, soulful version of "The Star-Spangled Banner," accompanying himself on guitar. In my memory, he sat among the crowd in the stands, but YouTube makes clear that he was standing on the field in front of an awkwardly motionless brass ensemble.

Game five was the turning point in the series. Down three games to one, the Tigers took the last three games and the series. Their number two pitcher, Mickey Lolich, won game five and somehow out-dueled future Hall of Famer Bob Gibson in game seven. (Gibson had just set one of the game's great records, with an earned run average of 1.12 for the season.) But in that tumultuous year, game five was remembered for Feliciano's avant-garde performance and the enraged reactions of traditionalists

Feliciano has said that he did not mean his version to be disrespectful, and the video bears this out: it was simply a non-martial arrangement. He was no Nina Simone and this was nothing like his incandescent version of "Light My Fire." If anything, the choice of Feliciano might have caused some local resentment in Motown, home of the musical hit factory; Black

Detroiters might have been forgiven for expecting an even more soulful anthem. The city had been engulfed in race riots the summer before. The Tigers, ironically, were one of the least integrated of baseball's elite teams, with just one regular Black starting player, the slugger Willie Horton. The Cards, in contrast, started future Hall of Famer Lou Brock and Curt Flood in a legendary outfield,[1] and Latino stars Orlando Cepeda and Julian Javier in the infield; most unusually for the time, Gibson was their number one pitcher. Indeed, almost every elite team of the era relied on Black (including Black Latin) regulars, and not just an isolated All-Star.

But 1968 was a year of traditionalist rage. Anti–Vietnam War demonstrations, compounded by the anguished reactions to the assassinations of Martin Luther King and Bobby Kennedy, provoked a conservative backlash we still feel. Richard Nixon won the presidency with his law-and-order message and his strategy of flipping southern states, but we should remember that Chicago Mayor Richard Daley was cheered at the Democratic National Convention for his harsh suppression of antiwar demonstrators, and Democrats nominated the candidate most identified with President Johnson's Vietnam War escalation, Vice President Hubert Humphrey.

I was still too young to pay much attention to politics, and in Portland, Oregon, there was not a lot of racial tension (due to some pretty shameful history that I also didn't know). Most of what I had learned about race was from my passion for baseball, including its history: Jackie Robinson's endurance of verbal abuse, especially in border cities like Cincinnati and St. Louis, when he started playing for the Brooklyn Dodgers in 1947; the emergence of Willie Mays and Hank Aaron from Jim Crow Alabama; the totemic wisdom of Negro League pitching legend Satchel Paige, who was denied access to the major leagues until age forty-two ("don't look back, somebody might be gaining on you"). But to an eleven-year-old watching The Game of the Week on NBC, these stories of discrimination already

---

1. Brock went on to set season and career base-stealing records and reach three thousand hits, but Flood, a wonderful hitter and center fielder, had a greater impact on the game. Traded to Philadelphia in 1969, Flood refused to report and instead challenged major league baseball's "reserve clause" in court for treating him like "a piece of property to be bought and sold irrespective of my wishes." His own suit was unsuccessful, but his position would be vindicated in later reforms that provided a path to free agency for all players (and indeed all professional sports).

The third outfielder was the white slugger Roger Maris, who had also offended traditionalists by eclipsing Babe Ruth's single-season home run record as a New York Yankee in 1961. Because he set the record in a slightly longer season, his achievement was given an asterisk in the official records.

seemed to belong to a different era. A true fan, I cared only that the game be played at its highest level.

Without realizing it, I had bought into the myth of meritocracy: now that civil rights laws were in the books, anyone with talent and drive (and maybe a little assist from affirmative action) could succeed. Recent scholarship, reinforced by so many cell phone videos of tragic police encounters, has thoroughly debunked that myth. In *The New Jim Crow*, Michelle Alexander documents the impact of mass incarceration from the 1970s forward; in *The Color of Law*, Richard Rothstein recounts the legacy of twentieth-century government-sponsored discrimination in the form of discriminatory zoning, redevelopment, and eligibility rules for government benefits. Many other essayists, memoirists, and poets have explored the stomach-turning ugliness of contemporary discrimination, in works like Isabel Wilkerson's *Caste*, Ta-Nahesi Coates's *Between the World and Me*, and Claudia Rankine's *Citizen*. But these correctives seem to have done nothing to stop the propagation of baseless claims of voter fraud and the wild fiction of replacement theory.

This essay explores the long history of American racial mythmaking, leading up to the brief, exceptional period of the 1960s, when just enough Americans saw past the myths to enable civil rights progress. In a country almost 90 percent white at the time, white attitudes dictated just how far the movement could go, before another set of myths emerged.

1. FLUIDITY

Today we know that race is no more than a social construct. Recent DNA studies confirm that, among other things, almost all of us descend from groups that walked out of Africa on the order of fifty to one hundred thousand years ago, more or less. More important, human groups have repeatedly interbred: "Present-day populations are blends of past populations, which were blends themselves."[2]

Yet family histories show that people had always understood the artificiality of race. Take the "one drop" rule adopted by state legislatures in Virginia and other southern states. A person with one great grandmother of African descent could have seven ancestors of European descent out of eight in that generation. What purpose could be served by assigning such a person a Black identity?

---

2. Reich, *Who We Are*, xxii, 28.

In the midst of the eugenics movement, just as Hitler was coming to power in Germany, William Faulkner provided a devastating answer in *Absalom, Absalom!* (1936). Faulkner's use of multiple narrators, slight inconsistencies, and branching sentences spanning several pages immerses the reader in the perspective of the Deep South's planter class. Henry Sutpen, son of the wildly avaricious, self-made Mississippi planter Thomas Sutpen, defends the engagement of his sister Judith to his college friend Charles Bon, even after learning that Charles is their half-brother. But when he learns that Charles is also an "octoroon" (that is, he had a Black great-grandmother), Henry will do anything to prevent the union. Bigamy, fornication, incest, murder, and arson are more tolerable in the novel's reflexively hierarchical society than the rise of a mixed-race person to the propertied class.

Faulkner was barely exaggerating. In the National Book Award–winning *The Hemingses of Monticello*, Annette Gordon-Reed recounts two hundred years of the Hemings family, house servants, in-laws, and descendants of Thomas Jefferson. Jefferson was no Thomas Sutpen, of course, but North American plantation slavery was cruel even in the most refined settings. He had inherited several members of the Hemings family from his late wife Martha, including young Sally Hemings. As the daughter of Martha's father John Wayles and Elizabeth (Betty) Hemings, a mixed-race house servant, Sally was Martha's half-sister and no more than one-fourth of African descent. By some accounts, Abigail Adams saw danger ahead when the beautiful fourteen-year-old arrived in London accompanying Jefferson's younger daughter, on their way to join Jefferson in Paris in 1787. Gordon-Reed ties the story together. Jefferson had promised the dying Martha that he would not remarry, so that their two daughters would not have to answer to a stepmother. When Sally became pregnant in Paris, at seventeen, the forty-six-year-old Jefferson promised her that their children would be freed after his death, in order to preserve the relationship and, quite possibly, to keep it secret. (Gordon-Reed explains that Sally could have walked away, because pre-revolutionary French courts did not enforce slaveholder ownership claims.) Jefferson found a way to keep his promises to both women and to abide by the norms of his race and class, while getting what he wanted.[3] Indeed, he followed through with that promise of freedom even though only two of their four surviving children were freed in his will; the other two, William Beverley Hemings

---

3. Gordon-Reed, *Hemingses*, 145 (Martha Jefferson's request), 175–76 (French law), 202 (Abigail Adams), 347 (Jefferson's motives), 285, 597 (Beverley and Harriet Hemings).

and Harriet Hemings, had been freed as young adults a few years before Jefferson's death, per their parents' long-standing plans. As no more than one-eighth of African descent, Beverley and Harriet "took white spouses and left blackness completely behind."[4]

It's tempting to see Beverley and Harriet as relatively fortunate, to be both free from slavery and able to assume white identities. But pause on that for a moment. In order to pass as white, Beverley and Harriet, at twenty-four and twenty-one, respectively, would have had to invent new life stories, move out of Virginia, have no further contact with their families, and make their way north into a new world of complete strangers. This must have been an unbelievably lonely and risky prospect. Yet their parents wished this life for them, giving them money and hoping never to see them again. Beverly and Harriet would have been obligated to hide the identity of their parents, one of whom was the third president of the United States and founder of the University of Virginia. Jefferson again did his part to protect (by denying) his children, making a careful record that these slaves "ran away." And this elaborate ruse was seen as better, far better, for them than living even as free black adults in the Virginia of 1822.

Gordon-Reed also emphasizes that Virginia had changed the rules of inheritance for Black families in the 1700s; children received the racial status of their mothers rather than their fathers.[5] Otherwise, as Faulkner's characters feared, plantations could be split between a patriarch's white and mixed-race children, and the social order upended. Much easier to regulate social class than the sexual prerogatives of planters. Gordon-Reed quotes the white Civil War diarist Mary Chesnut: "Unable to do anything about it, many a Southern white woman feigned ignorance of illicit, interracial relationships, at least those that occurred under her own roof."[6] This meant that enslaved Black women, already subject to their masters' life-or-death control, also had to employ their wombs to bear children for their masters' financial benefit.

The fluidity of race, then, was always pretty obvious, as were the social and financial prerogatives at stake. Faced with that reality, after slavery was abolished, even more explicitly race-based (as opposed to property-based) measures would be needed to sustain the existing social order.

---

4. Gordon-Reed, *Hemingses*, 601.
5. Gordon-Reed, *Hemingses*, 45–47.
6. Gordon-Reed, *Hemingses*, 346.

2. FOUR FICTIONS

The new racism included infamous measures that lasted until the 1960s: Black Codes and Jim Crow laws, prison labor camps and lynching. These were supported in white communities throughout the country by layers of long-held, widely accepted disinformation:

- The "states' rights" narrative of the Civil War—that the Confederacy fought against federal interference and not about slavery (and certainly not about abuses of basic human rights).
- Union virtue—that since the federal government had done what it could in winning the Civil War, blame for racial inequities could be deflected to the explicit laws and practices of the former Confederacy.
- The "Redeemer" narrative about Reconstruction—that the restoration of white control in the South in 1877 ended a period of chaotic rule by freed Blacks incapable of governance.
- Eugenics—a fake science of racial hierarchy that lent intellectual support to race-based policies, widely accepted for decades until Nazi atrocities thoroughly discredited it.

Princeton historian James McPherson provided a corrective view in *Battle Cry of Freedom* (1988). The Civil War was triggered by an economic impasse between white constituencies over the geographical scope of slavery. Northerners had long wanted to assure that new states were available for white settlement and paid white labor in the Northern economic model.[7] Unpaid slave labor could fatally undermine this still-racist goal: the newer states of Louisiana, Mississippi, and (nearly) Alabama had become dominated by a small number of massive plantations and had majority or near-majority Black (and nonvoting) populations. The sectional split became stunningly clear when party lines shattered over Democratic Pennsylvania congressman David Wilmot's unsuccessful 1846 proposal to bar slavery from territory acquired during the Mexican War. Regardless of party, almost every Northern congressman supported the Wilmot Proviso and almost every Southern congressman opposed it.[8]

---

7. A stark example of this Northern attitude: my home state of Oregon was admitted to the Union on Valentine's Day, 1859, two years before the Civil War began. It came in as a "free" state, and its constitution forbade Blacks from entering. Foner, *Reconstruction*, 26. Freedom from slavery meant excluding both Blacks and plantation owners.

8. McPherson, *Battle Cry of Freedom*, 54.

AN EVANESCENT COALITION

While McPherson's corrective view greatly complicates the story of Union virtue, it destroys the remnants of the states' rights theme. Southern politicians and their constituents could not, and would not, tolerate any effort to hem in their peculiar institution. Only at the risk of war did they agree to parity with the North in the Missouri Compromise (1820) and the Compromise of 1850: a new slave state for each new free one. The reason is clear enough: The Southern states had nearly half their wealth tied up in slave ownership, and the rest mostly in land, the value of which depended on the cost of labor.[9] Every additional slave state drove up demand for, and the market value of, enslaved persons. Southerners were the main supporters of the Mexican War, which added the huge slave state of Texas, and more adventurous efforts to annex Cuba and parts of Central America. Without those new markets, they worried, their property values, and the institution itself, would collapse. They did not seek merely to preserve the power of states to permit human bondage—they wanted a growing empire of slavery.

The exigencies of war then moved the Union toward full abolition, but largely for strategic reasons. Because former slaves consistently and courageously chose an uncertain fate with the Union Army (which may as well have arrived from Mars) over the supposedly benign rule of the planters, slavery—and the plantation economy—ended wherever the Union Army went, all the way to Juneteenth.[10] To help ensure that the old South would not rise again, Congress required the Southern states to ratify the Thirteenth and Fourteenth Amendments, abolishing slavery and guaranteeing equal protection of the law, as well as manhood suffrage (later the Fifteenth Amendment), as conditions for readmission to the Union.[11] The universal manhood vote, to include upcountry whites as well as Blacks, was seen as necessary to prevent restoration of plantation owner dominance; it did not pose political concerns outside the South since few Blacks lived there. Reconstruction clearly was intended to empower Black voters; it was also in the self-interest of the dominant Republican Party, which expected (correctly) to benefit from Black votes.

Reconstruction failed, as its preeminent historian, Eric Foner, concluded, but not for the reasons put forth by redeemers. To understand the twentieth-century civil rights revolution, it is essential to see that Reconstruction failed partly because of its own insufficiencies, partly because it

---

9. Piketty, *Capital*, 160.
10. Levine, *Fall*, 155; Foner, *Reconstruction*, 4.
11. Foner, *Reconstruction*, 276–77.

was abandoned by national Republicans, and partly because it was actively killed off by southern Democrats.[12]

Reconstruction was not a single coherent program but a series of compromise steps that gained majority support at the moment. With hindsight, we can see that its major omission was a meaningful economic program. While Blacks were initially allowed to earn wages, vote, hold office, and acquire property, they had been deprived of education and had essentially no capital; only the incredibly ambitious, and fortunate, could succeed with such handicaps. To make matters worse for all, the region's agrarian economy was underdeveloped and severely damaged by the war. In 1889, Atlanta newspaper editor Henry Grady could still complain that every item at a recent funeral, from coffin to wagon to clothes, had been made in the North from raw materials widely available in the South.[13] Reconstruction could have included economic reforms like straight land redistribution, but General Sherman's isolated wartime redistribution in Georgia ("forty acres and a mule") was soon reversed by President Andrew Johnson[14]—and/or a trade-financing program like the post–World War II Marshall Plan designed to revive and diversify the entire Southern economy. The Panic of 1873 and the deflationary economic policies of successive Republican administrations (the "Cross of Gold" derided by four-time Democratic presidential nominee William Jennings Bryan) further disadvantaged southern and western farmers, of all races, for a generation. An ebbing tide lowers all ships.

More important, white Southerners essentially rebelled again. Their Democratic Party advocated measures to keep the freedmen subjugated economically and socially, even to the detriment of regional economic development; the Ku Klux Klan and other violent white supremacist groups soon formed to keep freedmen from, among other things, voting. Congress and the federal government under President Ulysses S. Grant initially took decisive action to stifle the violence, passing the Ku Klux Klan Act (1871) and dispatching federal troops when necessary to stop what amounted to political insurrection.[15] But Grant's interventions proved unsustainable.

---

12. Foner, *Reconstruction*, 603.

13. Jacobs, *Cities*, 36–37, 93–94. Grady's point was that the South was by then adding the industrial capacity to make these items. The larger problem was that these items were not exactly cutting edge. At the US Centennial Exposition of 1876, new inventions had abounded: telephone, typewriter, electric light, the massive Corliss steam engine. Foner, *Reconstruction*, 564.

14. Foner, *Reconstruction*, 158–59.

15. Foner, *Reconstruction*, 454, 458, 551.

By the mid-1870s, he explained that "there was no sense in trying to save Mississippi if the attempt to do so would lose Ohio."[16]

In themes repeated in the twentieth century, the withdrawal of national support caused the freedmen's loss of personal safety and security and spelled the end of Reconstruction. The Democratic Redeemers swiftly suppressed Black voters and reasserted white power in every state of the former Confederacy. They left the Constitutional amendments and civil rights laws unenforced, with the blessing of several decisions by the US Supreme Court, leading up to the "separate but equal" doctrine of *Plessy v. Ferguson* (1896), which effectively encouraged systematic segregation. This was the most visible and visceral driver for the civil rights movement all the way through to the 1960s.

Amazingly, this history of local terrorism and nationwide neglect got repackaged into the Redeemer narrative of salvation. The landmark film *Birth of a Nation* (1915) reached a wide audience that included President Wilson's White House and helped to trigger a revival of the Ku Klux Klan throughout the 1920s, including in my native Oregon. And leading academic historians supported this narrative for decades until a generation of revisionists, inspired by W. E. B. DuBois's *Black Reconstruction in America* (1935), blew up its racist and narcissistic foundations.[17]

3. PROGRESS, CHILLED

The backlash did not make the Civil War amendments meaningless. As recounted in *The Warmth of Other Suns*, by Isabel Wilkerson, even the very unequal accommodations provided by interstate rail carriers enabled one crucial demographic change: the Great Migration. From the 1910s to the early 1970s, about six million Blacks moved out of the former Confederacy to cities in the North and West.[18] Many were pulled by industrial hiring during the First and Second World Wars, though migration continued even without this incentive. There the migrants experienced explicit discrimination and wretched economic and living conditions. This was neither equality nor real freedom, but it offered somewhat wider economic opportunities and some relief from the constant intimidation and threat of violence. It was enough that the migrants' friends and relatives, especially the young

---

16. Foner, *Reconstruction*, 563.
17. Foner, Reconstruction, xvii–xxi (DuBois and evolution of historians' views).
18. Wilkerson, *Warmth*, 8–9.

and ambitious, continued to leave their homes in remarkable numbers for sixty years.

It was enough freedom to allow a free Black culture to emerge in neighborhoods of the receiving cities, especially New York, Chicago, and Los Angeles. A few stars could shine, and white northerners began to notice. Musicians like Harlem-based Duke Ellington and Ella Fitzgerald, and athletes like the UCLA and Olympic sprinter Jesse Owens, became national icons in the 1920s and 1930s. Mississippi-born Richard Wright moved to Chicago as a young man and published the national bestseller *Native Son* in 1940. More concretely, the liberal wing of the Democratic Party began pressing vocally for new civil rights legislation during the Roosevelt administration, though they were stymied by southern Democratic senators whose support President Roosevelt needed to pass other New Deal legislation.

Thus, as World War II ended and Winston Churchill declared that an Iron Curtain was falling in Central Europe, the states of the former Confederacy still maintained what amounted to a system of apartheid. Not even the mildest civil rights legislation passed the southern-dominated Senate until the late 1950s. But the internal diaspora of the Great Migration had already created new possibilities and challenges: Blacks now had some political influence in the North; and whites outside the South now had to deal with race issues for themselves.

The Cold War did spark changes, but its impact was mixed at best. International criticism, from allies and foes alike, put a lot of heat on the US government. American leaders could not credibly hold up the country as a bastion of democracy and freedom, in contrast to totalitarian Communist regimes, as long as Black citizens were so visibly denied basic rights, including their supposed Constitutional right to vote. Jim Crow segregation embarrassed national leaders—even President Eisenhower, a little—both by fueling Soviet propaganda and by alienating diplomats from newly independent African nations, which were among the nonaligned countries, the free agents of the era.

But Cold War often eclipsed civil rights issues. Groundless Communist conspiracy theories were used to demonized left-leaning figures, including Black activists. And even welcome international attention did no more than amplify themes formulated by Black leaders. The actual case for justice had to be made right here in the USA.

Black-led organizations, including the NAACP and the Union of Sleeping Car Porters, gained some important victories in the 1930s and 1940s, as their voters gained visibility outside the South. Though he was not especially progressive, President Truman took action because he knew he would need northern Black voters in the 1948 election,[19] and he worried about both liberal challenger Henry Wallace and Republican Tom Dewey running to his left on this issue. In response to a wave of violence against returning Black servicemen in 1946–47, Truman sponsored a Committee on Civil Rights which concluded that in southern states "the white population can threaten and do violence to the minority member with little or no fear of legal reprisal."[20] Truman then pushed anti-lynching legislation (blocked by southern Democrats), issued an executive order integrating the armed forces and the federal civil service and, at the height of the 1948 presidential campaign, gave a speech in Harlem to a crowd estimated at 65,000.[21] The movement also achieved important court victories, well before *Brown v. Board of Education* (1954) overturned the separate-but-equal doctrine of the *Plessy* case. The Supreme Court banned segregation in interstate transport (1946) and voided racially restrictive real property covenants (1948), while the California Supreme Court ruled the state's anti-miscegenation statute unconstitutional (1948).

None of these things would have happened without Black activism. It is true that Truman cited Cold War concerns in advocating anti-lynching legislation, but NAACP petitions to the United Nations had already helped put it on the international agenda.[22] That Harlem crowd of 65,000 did not spontaneously assemble. These indications of Black political influence are even more remarkable when we remember that about half the country's Blacks, who still lived in the South, had effectively no say at the ballot box.

The progress of the late 1940s was not followed up. What happened to civil rights in the 1950s? One answer is: the Cold War. Beginning with to the Communist military victory in China (1949), followed by the Korean War and Soviet advances in nuclear weapons, fear of Communism dramatically escalated in the US. Even before Senator Joseph McCarthy's notorious inquisitions, the Truman administration moved on its own to "clean up" the State Department, draw a hard line in Korea, and vastly escalate

---

19. Borstelmann, *Cold War*, 59; Dudziak, *Cold War Civil Rights*, 26.
20. Borstelmann, *Cold War*, 56.
21. Dudziak, *Cold War Civil Rights*, 81–82.
22. Borstelmann, *Cold War*, 76–77; Dudziak, *Cold War Civil Rights*, 43–44.

defense spending. Nevertheless, Congressional Republicans swept into power in 1950, claiming that Democrats were soft on Communism, and Dwight Eisenhower was elected president in 1952. Unlike northern Democrats, Eisenhower-era Republicans relied on a white voting base outside the South and could afford to go slow on civil rights issues. The president himself seems to have hoped that these issues could be resolved locally, lifting a finger only when Arkansas Governor Orville Faubus pointedly refused to obey a 1957 federal court order integrating Little Rock schools. Even then, Eisenhower tried to steer a middle ground, praising the Confederacy while condemning white violence.[23]

Perversely, prominent civil rights activists were harassed for fear their criticism of the US would aid the cause of global Communism. In the early 1950s, the State Department prevented the singer Paul Robeson from leaving the country, and the dancer Josephine Baker, by then a French citizen, from entering the US and from performing in pre-Castro Cuba.[24] As George Orwell might have observed, freedom was denied in the cause of freedom.

The most powerful conspiracy-minded segregationist was FBI Director J. Edgar Hoover. Having cut his teeth during the first Red scare of the early 1920s, Hoover was a media-savvy operator who prioritized anticommunist espionage over the agency's ostensible job of enforcing federal law. (Attorney General Bobby Kennedy actually had to shame Hoover into investigating the Mafia.) Hoover was sure—quite wrong, but sure—that civil rights leaders were connected in some way to international Communism. He dragged his feet on requests to protect civil rights activists and to prosecute vigilantism in the South—effectively worsening the violence—but intentionally compiled dossiers on the sexual behavior of politicians and civil rights leaders, including President Kennedy and Martin Luther King, in service of his political goals.[25] An FBI conference agenda from late 1963 expressly stated that "we are most interested in exposing [King] in some manner in order to discredit him."[26] Even more shockingly, Hoover attempted to silence King by having excerpted hotel room tapes sent to him with a crudely worded blackmail message.[27] King did not need

---

23. Borstelmann, *Cold War*, 85–93; Dudziak, *Cold War Civil Rights*, 129–30; Newton, *Eisenhower*, 251–52.

24. Dudziak, *Cold War Civil Rights*, 61–62, 66–76.

25. Branch, *Pillar of Fire*, 148–50.

26. Branch, *Pillar of Fire*, 196.

27. Branch, *Pillar of Fire*, 294.

to be Sherlock Holmes to guess the real source of the wiretaps and, though shaken, he persisted.

Finally, US leaders consistently decided that Cold War concerns outweighed racial justice in many other parts of the world. The US needed South African uranium, so it said little and did nothing about apartheid. The US needed a jet refueling station on Portugal's Azores islands, so it said little and did nothing about Antonio Salazar's unapologetic colonial repression: "I cannot give in Africa what I cannot grant to my own people."[28] Worst, and most lasting, was Vietnam. As explained above,[29] the alliance with France in Western Europe and the ongoing Korean War had given the US two powerful reasons to support France's defense of its colonial holdings against Ho Chi Minh's Communist Party. After the French defeat in Northern Vietnam in 1954, the US stayed involved in order to fight the spread of Communism, but the ill-fated escalation of the 1960s would play a major role in limiting the success of the domestic civil rights movement.

4. OUT OF SIGHT

Unlike the nuclear threat, civil rights issues got almost no attention from Hollywood, and Black American stories got only very little. The Production Code, in effect from the 1930s the mid-1960s, limited national distribution to films that would not offend sensitive white audiences; McCarthy-era blacklisting of supposed Communist sympathizers reinforced this self-censorship by driving politically active artists underground or overseas.

For these and other reasons, during the key decades 1950–70:

- Only one Black actor, Sidney Poitier, and two Black actresses, Dorothy Dandridge and Juanita Moore, were even nominated for Oscars.[30]
- *1001 Movies to See before You Die*, Barron's fairly inclusive critics' list of American and foreign titles, includes by my count only five American movies with Black leads.[31]

28. Borstelmann, *Cold War*, 152.
29. Chapter 2, "Vietnam."
30. Poitier was nominated for *Defiant Ones* (1958) and won for *Lilies in the Field* (1963); Dandridge won for *Carmen Jones* (1954); Moore was nominated for her supporting role in *Imitation of Life* (1959). No Black directors would be nominated until the 1990s.
31. Schneider, *1001 Movies*. The films are *Carmen Jones* (1954), *Defiant Ones* (1958), *Shadows* (1959), *Cool World* (1963), and *In the Heat of the Night* (1967) (yet another

- Most tellingly, only one film from those two decades made the 2016 *Slate* critics' survey of greatest movies by Black directors, *The Learning Tree* (1969) by the acclaimed photographer-director Gordon Parks.[32]

Sidney Poitier's rise to A-list stardom was an amazing achievement at the time, but it could also seem as though he was the only Black leading man in Hollywood. What's more, he was often cast as a nearly flawless hero, in roles designed to make white audiences comfortable. For example, Poitier's Philadelphia homicide detective is miles smarter, cooler, and braver than any of the whites in small-town Mississippi in *In the Heat of the Night*. The film (just) avoids caricature by allowing Poitier's character a moment of anger ("They call me *Mister* Tibbs!"), and by casting Rod Steiger as a racist, but pragmatic, local police chief who resists political pressure for the larger purpose of solving the crime. The Black cotton field workers, whom Poitier's character sees on the way to meet the local patriarch, remind us how little had changed.

The Learning Tree, a semi-autobiographical coming-of-age film set in rural 1920s Kansas, also dramatizes discrimination—but settles for a morally straightforward story. The white sheriff murders fleeing suspects in three separate incidents; the teenage protagonist's girlfriend moves away after she is impregnated by a rich white boy; and the Black teens can only order their after-school Cokes to go. But the young protagonist's almost saintly behavior, and the fairness of the local judge releasing a wrongly accused Black farm worker in reliance on the protagonist's testimony, suggest that Parks (or the studio) was still very cautious about white audience reaction. It wasn't because of the Production Code: much edgier films like *Easy Rider*, *The Wild Bunch*, and *Midnight Cowboy* came out that same year. Not until 1971–73 was a small wave of Black-led films more widely recognized, a result of rather than a contribution to civil rights reforms: the action movies *Shaft* (also directed by Parks), *Superfly*, *Sweet Sweetback's Baadasssss Song*, and *The Spook Who Sat by the Door*, as well as award magnets *Sounder* and *Lady Sings the Blues*.

In music, Black artists had career opportunities, and they used forms they'd inherited to mount a revolution. It would be enough to say that the 1940s–60s was a golden age for jazz; Charlie Parker, Dizzy Gillespie, Miles Davis, John Coltrane, Thelonius Monk, Billie Holiday, Nina Simone

---

Poitier film).

32. Harris and Kois, "Black Film Canon," 1–5.

supplanted the high energy big bands with a full spectrum of innovative personal expression, from introspective to angry to soaring. This is American classical music, every bit as much as Bernstein, Copland, and Gershwin (another group of outsiders), and much of it will be played for centuries.

But jazz can be difficult, an acquired taste. The popular revolution was rock and roll, a blues-based form adopted or co-opted by white artists. The mass appeal of Elvis Presley in the 1950s and the Beatles in the 1960s created a generational watershed. Baby boomers of all colors and classes, and every generation since, have found it hard to enjoy older forms. Frank Sinatra, an A-list celebrity since his own years as a teen heartthrob in the 1940s, released his most acclaimed work in the mid-1960s, such as "Strangers in the Night," but he may as well have been singing in Latin. We couldn't understand what our parents saw in Sinatra; in contrast, our kids would always love the Beatles.

Recent documentaries now give us the chance to see Black artists at work in the 1960s. Netflix and other platforms have made it a point to carry documentary or fictionalized biopics (both, in some cases) of individual stars, all of them pioneers and survivors of official and de facto discrimination: Billie Holiday, Nina Simone, Charlie Parker, Sam Cooke, Ray Charles, Miles Davis, Quincy Jones, Aretha Franklin.

But the best films widen their lenses. *Twenty Feet from Stardom* (2012) profiles the predominantly Black, predominantly female singers who—with almost no recognition and very little reward—provided the church choir-like counterpoints for everyone from Ray Charles to the Rolling Stones, David Bowie, and, yes, Lynyrd Skynyrd. It's a testament to their artistry and perseverance and an example, if another were needed, of how Black contributions to our culture have been overlooked.

And now we have *Summer of Soul* (2021). In collecting and editing somehow-forgotten tapes of the summer-long Harlem music festival of 1969, with reflections from artists and attendees, the producer Questlove has given us an indispensable history of that creative, tumultuous, and now distant time. (Filmmakers have had little trouble finding footage of the Woodstock festival that same summer.) The Harlem festival, backed by the liberal Republican mayor John Lindsay, ran several weekends over the summer as a sort of escape valve to the Harlem community, which had endured occasionally violent demonstrations during the terrible summer of 1968. Naturally there were pop stars like the teenage Stevie Wonder, Sly and the Family Stone, Gladys Knight and the Pips, David Ruffin (recently of the Temptations), and the Fifth Dimension, but festivalgoers also got to see gospel legends Mahalia Jackson and the Staples Singers and the political advocacy of Nina Simone. I got a chill to see the dozens of choir members of the Ephesian Church of God in Christ, from Berkeley, California, assemble on stage and sing "O Happy Day." I remembered the song of course—it's mesmerizing and life-affirming even for a committed agnostic—but only from the radio. In those years before MTV, and in my ignorance of gospel music, I had no idea what the group looked like. The true fan cares only that the music be performed at the highest level.

5. REACHING THE STAGE

With due regard for many fascinating and charismatic political leaders—Jack and Bobby Kennedy, Malcolm X, Bobby Seale, Barry Goldwater, George Wallace—the Shakespearean triumphs and tragedies of the 1960s would be played out by Lyndon Johnson and Martin Luther King. Enormously ambitious and unbelievably energetic, Johnson and King attained leadership at the time when decades of protest and political groundwork by many thousands could finally be realized. They shared a brief, glorious triumph. Within a week in the spring of 1968, one had surrendered, the other was murdered. But in the early 1960s, several things came together to push real breakthroughs.

A peaceful and morally grounded campaign. King came to be the most widely known and respected leader because he framed the movement as a moral struggle. King was a young minister in a Montgomery church when he was elected to lead the local bus boycott after Rosa Parks was arrested for sitting in white section of a city bus in late 1956. As cultural historian Louis Menand has written, King framed the boycott not as striking back in anger—an un-Christian response—but as withdrawing support from an evil system, of which the bus company was just a part. Thurgood Marshall, who had argued the *Brown* case and many others as the NAACP's lead attorney, thought the bus strike was a waste of resources: the policy was illegal, why not just sue? (The strike would in fact be resolved in court.) But King's insight was that court cases did not demonstrate the Black community's values or its commitment to justice. As Annette Gordon-Reed has observed, they wanted more than legal recognition; they wanted to be seen as human beings, as Jesus had said they should. And they were willing to continue to demonstrate, peacefully and in the face of violent resistance, until they achieved that goal.

Menand has explained that King was in this respect unlike Marshall, who had worked for so long and so successfully to change the law; unlike the writer and public intellectual James Baldwin, who used his own writing and media appearances to change minds; and unlike Malcolm X and the Black Panthers, who sought to form an exclusively Black movement that asserted its rights without apology and without promising to turn the other cheek. All of these avenues of advocacy were important and, despite intramovement tension, reinforced each other.[33] But it was the public demonstration of ordinary Black people simply seeking to behave like ordinary people that gripped the nation.

A young population that sought changes in their lifetimes. King was only the most visible member of a complex movement that featured a lot of independent young activists. For example, King had nothing to do with the student lunch counter sit-ins that swept the upper South in 1960; four freshmen at North Carolina A&T in Greensboro had seen little tangible progress from *Brown* and other court rulings, and they had had enough of waiting.

King was also not initially a strong supporter of the very dangerous Freedom Rides in 1961, led in large part by college students of both races. King's younger colleague, James Bevel, had the brilliant and very dangerous idea to have schoolchildren march in Birmingham in 1963 when the adults weren't eager to face Sheriff Bull Connor's truncheons and firehoses; Bevel also initiated the march from Selma to Montgomery in March 1965.[34] King came to support these actions—for example, he wrote his famous letter from the Birmingham jail at the outset of the Birmingham protests and walked with other leaders in the second, successful march from Selma. But the impatience of youth created much of the energy.

Predictable and unsympathetic villains. By the mid-1950s, it should have been apparent that the harshness of segregation would not survive national attention. Yet southern Democrats continued to defend the extreme perimeter of their states' segregation policies, to the point of filibustering every civil rights bill, including anti-lynching legislation, the most neutral reform imaginable, until the late 1950s. Their rationalization was

33. On the respective contributions of Baldwin, King, Malcolm, and Marshall, see Menand, *Free World*, 620–22; Boyle, *Shattering*, 89–91, 109–11.

34. Boyle, *Shattering*, 188; Branch, *Pillar of Fire*, 78.

that, despite all evidence to the contrary, local laws were sufficient to deter wanton murder.

Likewise, regional politicians and citizens reflexively resisted every step toward integration, with increasing levels of violence: from King's first campaign boycotting Montgomery's municipal bus system (1956), to Little Rock public schools (1957), a Woolworth lunch counter in Greensboro (1960), the interstate Greyhound bus station in Montgomery (1961), the steps of the University of Mississippi in Oxford (1962), Birmingham's downtown streets (1963), a Black church in Neshoba County, Mississippi (1964), and the Edmund Pettis Bridge in Selma, Alabama (1965), among many others.[35] Despite losing every political and public opinion battle until the passage of the Civil Rights Act of 1964 and the Voting Rights Act in 1965, reactionary behavior was so predictable and egregious that civil rights leaders had a bottomless well of opportunity for action whenever progress seemed to slow. When civil rights leaders turned to face north, wily Chicago Mayor Richard Daley stalled far more effectively by agreeing with them, in principle.[36]

A slain ally and a would-be FDR. Despite his support from Black voters, President Kennedy was initially reluctant to make civil rights a priority. Other Cold War firestorms bedeviled his administration from the very start: the Bay of Pigs fiasco, a botched summit with Khrushchev, a military standoff in Berlin (ending with construction of the Berlin Wall) all in 1961. The Cuban missile crisis took place in October 1962, the ill-fated overthrow and murder of South Vietnamese president Diem in November 1963. It was only the persistence of civil rights demonstrations that forced Kennedy and his brother, Attorney General Robert Kennedy, to get involved, particularly in the cases of the Freedom Riders in that eventful summer of 1961 and the James Meredith admission to the University of Mississippi in the fall of 1962.

By the time TV cameras caught Bull Connor turning firehoses on schoolchildren in May 1963, the Kennedys had seen enough. The president introduced civil rights legislation that summer and green-lighted the march on Washington that August, providing King (among many others) the national platform they needed.

---

35. For key episodes of civil rights movement, see Boyle, *Shattering*, 97 (Montgomery bus resolution), 102 (Greensboro), 114 (Freedom Rides), 124–25 (JFK and Birmingham); Branch, *Pillar of Fire*, 87 (JFK and Birmingham).

36. Boyle, *Shattering*, 218–20.

AN EVANESCENT COALITION

After John Kennedy's assassination, Lyndon Johnson, a former Texas senator and Senate majority leader, sensed what he could accomplish in that New Deal–like moment. Johnson threw his support behind a stronger civil rights bill, which passed in the summer of 1964, then swept to victory in the 1964 election with a huge congressional majority. The only dark cloud was the Gulf of Tonkin incident, a possibly made-up exchange of fire off the coast of North Vietnam that Johnson leveraged for congressional approval of military action (and to deprive his Republican opponent Barry Goldwater of a campaign issue).

Then in March 1965, just weeks after Johnson's inauguration, James Bevel's peaceful march for voting rights was violently halted by Alabama state troopers at the Edmund Pettis Bridge. Johnson was apoplectic. He addressed a joint session of Congress the following week, calling for swift action on the Voting Rights bill. And closed with the song lyrics "we shall overcome."[37] Watching on television, King reportedly teared up.

6. MUTUAL MISUNDERSTANDING

This was their finest hour. It was so much—too much for a lot of white voters—and yet it was also not enough, as events quickly showed.

Just five nights after the passage of the Voting Rights Act in August 1965, riots erupted in the Watts neighborhood of Los Angeles. The trigger had been a police traffic stop of a young Black driver that escalated unnecessarily.[38] Large-scale rioting broke out in Black neighborhoods every summer from 1964 (beginning in Harlem) through 1967 (beginning in Detroit), even before King's assassination in April 1968. The cause was almost always the use of excessive force by police. Voting rights were important, but Blacks also wanted to be safe on the streets: safe from criminal behavior and from police misconduct. They were not—not in the south, north, east, or west.

This proved to be the issue that really split the country. The rioting was terrifying to Black residents as well as alarming to white viewers. But most whites trusted and felt protected by their local police; the dramatic difference in police behavior in Black neighborhoods created a climate of fear that echoed Jim Crow. This did not persuade many whites that their own local police might be part of the problem. As we now know, it took the circulation of many cellphone videos, beginning with the 2008 killing

37. Branch, *Pillar of Fire*, 192 (Johnson speech).
38. Boyle, *Shattering*, 208.

of Oscar Grant III by transit police at Oakland's Fruitvale BART station, for the pervasiveness of this problem to become undeniable.

Vietnam further polarized opinions along racial lines. Black leaders almost universally condemned US involvement as, among other things, a wasteful effort that perpetuated a form of racist colonialism. King, after some delay and considerable introspection, announced his opposition with clarity in early 1967. Heavyweight boxing champion Muhammad Ali risked jail to avoid the draft that same year, calling out the racial lines of a war in which US troops were killing Vietnamese while Black Americans were still subjected to racist epithets, or worse.

Many white liberals also opposed the war, of course. Johnson's critics included those who hated losing, those who couldn't support more US casualties, and those who opposed the war itself. But most Americans favored the war effort as part of the larger fight against Communism and would have punished President Johnson's party for backing out.[39] As late as October 1969, polls showed large majorities—necessarily white majorities[40]—opposed to antiwar demonstrations and withdrawal from Vietnam after President Nixon appealed to the "Silent Majority" in a nationally televised speech.[41]

The year 1968 would be the beginning of a political exile for progressives. White voters vastly outnumbered Blacks, as Black leaders well knew. Nixon's law-and-order message would be racially neutral on its surface, a tacit acknowledgment of civil rights achievements, and would sound moderate in comparison to third party candidate George Wallace's explicit segregationism. The message also resonated with many voters, the so-called Silent Majority, who disagreed with Vietnam War protesters, feared racial disturbances in the cities, or were culturally unready to fully accept new ideas. It was effective enough to win a narrow electoral victory over the Democrats' most centrist candidate and to stop the tide of reform.

Nixon went on to declare a War on Drugs, a tough-on-crime move that would be emulated, under different names, by presidents of both parties with disproportional and devastating effect on Black communities. He won reelection with 70 percent of the white vote in 1972.[42] A new era of mythmaking had begun.

39. Menand, *Free World*, 689; Boyle, *Shattering*, 264–65.
40. Boyle, *Shattering*, 150 (White voters outnumbered Blacks nine to one).
41. Boyle, *Shattering*, 321–22.
42. Boyle, *Shattering*, 384.

Two takes. Top, from left, Vice President Spiro Agnew, the shah of Iran, and President Richard Nixon with a delegation of Soviet cosmonauts, October 1969. Nixon and Agnew were in their first year in office and were flush from the American astronauts' moon landing in July; the shah owed his position to the 1953 US-backed coup. But Agnew, Nixon, and the shah would each leave office in disgrace in the 1970s.

Bottom, President Nixon signs the Clean Air Act of 1970, December 1970. At left is William Ruckelshaus, the first Administrator of the Environmental Protection Agency. Ruckelshaus would later issue the order banning most domestic use of DDT in 1972, about ten years after Rachel Carson's *Silent Spring* brought public attention to the harms caused by some pesticides.

Credits: (Top) Warren Leffler, Library of Congress. (Bottom) Nixon White House Photo Office, U.S. National Archives.

5

Decade of Reckoning
Two Takes on the US Experience of the 1970s

I WAS BORN IN 1957 and became a teenager and young adult in the 1970s. It can be easy to see the uncertainties as well as the promise of this period as dated and anachronistic, but of course we couldn't have known what was coming. That's one reason to read history: to remind ourselves that things can always change dramatically. To try to convey the perspective of the time, this essay, much more than the others, reflects my personal views of events I lived through and remember.

TAKE ONE

1979 would be the worst.

Sure, we had experienced many setbacks by then and had plenty of reasons for skepticism about our leadership and the country's direction. And direction is a proxy for how many people felt about their own prospects.

Vietnam had been the watershed, of course. That war had differed in so many ways from the Good War paradigm—Americans as the liberators of World War II—that from the mid-1960s moderate and conservative adults had begun to join liberals in questioning its purpose and/or the means of its prosecution. While there was always broad agreement about opposing the spread of Communism—after Republicans had successfully tagged Harry Truman with losing China, Democratic Presidents Kennedy and Johnson were not about to get outflanked by the anti-communist right—Vietnam itself kept posing problems. The war was undeclared; the South Vietnamese government, or governments, had issues of legitimacy and popularity, and their commitment to the fighting seemed to be limited by what the US Army could provide; the countryside to be saved from Communism already seemed to contain a lot of, well, Communists (Vietcong). These were problems that firepower might not solve, and even the rosiest of military reports did not promise an early end to the conflict. The erosion of support from a historically conservative, newly affluent middle class was the real watershed. The federal government, especially under President Johnson, had pushed through some very progressive reforms—major civil rights legislation, Medicare, and anti-poverty programs—in part under the banner of Cold War competition about human rights and living standards. But his administration's institution of a military draft, and its escalation of the war to include over half a million troops, dissipated the goodwill from Johnson's crucial allies on the left.

To make matters worse, Vietnam blew open the nascent generation gap. During Johnson's post-1965 escalation, few in the Baby Boom generation (born 1946–64) had reached the voting age of twenty-one. But as the cohort's oldest members turned eighteen, they faced the most agonizing personal choices about Vietnam: whether to enlist, await a lottery number, seek a college deferment, support or protest against the war, and/or seek to avoid service altogether (as a conscientious objector or in Canada). As we would much later learn, many future political leaders avoided risky service, including Dan Quayle, Bill Clinton, Al Gore, George W. Bush, and Donald Trump. Future presidential candidates John Kerry and John McCain did see dangerous combat, though both lost their elections, and Kerry even got slimed in the process. The younger boomers, basically anyone born after 1954, mostly escaped those choices, but almost all would grow up knowing about the public discontent.

Well before 1979, then, the boomers came of age just as the mirror started to crack:

- By March 1968, the war was so unpopular that President Johnson stunningly decided not to stand for reelection. Within weeks, the nation was shaken internally by the assassinations of Martin Luther King and liberal presidential candidate Robert Kennedy. Republican candidate Richard Nixon felt obliged to declare, falsely, that he had a secret plan to end the war; as president, he continued to fight it.

- In November 1969, *New York Times* freelancer Sy Hersh broke the story of a massacre of Vietnamese civilians by a US Army division at My Lai village the year before. The news prompted a nationally televised congressional inquiry and captured overwhelming public attention. But eventually, just one participant, the unit leader Lieutenant William Calley, was convicted. Nixon commuted his sentence.[1]

- Poorly supervised national guard troops, called out to control antiwar demonstrators at Kent State University in Ohio, shot and killed four students there in May 1970, setting off another round of demonstrations. Another student protester was killed at historically Black Jackson State University in Mississippi just a few weeks later.[2]

- Military consultant Daniel Ellsberg leaked the classified Pentagon Papers to the *New York Times* and *Washington Post*, which published them in May 1971. This internal Defense Department history of US involvement in Vietnam revealed that administrations from Truman through Johnson had, among many strategic errors, consistently misled the public about the cost, nature, and extent of US military involvement in the conflict. Even worse, the government had long concealed frank—and highly unfavorable—appraisals of the political and military situation at the time.[3]

- On the occasion of Yom Kippur, 1973, Egypt and its Arab allies invaded Israel in a surprise attack, seeking to take back territory Israel had occupied since the famous 1967 Six-Day War. Israel recovered militarily, but the West suffered collateral damage for its support of Israel. OPEC, a Saudi Arabian-led consortium of mostly Arabic oil producing nations, announced an oil embargo against the US and a 70 percent price increase, driving the US economy (and others) into its worst recession since the Great Depression.[4]

- Nixon, unnerved by the Pentagon Papers leak (even though the study did not cover his presidency), created an in-house counterespionage unit called the "plumbers" who proceeded to break criminal laws, including the truly idiotic campaign burglary of Democratic headquarters in the Watergate building complex. After two years of slow-drip

---

1. Boyle, *Shattering*, 329–32, 353–54.
2. Boyle, *Shattering*, 345–46, 359.
3. Greenfield et al., *Pentagon Papers*, viii–x.
4. Judt, *Postwar*, 454–55.

revelations and televised congressional hearings, Nixon resigned in August 1974, facing certain impeachment. He would have been charged with obstructing justice, not for planning but for covering up the Watergate incident. His political crime, though, was losing the trust of fellow Republicans. When tape recordings of Oval Office meetings became public, even the hard-right former presidential candidate Barry Goldwater dropped him; Nixon had been lying to them, too.

- The North Vietnamese army swept into Saigon in the spring of 1975, in this period of deep US distrust of military commitments, thus mooting every drop of blood and every dollar the US had spent there.[5]
- In the wake of the Watergate scandal's uncomfortable revelations about covert CIA activities, the Senate launched a more systematic review of US intelligence activities. According to the Senate Church Committee report, the review was prompted by, among others, concerns over the secret war in Laos, spying on US civilians, and the covert destabilization of the democratically elected socialist government of Salvador Allende in Chile. It mentioned, barely, the 1953 covert action that had successfully installed the shah of Iran, then still in power.[6]

Then there was the economy. Improving living standards had been a key factor in the West's favor during the Cold War. Western Europe, especially Germany and France, had become wealthy since the end of World War II. Soviet leader Nikita Khrushchev, who had been embarrassed in the so-called kitchen debate over consumer living standards during Vice President Richard Nixon's 1959 visit, worried instead about shortages of housing, eggs, and other basic foods.[7] And that had been a period when the Soviet economy was doing comparatively well.

But the US economy seemed to have run out of gas. In the late 1970s, I sometimes rode to and from college on commercial buses, which stopped with agonizing inevitability at every little mill or port town in New England. These tired places, which had once displaced agriculture as engines of employment, had themselves been displaced by larger scale operations in the Midwest and elsewhere and could have told a cautionary tale for the Detroit and Pittsburgh of the time.

5. Lawrence, *Vietnam War*, 166–68.
6. U.S. Senate Select Committee, "Final Report," 35, 111.
7. Kempe, *Berlin 1961*, 4, 6; Newton, *Eisenhower*, 296–97.

More recently, economists have pointed to 1973 as a turning point, to show that the US middle class has since fallen ever further behind the very wealthy. That is not surprising: the 1973 downturn was certainly noticeable at the time. With the OPEC oil embargo, high inflation, low growth rates, and high unemployment suddenly plagued the US. The stock market plunged 40 percent in 1973–74, a drop similar in magnitude to 2008–09. But the troubles couldn't have been more different. It was not just the financial sector but the entire economy that seemed to have become ill. Worse, it was not at all clear what to do about it.

Unlike in the Soviet Union, US voters and consumers were able to demand change, but political change could not provide a quick fix. Jimmy Carter's successful 1976 presidential campaign pointed to an alarming measure called the Misery Index, a mashup of the annual inflation and unemployment rates. While these two figures measure very different things, they were generally thought to be *inversely* related—high unemployment usually reduces consumer spending, making it hard to raise prices—so it was quite disturbing when the two rose together. Unemployment ranged between 6 percent to 11 percent from 1974 through 1986, inflation between 6 and 13 percent per year between 1974 and 1982. These figures would be almost shocking today. Unfortunately for Carter, the Misery Index actually rose at the end of his watch, to over twenty (slightly higher than the Nixon-Ford peak of around eighteen).[8] Having blamed Republicans for short term economic results before, Carter shouldn't have been surprised when the Misery Index was turned against him in 1980.

Although 1973 was clearly a turning point, it's vital to acknowledge that serious problems had arisen by the end of that postwar growth period that the French call the *Trente Glorieuse*. US budget deficits were driven up by the cost of the Vietnam War, providing a security guarantee to Western Europe and Japan, and the continued development of nuclear weapons that were meant never to be used. These deficits, plus the increasing wealth of US trading partners in Europe and East Asia, made it impossible for the US to continue its promise to redeem dollars for gold at thirty-five dollars per ounce under the postwar Bretton Woods arrangements. While this showed the success of the alliance reconstruction strategy, its immediate impact was to devalue the dollar and increase the price of imported goods. Those imports included most of the country's oil needs, then a far greater percentage

---

8. Average annual unemployment rates: U.S. Department of Labor, "Household Data, 1953–2023"; inflation rates: US Inflation Calculator, "Historical Inflation Rates."

of the country's expenses than today, making the country more vulnerable to OPEC's price increases. Energy, we abruptly learned, is a component of almost all goods and services, which accordingly rose as well. These price increases hit the middle and lower classes hardest and de-stimulated the economy by sending currency abroad. Interest rates rose as lenders defensively recognized they needed to make a higher return on their money to keep pace, effectively tightening credit by increasing the cost of borrowing and making the stock market look much less attractive. Labor unions and other workers with bargaining power demanded wage increases to keep up with inflation. These interdependent factors, called the inflation spiral, drove consumer prices up by over 100 percent from 1972 to 1980, creating uncertainties that are difficult to imagine today, even with the hopefully brief spike in 2021–22.

These economic developments don't fully convey the sense of fading competence. Ralph Nader's 1965 book *Unsafe at Any Speed*, best known for its critique of the Chevrolet Corvair, exposed the entire auto industry's failure to integrate safety features and led to national transportation safety regulation. The Corvair came off the market, but the arrogance and incompetence of the bottom-line driven Detroit culture would continue for two full decades. My family made the mistake of purchasing a late-1970s Chevy Monza that often stalled, like a novice driver in a stick shift, when starting on hills. But it had an *automatic transmission*. A Cadillac or a Lincoln, the top of the line, may have featured powerful (and gas-guzzling) engines, but also the ride and handling of an oil tanker. My parents briefly owned one of those, too. The country was only beginning to feel the effects, positive and negative, of competition from foreign manufacturers, at first mainly from Japan. In an ironic echo of the lack of incentives for productivity in the Soviet Union, the limits of foreign competition had reduced incentives in the US by the 1970s.

The malaise was hardly limited to the auto industry or to the practices of management in industries dominated by few companies. At a time of unprecedented gas price increases for drivers, the Penn Central Railroad, operating in the most densely populated part of the country, went bankrupt; at the same time, American visitors to Europe marveled at the convenience of the Eurail Pass. East Coast dockworker strikes delayed for years the introduction of container shipping; this revolutionary improvement in labor and energy productivity violated union work rules.

The problems of quality and innovation extended even to matters of taste. Coffee sales were dominated by Folgers and Hills Brothers; coffee could also be purchased on the East Coast at the chains Dunkin Donuts and Chock Full o' Nuts (the latter referring to store's origin as a nut roastery and not, as some would have it, to the customers). Budweiser and Miller were premium beers. Baskin Robbins 31 Flavors was a big ice cream treat. The glimmers of hope illustrated US cultural dependence on Europe: Alice Waters started a food revolution by opening the French nouvelle cuisine–inspired Chez Panisse in the radical utopia of Berkeley, California, in 1971, a long way from Kansas, you might say. A chardonnay and a cabernet from California stunned the world by winning an international blind tasting competition in Paris in 1976, a time when no one saw the Gallo-dominated wine industry in Napa County as a tourist destination.

Cynicism and irony percolated through the culture. Crosby, Stills and Nash had once invited fans to the 1968 Democratic National Convention in Chicago in order to change the world. But the event sharply disappointed liberal expectations, concluding with the defeat of the "peace" candidate Eugene McCarthy and violent suppression of antiwar demonstrations by Mayor Richard Daley's police department. The *Rolling Stone* correspondent Hunter S. Thompson, one of the New Journalists who did not shy away from expressing his personal views, would later describe Democratic nominee Hubert Humphrey as "a treacherous, gutless old ward-heeler who should be put in a goddamn bottle and sent out with the Japanese current."[9] Nixon came in for worse—and that was before Watergate. Not long after, joined by the more radical Neil Young, CSN was singing "Four Dead in Ohio" and "Alabama."

This turn had roots well beyond Vietnam and Watergate. The period was riddled with pointless violence. Of the string of murders by members of the Charles Manson cult, Joan Didion famously wrote:

> Many people I know in Los Angeles believe that the Sixties ended abruptly on August 9, 1969, ended at the exact moment when word of the murders on Cielo Drive spread like brushfire through the community, and in a sense this is true. The tension broke that day. The paranoia was fulfilled.[10]

---

9. Thompson, *Fear and Loathing*, 118.
10. Didion, *White Album*, 47.

Didion's point, brilliantly established in her essay, was that the tension had been building for a long time. But it is hard to agree that it broke. Many remained angry, armed, and on edge. In December 1969, Chicago police, aided by the FBI, assassinated twenty-one-year-old Black Panther leader Fred Hampton in a hail of gunfire. In September 1971, New York State officials abandoned efforts to negotiate with striking prisoners who had taken control of the Attica Correctional Facility in protest over prison conditions; frustrated officers, sent in to regain control, opened fire into a cloud of tear gas, killing thirty inmates and nine correctional officers who had been held as hostages. The radical left Weather Underground carried out a series of bombings of government buildings in the early 1970s, including the office of the New York Commissioner of Corrections (in response to Attica), the US Capitol building, and the federal Defense and State Departments (primarily in opposition to the Vietnam War effort). A bizarre offshoot, the Symbionese Liberation Army, kidnapped media heiress Patricia Hearst in 1974 and later involved her in an armed bank robbery. President Gerald Ford's efforts to move the country past the Watergate scandal were met with two assassination attempts seventeen days apart in September 1975, in Sacramento and San Francisco. The unimaginable mass murder of nine hundred People's Temple cult members (and others) in Jonestown, Guyana, took place in November 1978. The People's Temple had moved to Guyana from the San Francisco Bay Area, to free themselves of outside interference, so most members had Bay Area connections. Less than two weeks later, former San Francisco Supervisor Dan White shot Mayor George Moscone and Supervisor Harvey Milk to death at close range inside City Hall. Milk was likely the first openly gay elected official in US history, and he had sponsored one of the country's first successful gay rights measures. White, a conservative former firefighter, had made a huge political error, offering his resignation after a salary measure he promoted had failed, and was angry that he couldn't get his position back. True to the era, he couldn't think of a more productive way back into power. His lawyers would later argue, in mitigation, that he was too depressed to premeditate the killings, as evidenced by his increased consumption of junk food, and the jury returned the lesser verdict of voluntary manslaughter; this became known, somewhat misleadingly, as the Twinkie Defense.

Skepticism seemed the only sane response. Smart-mouthed iconoclasts were the heroes of the first popular Vietnam movie, *M*A*S*H* (1970), ostensibly set in the Korean War but filmed in a tropical setting to make the allusion to Vietnam unmistakable. Anti-establishment themes took many forms. Movies like *Easy Rider* (1969), *A Clockwork Orange* (1971), *Chinatown* (1974), *One Flew Over the Cuckoo's Nest* (1975), *Taxi Driver* (1976), and, in a different vein, the *Godfather* films (1972 and 1974) dominated a period many critics see as the golden age of American cinema. We heard similar themes in popular music, with a panoply of increasingly hopeless loners, as in "Don't Take Me Alive" from Steely Dan's *The Royal Scam* (1976) and "Psycho Killer" by the Talking Heads (1977). In less mainstream quarters, punk and reggae groups like The Clash and Bob Marley and Wailers simplified the message of protest, loud and clear.

This kind of thing might have gotten old by 1979, if it had not continued to resonate. In particular, the country was still struggling to come to terms with the disaster of Vietnam. *M*A*S*H* went on to become the most successful TV series of its era, from 1972–83. At the Academy Awards in April 1979, *The Deer Hunter*, a bitter saga of young working-class men drafted into the war, won the Best Picture award; Best Actor awards went to Jane Fonda and Jon Voight for the wounded-veteran drama *Coming Home*.

The Cold War seemed to have settled into permanence, or entrenchment. There were serious people who already described the Cold War in the past tense.[11] This attitude presumed the success of the 1970s policy of negotiated détente, which had for a time improved the tone of relations. Nixon's famous 1972 outreach to China had drawn the Soviets into discussions; the Helsinki Final Act (1975) on the Conference of Security and Cooperation in Europe was an important success, with accords on borders, military communications, trade, and human rights. But mainstream US politicians could not rely on diplomatic pretense. President Ford committed a huge gaffe in a 1976 presidential debate by stating that Poland was independent, implicitly free of Soviet influence, an Orwellian fiction underlying Helsinki. The Democratic nominee Jimmy Carter jumped on the error, using it to suggest that he would hold a tougher line.[12]

This showed, at least, that American setbacks had done nothing to improve the Soviet Union's even more dismal image, still almost that of a pariah state. Those who criticized the US at home did not thereby accept the worse behavior of its rival—quite the opposite, I would think. Even if Stalin's program of murder, genocide, and mass incarceration, and the Red

---

11. Braden, "What's Wrong with the CIA?," 1 (attached as Exhibit H to Church Committee Report).

12. Menand, *Free World*, 720.

Army's vicious suppression of dissent in East Germany, Hungary, Poland, and Czechoslovakia over two decades had not been well known, which they were, and even if George Orwell's *Animal Farm* and *1984* (his unthinkable future date by then just five years away) had not been standard high school reading for two decades, and even if the Soviet government had seemed less threatening since the end-of-days emergency of the Cuban Missile Crisis, the simple fact that the Soviet allies had to maintain armed prison walls to keep East Germans from fleeing *en masse* was an unmistakable sign of conditions behind the Iron Curtain. Though the Kremlin had participated in the Helsinki accords, bad news kept leaking out: Solzhenitsyn's *The Gulag Archipelago* about the Soviet political prison system was published in 1974; nuclear-physicist-turned-dissident Andrei Sakharov was awarded the Nobel Peace Prize in 1975 for his brave civil rights activism within the country; superstar dancer Mikhail Baryshnikov and poet Joseph Brodsky were among the talented Soviet citizens who escaped to the West whenever they could. For students and tourists, the Westerners most likely to want to learn about and understand foreign cultures, the Eastern bloc and China remained virtual no-go zones. We might hope, in optimistic moments, that the superpowers would continue talking, stand back another step or two from their nuclear missile triggers, and cut down on the Third World adventures.

All of this was a mere prelude to 1979, proof of the corollary of Murphy's Law: things are never so bad that they can't get worse.

January. In the wake of mass demonstrations against his regime, led by Islamists spouting anti-American vitriol, the shah of Iran leaves his country. He is never able to return. In February, the Ayatollah Khomeini returns from exile in France to lead the revolution and demands the return of the shah, which makes it very difficult for the shah to find a new home. Even his longtime ally, the United States, is initially reluctant to offer him assistance.[13]

The public begins to learn why. Iranian revolutionaries demonize the US and blame it for the shah's repression because of that little-known 1953 CIA operation that put the shah in power. Notwithstanding his ancient-sounding title, the shah's father had been a military strongman who took power in a British-sanctioned coup and assumed the title *shah* in the 1920s. His son lost power to the elected prime minister, Mohammed Mossadegh, who had nationalized the British-owned oil company in 1951 for its refusal to renegotiate pricing and improvements to the horrible conditions of local

---

13. Westad, *Global Cold War*, 295; Kinzer, *All the Shah's Men*, 197.

oil workers. The British then imposed an embargo on Iranian oil and took an increasingly hard line in negotiations after Winston Churchill replaced Clement Atlee as British prime minister later that year.[14] (Churchill snorted that "a splutter of musketry would have ended the matter."[15]) The Truman administration's effort to broker a compromise failed.[16] The new Eisenhower administration, led by the fiercely anti-Communist Dulles brothers, persuaded the president to authorize the CIA coup not to resolve the British-Iranian economic dispute but over concern of Soviet intervention.[17]

The CIA had often cited the 1953 Iran coup as a major success in support of the covert action program, as the Church Committee seemed to acknowledge just three years before the revolution.[18] Although this was a covert action, Iranians widely understood the shah to be a US client and blamed the US for the excesses of his regime. Even Eisenhower had privately expressed concern that disclosure of US involvement would have "embarrassed [the US] in the region" and closed off chances of future operations.[19] It was a hidden risk that the Eisenhower administration had visited upon the US of 1979.

March. In a remarkable case of art anticipating events, *The China Syndrome* with Jane Fonda and Jack Lemmon appears in theaters twelve days before the worst-ever US nuclear power accident at Three Mile Island in Pennsylvania. The core is badly damaged, and the reactor has to be permanently shut down, but no one dies and the radioactive release that greatly concerned the public turns out not to be especially alarming. In October, a presidential blue-ribbon panel headed by Dartmouth president and computer scientist John Kemeny finds that the accident originated with an equipment error but was made much, much worse by the response of the inadequately trained staff, such as their failure to keep emergency cooling systems on through the early stages of the accident.[20] The attribution to human error does not promote confidence. The civilian nuclear power industry never really recovers; higher safety standards and local opposition

---

14. For the British-Iranian oil dispute, see Kinzer, *All the Shah's Men*, 80–98.
15. Kinzer, *All the Shah's Men*, 132.
16. Kinzer, *All the Shah's Men*, 128–31.
17. Kinzer, *All the Shah's Men*, 157–58; Newton, *Eisenhower*, 102–5.
18. U.S. Senate Select Committee, "Final Report," 111; Westad, *Global Cold War*, 122–23.
19. Newton, *Eisenhower*, 102–5, 108.
20. President's Commission on the Accident, "Report," 10.

groups stop most new projects. One hopes that the military has much better control over its nuclear operations, but that information is highly classified.

Spring and Summer. More fallout from Iran: Shrinking production from this major producer leads to near panic in oil markets. The price of oil doubles from April 1979 to April 1980.[21] The US economy was no better prepared than in 1973. Gas lines return. Inflation returns. Saudi princes acquire more US real estate and flashy cars. President Carter appoints the hawkish Paul Volcker as Fed chair to get inflation under control, and Volcker sharply raises interest rates. Unemployment rises and another recession begins.

November. Iranian "students," furious with President Carter's decision to allow the shah to come to the US for medical treatment, and with the implicit sanction of revolutionary leaders, take fifty-two American hostages at the US embassy. This blatant breach of international law grabs and holds the attention of the US public, in a way nearly comparable to the 9/11 attack two decades later. ABC launches very successful late-night TV coverage, hosted by Ted Koppel, under the banner "America Held Hostage: Day XXX." The crisis would last throughout 1980, ending with the hostages' negotiated release hours before Ronald Reagan took the oath of office.

Christmas Eve. The Red Army takes over the airport in Kabul, Afghanistan. This comes as a great surprise to US intelligence agencies.[22] Detente, too, seems to have failed unexpectedly.

TAKE TWO

There was so much to admire in the United States, and not just progressive totems like great movies and music and integrated sports teams,[23] though those things were cool enough.

---

21. Gross, "What Iran's 1979 Revolution"; Judt, *Postwar*, 456.
22. Stone, *Atlantic*, 363, 367–68.
23. For example, the hard-hitting 1979 Pittsburgh Pirates adopted as their theme song the soul/disco hit, "We Are Fa-mi-ly" by Sister Sledge, a group of four sisters from the "Philadelphia sound" scene that included crossover stars Patti LaBelle, the O'Jays, Harold Melvin, and others. In baseball, the least integrated of the major professional sports, all the World Series champions of the decade were led by second-wave Black stars, including legends Frank Robinson (1970 Orioles); Roberto Clemente, Willie Stargell, and Dave Parker (1971 and 1979 Pirates); Reggie Jackson (1972–74 A's and 1977–78 Yankees); Vida Blue (1972–74 A's); and Joe Morgan (1975–76 Reds). Latin stars featured prominently on these teams as well: Mike Cuellar (Orioles); Clemente, Manny

Americans were loud, critical, and demanding. More important, they were not afraid of change. They had chased out Lyndon Johnson, thrown over Nixon just two years after overwhelmingly reelecting him, and switched to the novice politician Jimmy Carter two years after that. He wouldn't last either. They investigated the once-sacrosanct CIA and FBI for shocking abuses. They let their greatest city teeter on the edge of bankruptcy ("Ford to City: Drop Dead" ran the 1975 *New York Post* headline) to force it to make fiscal reforms. Major corporations went bankrupt (Penn Central Railroad, Franklin National Bank), were sued under antitrust laws (AT&T, IBM) and were deregulated (the New York Stock Exchange, savings and loans, airlines)—all events that forced changes in calcified industries. Major environmental laws for cleaner air and water, and the protection of endangered species, were enacted by Democratic Congresses and signed by Republican presidents—and the laws worked and continue to work. Entrepreneurs and policymakers had already proposed dozens of responses to the energy crises, some with long-lasting benefits, like car mileage standards and reflective glass for office buildings. (The oil price plunge of the 1980s would make many other ideas financially impractical.) They embraced, to an extent scarcely imaginable beforehand, liberalized divorce laws. The religious right asserted itself as a counterrevolutionary political force, especially on social issues, influencing elections and setting teeth on edge by calling itself the Moral Majority. If the American Dream was no longer a birthright, the country still had an exciting and youthful society of high expectations, sharp elbows, and serious consequences. You had better do your job well, it seemed, or someone would call you out and replace you.

Americans were also young. The midpoint of the huge baby boom cohort turned eighteen in 1975; recently expanded immigration from non-European countries also nudged the country younger and a bit less overwhelmingly white. Even as Vietnam's tragic endgame dissipated the energy of the late 1960s antiwar movement, Watergate and the oil shock–induced recession of 1974–75 blew holes in the façade of American institutional and economic superiority. There were plenty of reasons for cynicism and malaise, reasons to retreat into personal rather than political concerns. Yet, young people being young, there was still the capacity for joy.

Sanguillen, Rennie Stennett, Omar Moreno (Pirates); Bert Campaneris (A's); Tony Perez, Dave Concepcion, and Cesar Geronimo (Reds). Even the Boston Red Sox, shamefully late to integrate, became contenders with future Hall of Famer Jim Rice and the inimitable cigar-smoking pitcher Luis Tiant (El Tiante).

Instead of summoning the collective to Chicago or Woodstock like CSN and Joni Mitchell, or plaintively reflecting on the war and social troubles like Marvin Gaye in "What's Goin' On" (1971), we began to hear themes of individual escape in some of the best and most innovative popular music. Bruce Springsteen, echoed by Clarence Clemons's unforgettable sax, appealed to a romantic idea of the American road and its opportunities in songs like "Born to Run" and "Thunder Road."

Likewise, Earth, Wind and Fire's signature track, "September," asked a lover—with the group's incomparable harmonics—to remember a magical night. Even the loners and addicts of Steely Dan's elaborate studio productions got remarkably upbeat jazz-infused tracks. Long before *Breaking Bad*, the group recounted the rise and fall of a drug dealer (implicitly Black) in "Kid Charlemagne," the plight of Puerto Rican immigrants in "The Royal Scam," and an addict's delusions in "Doctor Wu."

This was all a surprising amount of fun. But individualism could have an edge. Not long after, Tom Petty sang, a bit hyperbolically, that he didn't want to live like a refugee. Petty, who'd grown up poor in rural Florida, had just won a long battle to extract his band from a harsh recording contract, leading the way for many other artists, at least those near the top of the charts. His quest followed the ultimately successful efforts of professional baseball players to gain the right of free agency. After St. Louis Cardinals' All-Star center fielder Curt Flood lost his groundbreaking effort to void a trade to the Philadelphia Phillies—he'd compared it to the purchase and sale of slaves—the players' union filed arbitration proceedings under the collective bargaining agreement to challenge the standard "reserve clause" that bound players to their teams. By 1976, white pitchers Catfish Hunter (A's), Andy Messersmith (Dodgers), and Dave McNally (Orioles) had been declared free agents; Reggie Jackson of the A's signed an unprecedented contract with George Steinbrenner's Yankees; and professional sports were never the same.

This may sound like special pleading for a comparatively elite group of workers, but their successes, coupled with the revolution of the civil rights movement, led the way for many marginalized groups to seek recognition.

Before there was *Roots*, Alex Haley's very popular African-American family history (and TV miniseries), there was *Bury My Heart at Wounded Knee* (1970). A surprise bestseller by Dee Brown, a university librarian, *Bury My Heart* retold the history of 1860–90 from the American Indians' perspective. In story after story, Brown made clear that the removal of

American Indians from their homelands was a military operation, often carried out by Union Army heroes of the Civil War using the same tactics of total war—destroying villages, property, and means of support. The deliberate destruction of 3.7 million buffalo in 1872–74 is horrifying to us today, but Union General Phil Sheridan described it as "the only way to bring lasting peace and allow civilization to advance."[24] Nothing, and no one, would be allowed to get in the way. The official US population more than doubled from 31 million to 63 million over the period, a tidal wave, especially in comparison to the country's American Indian population, which plummeted to about 250,000 according to the 1900 census.[25]

Brown's popular history stopped short of the American Indians' twentieth-century traumas under the subjugation of Congress and the Bureau of Indian Affairs: English-only boarding schools; "allotment," which permitted the partition and sale of reservation lands to outsiders; and the later policy of full termination of reservations, among other measures. However, by the early 1970s, the efforts of tribal civil rights leaders were beginning to chart a path upward from mid-century poverty, as Charles Wilkinson recounts in the modern history *Blood Struggle*.[26]

Public attention focused on highly visible demonstrations in the spirit of Black civil rights protests a decade earlier. These included the occupations of Alcatraz Island in San Francisco Bay beginning in late 1969 and Wounded Knee at the Pine Ridge Reservation in South Dakota in 1973. When Marlon Brando's name was announced at the 1972 Oscar ceremony, one of TV's most-watched broadcasts, actress Sacheen Littlefeather (Apache/Yaqui/Arizona) walked to the stage in ceremonial Apache dress to refuse the award on his behalf, due to Hollywood's frequently insulting characterizations of American Indians. But the tribes' strategic objective of regaining sovereignty was mostly achieved through legal channels. In perhaps the most prominent among a number of court decisions recognizing historic treaty rights, in 1974 US District Judge George Boldt interpreted a nineteenth-century treaty between the federal government and tribes in pre-statehood Washington, which provided for the Indians to retain "the right of taking fish, at usual and accustomed grounds and stations . . . in common with all citizens of the Territory" to give a 50 percent allocation to

---

24. Brown, *Bury My Heart*, 265.
25. Brown, *Bury My Heart*, 13, 415.
26 Wilkinson, *Blood Struggle*, 27–56.

the tribes.[27] Congress acted as well, reversing its own prior termination of the Menominee reservation in Wisconsin in 1973 and enacting the Indian Self-Determination and Education Assistance Act (1975), a centerpiece of President Nixon's legislative agenda, to reverse the policy of termination.[28] This laid the groundwork for later economic development of forest, mineral, and casino businesses. It has not, as Wilkinson makes clear, been a smooth or completely successful road, but the American Indian population rebounded to around 2.5 million by the year 2000, a remarkable recovery from the dire situation of a century before.[29]

In the wake of the civil rights movement, other marginalized groups found their voices and made foundational progress as well. The recent Oscar-nominated documentary feature *Crip Camp* (2021) highlights the three-week occupation the San Francisco office of the US Department of Health, Education and Welfare by disability rights activists in 1977, to demand adoption of employment regulations for federal contractors. Perhaps more important, Congress enacted the Individuals with Disabilities Education Act (1975) which required that public schools provide a free and appropriate public education to individuals with disabilities, ending an era of officially sanctioned segregation and neglect.

At about the same time, gay rights activists gained a vital objective in convincing the American Psychiatric Association to end the characterization of homosexuality as a psychiatric disorder.[30] By the mid 1970s, gay themes were also emerging in popular culture, still mostly coded and/or closeted. Before they were out, Elton John and Freddy Mercury of Queen filled stadiums; disco ruled the radio airwaves for a couple of years. As with *The Rocky Horror Picture Show* (1975), straight America—at least those of us who couldn't dance—completely missed the point. Many of us were so serious, even defensive, about our musical tastes that a little humor, or a secondary meaning, may as well have been in a foreign language.

Second Wave Feminism was nothing new by the 1970s, but it was still inspiring a lot of heat and light. Most histories date this wave to Simone de Beauvoir's *The Second Sex*, published in English in 1953, which led on to Smith College alumna Betty Friedan's *The Feminine Mystique* (1963). Women's groups had won sweeping legislative victories in the 1960s, most

---

27. Wilkinson, *Blood Struggle*, 200, 202.
28. Wilkinson, *Blood Struggle*, 177–205.
29. Ogunwole, "American Indian."
30. Lyons, "Psychiatrists, in a Shift," 1.

prominently in the Equal Pay Act signed by President Kennedy in 1963 and the last-minute inclusion of women in the Civil Rights Act of 1964.[31] Women (and men as well) gained greater autonomy in family matters throughout the sixties and seventies, with the increased availability of contraception, the Supreme Court's privacy-based rulings granting rights regarding contraception and abortion, and the gradual, state-by-state adoption of no-fault divorce laws.[32] As with the experience of Black Americans, however, winning the legal and rhetorical battles changed the culture only very slowly.

I remember. Moms with professional careers were still something of an anomaly when I was growing up in the late sixties and early seventies in ostensibly progressive Portland, Oregon. The girls at my upper middle class public high school did at least as well academically (or so it seemed to me), and girls' sports programs were expanding, though nowhere near equal. Things were considerably worse when I arrived at Dartmouth College in 1975. A wonderful institution, the formerly all-male college had just embarked on an ill-advised and ill-fated experiment with partial co-education. In a compromise with resistant alumni, men outnumbered women by three to one. As a result, the well-established fraternities dominated the social life, alienating many of the women, while most of the men necessarily, indeed mathematically, had to date either off-campus or not at all. Misogyny and homophobia were widespread and often very public. Somebody told me that every year a man spent at Dartmouth set him back a year socially, which was mordantly funny only because it we could see it in ourselves. But: the PEN/Pulitzer/National Book Critics Circle award winning novelist Louise Erdrich (class of 1976), whose books are mostly set in American Indian communities, and National Book Award winning historian Annette Gordon-Reed, '78, who studies colonial period slavery, came through that male-dominated and overwhelmingly white environment. College President John Kemeny, who had led the opening of co-education, recognized the first female valedictorian at my graduation in 1979, by reversing his usual opening: "Women and men of Dartmouth." (The college finally moved to sex-neutral admissions in the early 1980s and the gender ratio soon evened.)

Still, the feminists' victories had not exactly permeated the culture, not even the upper class white settings that the second wave was criticized for favoring. More work was needed, and some pushed their arguments further. Legal scholar Catherine MacKinnon's groundbreaking definitions

---

31. Menand, *Free World*, 566–72.
32. Borstelmann, *1970s*, 88, 92–93.

of workplace sexual harassment—including both *quid pro quo* demands for sexual favors and hostile work environments—would later be adopted by the Supreme Court.[33] Susan Brownmiller wrote that men have systematically used force, that is, rape and sexual assault, to subjugate women.[34] Andrea Dworkin denounced pornography for demeaning women by showing them principally as sex objects and for eroticizing sexual abuse and instilling terror.[35] (This was when it took some effort to view explicit pornography, either going into a sleazy movie theater or buying an 8 mm reel-to-reel tape.) These views would later be criticized, even by allies, as generalizations regarding the roles of women and for failing to encompass the views of women of different races and classes and sexual orientation.

But these criticisms didn't affect the main points of the second wave. Even conceding early issues with inclusivity, and some rhetorical overbreadth, the objections to stereotypical gender roles and sexually exploitive portrayals of women seemed indisputable. So much of fashion, advertising, and popular entertainment was designed to attract male attention. And avoiding these stereotypes could not mean cloistering: women who wanted education and careers, either instead of or in addition to traditional roles, had to be out in the world. So it became okay for young women, at least in college settings, not to adhere to those standards, and even a little uncool to conform, much less to dress up. My fellow college and grad school students of all genders dressed in an equally unflattering manner—that is, we all looked like hell—in the late 1970s. Bulletin: This did not cause us to lose interest in sex. Nor was it true that second wave activists must be anti-sex or anti-family. (Reader, I married one.) Rather, the message was more that, following Beauvoir, women wanted to be able to act like human beings without being accused of acting like men.

As with race issues, not everyone was ready for these arguments. My late wife recalled that, as a VISTA volunteer in the Quad Cities, she traveled with a group to Springfield, Illinois, in 1979 or 1980 to lobby the state legislature to adopt the Equal Rights Amendment. On the other side was a Phyllis Schlafly–organized battalion of well-scrubbed young women in matching red dresses and heels, whining about the prospect of gender-neutral bathrooms. (Every home has gender-neutral bathrooms, made safe from embarrassment by the locks on their doors.) Stunts like this provided

---

33. Duberman, *Andrea Dworkin*, 136; Meritor Savings Bank v. Vinson.
34. Borstelmann, *1970s*, 93.
35. Duberman, *Andrea Dworkin*, 126–27.

cover for male insecurity and stalled the ERA. I suppose that the increasing influence of white Christian nationalists, the self-described Moral Majority, and the election of Ronald Reagan should have prepared us for a backlash. But the later popularity of, for example, the bustier-clad Madonna came as something of a shock, at least to me. She may have meant to be campy, to satirize and poke fun at a stereotype, but she was also using it the old-fashioned way: advertising her sexuality to sell records—complicating the feminists' messages, perhaps beyond recognition. The resulting freedoms of individual choice, for men and women, has meant that women can pursue an incredibly wide, if not bewildering, set of life choices; it has not, however, resulted in a notable reduction in sexual harassment or the elimination of pay disparities, much less in the ubiquity of exploitive images.

Fortunately, the main achievements of the second wave live on. One of the most lasting, and most generous, products of the era was *Our Bodies, Ourselves* by the Boston Women's Health Book Collective, a group of young women including doctors, social workers, and other activists, who aimed to free basic facts about women's bodies and sexuality from the grip of mostly male doctors and psychologists. In a careful, measured tone, it covered topics from basic anatomy and health concerns, to sexuality, relationships, birth control, pregnancy, and menopause. This knowledge clearly had power. The book was an underground bestseller in Boston before it got picked up by Simon & Schuster in 1973, and it has been expanded and updated many times in the fifty years since. I learned about it in the late 1970s from a quite possibly exasperated girlfriend. "Read this," she said.

As historically disadvantaged groups spoke up, so too did evangelical Christians. Predominantly white, traditionalist, and nationalistic, the evangelicals nonetheless acted like aggrieved outsiders because their beliefs were not represented by mainline Protestant denominations and because the nation and the West as a whole had become much more secular in the wake of twentieth-century brutality. "Is God Dead?" blared the cover of *Time* magazine in 1966.

Regardless of one's belief in God, it became abundantly clear that religion was thriving in many parts of the US. Garry Wills has written that by guaranteeing religious freedom and forbidding the state establishment of religion, the First Amendment fostered a vibrant and successful competition among religions and enabled them to appeal to many more people.[36]

---

36. Wills, *Under God*, 19, 25.

The entrepreneurial spirit included, but was not limited to, sects in which financial success was considered a sign of divine approval.

As this movement emerged into the political sphere, it did seem anachronistic and out of touch to many. It aimed to block the Equal Rights Amendment and decried abortion and gay rights, which liberals read as ill-disguised bullying. The evangelicals were underestimated, and misunderstood, in part because Jimmy Carter, the first born-again Christian in the White House, successfully carried almost all of the South and Midwest as a moderate liberal. In the 1978 midterm elections, the Democrats lost seats but retained control of both houses of Congress. The political impact of the Moral Majority was not yet fully appreciated.

Beyond established industries, a real revolution had its beginnings. The emergence of Bill Gates, Steve Jobs, and other founders can be framed as stories of individual triumph, like those of King Arthur, Luke Skywalker, or Ayn Rand's corporate titans—and such stories would be equally fictional. The Department of Defense had kept computational research alive for most of the Cold War in support of aerospace and telecommunications applications. It fostered companies like Fairchild Semiconductor, Hewlett Packard, and Intel, and a community of skilled employees, in what became Silicon Valley. The first internet protocols emerged from the Defense Department's ARPANET in the late 1960s. (This genesis was born of practicality. During the much later dot-com boom, a presenter to a conference of non-experts played down the technical achievement: "the internet is just a request for a file from another computer." The rest, I guess, is infrastructure.)

Jobs and Gates each had prominent collaborators—most prominently Steve Wozniak and John Sculley at Apple and Paul Allen at Microsoft—and their companies emerged from work with large, established bureaucratic corporations with serious concerns about antitrust laws—Xerox (through its PARC research center) and IBM. This is not in any way to deny the entrepreneurs' creativity, vision, and intensity. If anything, it's impressive that they broke through in an industry dominated by establishment behemoths, and that they saw the way to new markets and better products.

But they didn't work alone. For example, John Kemeny, a mathematician who'd worked with Einstein and had developed an early, easy-to-use programming language called BASIC, often told Dartmouth students in the 1970s that in the future people would be sharply divided into those who could use computers and those who couldn't. This didn't come true in quite the way he meant it—that everyone should learn to code—but only because he didn't state his prediction broadly enough. Computers would turn into consumer appliances inside mobile phones and on desktops and would isolate those who couldn't afford them. Even though I majored in math, and briefly had a TA job for one of Kemeny's collaborators, I lacked the vision too. In my one programming class in 1976, I wrote a working program that could perform simple calculus functions (it could take the first derivative of common functions), but the late nights and mind-numbing repetition ruined a perfectly good term. I couldn't see doing it for a living.

By then Gates had judged the opportunities differently and dropped out of Harvard to take advantage of them.

On July 15, 1979, President Carter gave a televised address, prompted by the ongoing energy crisis. The US still depended very heavily on imported oil, and the latest OPEC embargo had reduced supply and fueled raging inflation. But the speech is better remembered as the Crisis of Confidence speech. Even though the US had unmatched economic power and was "at peace everywhere in the world," he observed that American workers' productivity was actually dropping and that a majority of people believed that the next five years would be worse than the last. Like a preacher, he counseled that "owning things and consuming things does not satisfy our longing for meaning. We've learned that piling up material goods cannot fill the emptiness of lives which have no confidence or purpose." All this was meant to empathize and explain his real objective: a six-point plan to reduce dependence on oil imports and increase domestic energy production. The last point included a fateful request for Americans "to build conservation into your homes."[37]

As we now know, the electorate did not respond warmly. (Ronald Reagan would get himself into a similar kind of trouble a few years later by proposing cuts to Social Security.) But Carter's speech was not about passive acceptance of the status quo. Although the Cold War and the energy crisis continued, the youthful nation had learned quite a bit in the 1970s and proven itself capable of great changes. We could have taken many paths forward.

---

37. Carter, "Crisis of Confidence," para. 37.

US General Smedley Butler (left) with President Warren Harding and Generals John Pershing and John Lejeune, July 1922. Although less famous than the president and the other World War I leaders, Butler had led US military interventions in Nicaragua and Honduras in the 1900s and 1910s to protect US corporate interests and later expressed regret for his actions. During the Cold War, anti-communism replaced financial interests as the leading reason for US covert and overt interventions in Central America and the Caribbean.

Credit: Harris & Ewing, U.S. Library of Congress.

6

The Long Memories... of Others
US Intelligence "Projects" in the Cold War

IN THE LATE 1960s, my sixth-grade class had a unit on Latin America. Every few days, we would turn to a different country. The textbook provided basic facts: date of independence, capital city, population, major industries, literacy rate, and per capita income in dollars. These disclosures must have been intended in part to help us empathize, and we did understand that the literacy and income figures were quite low in comparison to the US. But for preteens with few if any financial responsibilities, who barely understood what our parents did for a living, the week after week repetition of dismal numbers did not make much of an impact. I'm still pretty good with capital cities though. Caracas, Managua, Quito, Tegucigalpa!

Among the shortcomings of this pedagogical approach, the greatest was its context: it was delivered in the middle of the Cold War. Countries were either allies, enemies, or potential problems for the US, and countries in the Americas didn't have much of a choice. The Monroe Doctrine had long ensured that the US would "protect" the Western Hemisphere from outside influence. Cuba had shown what might happen without vigilance.

1. SIDE EFFECTS

In light of the Cold War's result, it might seem petty for a fortunate US citizen to belabor the adverse side effects—toxicities, to borrow the medical term—of many foreign interventions. But in places like Cuba, El Salvador, Guatemala, and Iran, we are still living with the consequences. It's part of a longer history of exported violence with terrible outcomes. These outcomes rarely become election issues in the US until the fallout becomes visible: when poor people reach our borders or former allies start building nuclear weapons.

To be sure, the Soviet Union also left wreckage all over the world. In *The Global Cold War*, historian Odd Arne Westad concluded that "the Soviet leaders who had brought about the intervention [in Afghanistan] were, by the end of the 1980s, seen as fools or knaves.... For many, Soviet allies in the Third World seemed to perform a mockery of the advanced socialist humanism that they viewed themselves as representing."[1] This could have been the epitaph for any number of US alliances as well. The difference, as Westad has observed, is that the Cold War's favorable outcome for the US could more easily be used to explain objectively awful results as mere collateral damage.[2]

Despite a number of dramatic failures, CIA-sponsored military projects continued all the way through the Iran-Contra scandal, the last misbegotten intervention before the Cold War's end in 1989–91. But the CIA did not come out of nowhere. The US had been declaring its overseas interests and sending the marines, in some incarnation, almost from the beginning of the republic. It's a part of our history that gets overshadowed by more dramatic conflicts, the Civil War and world wars. As with the legacies of slavery and Indian displacement, we may find it uncomfortable to recall that the US often benefited from exploitative business arrangements, especially in the Caribbean and Central America. But our failure to recall puts us at a distinct disadvantage, because the countries on the receiving end have proven to have very long memories.

2. SUGAR, COFFEE, BANANAS

At the time of independence, the new United States was small and isolated in the Americas. Spanish colonies had been pulling silver out of the mountains of Peru and Mexico for centuries. Most of the other European settlements, as well as the southern US states, were plantation economies, growing crops for export. Vast stretches of both American continents were

1. Westad, *Global Cold War*, 402.
2. Westad, *Global Cold War*, 404.

still populated exclusively by indigenous peoples. The US was also different. It was a republic with elected leaders, unlike almost anything in the world. Some of its northern states were the first in the Americas to have diversified economies that did not depend almost exclusively on slavery or other less-than-voluntary labor.

In context, the United States' early expansion—acquiring the Old Northwest, trans-Appalachia, Florida, the Louisiana Purchase—did have a defensive aspect, removing powerful European rivals from the borders, although this was hardly the sole motivation. The same was true of the Monroe Doctrine. Following the Bolivarian independence revolutions, the new South American countries were friendly to the US (and less powerful than Spain). In 1823, President Monroe warned European states against future interference in the Americas. At the time, the US did not have remotely enough firepower to enforce this presumptuous pledge, probably not even enough to control all of its own territorial claims, but as a statement of national policy it had to be seen as a gesture of support for the new countries and a complicating factor for European powers (especially Spain). The policy was crafted by Secretary of State John Quincy Adams, who was not an unrestrained supporter of expansion; two decades later, he was one of very few House members to vote against the Mexican War.

The country's priorities soon changed, and the Monroe Doctrine would get a much different interpretation. US expansionists dominated the nineteenth and early twentieth centuries. The Mexican War (1845–46), the final wars against the American Indians (1860–90), and the Spanish-American War (1898) completed American transcontinental expansion and added official overseas territories in Puerto Rico, the Philippines, and Guam, plus hegemony in Cuba and Central America. All were to some extent wars of aggression, or at least of choice; none of these enemies had posed a threat to US territory.

In newly independent Cuba, the US did not withdraw its occupying forces until Cuba added the Platt Amendment to its new constitution in 1901. As Ada Ferrer explains in *Cuba: An American History*, Connecticut Senator Orville Platt insisted that the Cuban constitution acknowledge a US right to intervene military in order to preserve its own concept of Cuban independence and an orderly government.[3] The subjectivity of these conditions would hobble Cuban leaders for decades. (Noting that the Americas is the entire the Western Hemisphere, Ferrer also points out the

---

3. Ferrer, *Cuba*, 178–79.

linguistic arrogance of those who use the word Americans to refer to US residents, something I must confess to have done many times.) The US also engineered the separation of Panama from the stubborn Colombian government, paving the way (pardon the expression) for American completion of the Panama Canal from 1904 to 1914.

Overall, the US protected its economic interests, as much or more than its security interests, with twenty military interventions in nominally independent Latin American and Caribbean countries (including French-speaking Haiti) in the period 1898 to 1920 alone.[4] Even President Wilson, the famous proponent of self-determination (for some), ordered or continued military interventions in Haiti, Nicaragua, and Santo Domingo (Dominican Republic).[5] The US had boots on the ground in Nicaragua for over twenty years, withdrawing only in 1933, in the depths of the Depression, and only after the US military had chased Augusto Sandino's insurgents into the mountains and trained the domestic Guardia Nacional to preserve order. The Guardia's commander, Anastasio Somoza, had Sandino assassinated the very next year, and the Somoza family would dominate the country for the next forty years.[6]

Similarly, despite the country's turn to extreme isolationism in the 1920s and 1930s, the US sent a battleship and two destroyers to Havana harbor in September 1933, after the Sergeants' Revolt put the reformist Ramon Grau San Martin briefly into the Cuban presidency and formally eliminated the Platt Amendment. Although the Roosevelt administration did not put soldiers onshore, US ambassador Jefferson Caffery delayed diplomatic recognition, threatening to strangle the economy, until a countercoup by Cuban military leader Fulgencio Batista put a more acceptable administration in place in 1934.[7]

These interventions, and the implicit threat of others, enabled even more thorough economic dominance. In 1929, just before the Depression, of the five Central American states' collective 97 million dollars in exports, 54 million dollars were from coffee and 31 million dollars from bananas. The US was the leading export market for each country except El Salvador (where Germany led). The profits of each country's export business accrued mostly to US companies, especially the United Fruit Company,

---

4. Ferrer, *Cuba*, 241; LaFeber, *Inevitable Revolutions*, 81.
5. LaFeber, *Inevitable Revolutions*, 55.
6. LaFeber, *Inevitable Revolutions*, 66–71.
7. Ferrer, *Cuba*, 239, 246–47.

known locally as *La Frutera*, and US banking, utility, and rail interests, which dominated in every country. Similarly, in 1926, US-owned mills produced 63 percent of Cuba's principal export, sugar.[8] These are stunning statistics. That domination enabled the companies to displace local—in Central America, largely Indian—farmers from much of the agricultural land and to set prices for labor in agricultural industries not noted for generous wages or comfortable working conditions.

Smedley Butler, a top Marine Corps commander, later regretted his role: "I helped purify Nicaragua for the international banking house of Brown Brothers in 1909-12 [and] helped make Honduras 'right' for American fruit companies in 1903 . . . I might have given Al Capone a few hints."[9] This was not ancient history in 1945-46, at the start of the Cold War. In 1948, nearly 80 percent of Central American exports went to the US, and US military and economic power dominated the region.

During the Cold War, the US government would quite rightly, and without evident self-consciousness, object to Soviet dominance over its Eastern European neighbors, especially Soviet military interventions to suppress uprisings in East Germany (1953), Hungary (1956), and Czechoslovakia (1968).

3. OVERSHADOWED PROJECTS

All US anti-communist projects were overshadowed by the Vietnam War, the Ahab-like obsession of two generations of US leaders of both parties, and a tragedy for victims and victors alike. Vietnam, the extreme result, did prompt a brief period of cautious reconsideration of foreign interventions. Beyond the highly visible spectacle of Vietnam, however, it was not until the 1980s that two widely released movies dealt with US-sponsored anti-communist activities in other developing countries.[10] Like the Ameri-

---

8. LaFeber, *Inevitable Revolutions*, 62-63, 93; Ferrer, *Cuba*, 191.

9. LaFeber, *Inevitable Revolutions*, 81.

10. This is based on my own, concededly informal, research. There were earlier films with similar themes that did not portray interventions by the US. *Battle of Algiers* (1966) dramatizes the ultimately unsuccessful French effort to suppress the Algerian independence movement and to preserve Algeria as a "department" of France. Costa-Gavras's *Z* (1969) is based on the real assassination of the liberal Greek politician Gregorios Lambrakis in 1963. The US and Britain had been very active in defeating the Greek Communist Party in the 1948 civil war, and the country was for decades dominated by a deeply anti-communist and eventually anti-democratic regime. However, this particular incident is

can films about Vietnam, both films have the limitation that they tell their stories from the perspective of Western protagonists; coincidentally, both feature Michael Murphy, a reliable player of unreliable characters, in supporting roles that do not cast the American presence in a flattering light.

The better film is *The Year of Living Dangerously* (1982), by Australian director Peter Weir, with Mel Gibson in the lead as Guy Hamilton, a young Australian reporter in his first overseas assignment amid the political turmoil in Indonesia in 1965. Billy Kwan, an Indonesian photographer with dwarfism (played by Linda Hunt in an Oscar-winning performance) befriends Guy and gets him access to important sources (as well as a meeting with Jill Bryant, a beautiful British attaché played by Sigourney Weaver), while trying to educate him that Indonesian culture prizes a balance between the rational and the spiritual. Guy values the introductions but, to Billy's frustration, the message of balance does not sink in; instead, Guy uses information received in confidence from Jill in a news story that advances his career.

Indonesia's poverty is repeatedly contrasted with the gilded and carefully guarded life of the Western expats. Guy and Jill flirt at the British embassy's swimming pool, and the Western reporters party at the house of a British journalist and his Indonesian male partner. Guy later learns that his driver is a member of the Indonesian Communist Party (PKI), who explains his motivation by asking why an intelligent man can live well in Australia but not in Indonesia. In the end, Guy narrowly escapes the imposition of martial law following the military takeover and reunites with Jill as the last airplane out closes its doors. And without any need to show the bloodshed that followed.

While the actual political events may not be fully understood by historians, it is clear that General Suharto, a close Washington ally, took power from the elected President Sukarno on October 1, 1965, ostensibly to protect Sukarno and the country from a Communist uprising, or possibly as part of a pre-planned coup. In any case, the movie ends before the real crime began. In the ensuing years, perhaps half a million Indonesians were murdered in the name of anti-communism, and Suharto did not relinquish

---

not visibly tied to US agitation. Finally, *The Quiet American* (1958), released during the period when alleged Communist sympathizers were still blackballed in Hollywood, goes against its source material, a Graham Greene novel, by suggesting that street-level unrest in Saigon—an excuse for intervention—was sponsored by Communist activists rather than the CIA. A 2002 remake of the film reverses this, implying that the CIA sponsored the unrest and blamed the Communists for it.

his position or restore democracy.[11] Josh Oppenheimer's remarkable documentary *The Act of Killing* (2012) shows the officially repressed history of this near genocide in the clearest way imaginable, by interviewing aging perpetrators who calmly recount how and where they did their work.

The second movie is Oliver Stone's *Salvador* (1986), based loosely on true events that took place around 1980. Stone is not known for subtlety, and I cannot recommend the film as a cinematic experience. But Stone deserves credit for his unflinching portrayal of real-life violence by the Salvadoran military and government-aligned death squads, including the murder of liberal Archbishop Romero and the abduction and murder of four American nuns who provided aid to the *campesinos*. The film also highlights the US role, with most of the American officials parroting incoming President Reagan's line that leftist insurgents were terrorists or outside agitators from Communist governments in Nicaragua and/or Cuba, and that eventually a series of Communist takeovers might present a threat to the US. In the film, the insurgents' push for the capital nearly succeeds, only to be turned back by US-supplied tanks and aircraft. The economic desperation that motivated the rural FMLN groups is left mostly unexplained. "They're not just killing Indians," a veteran photographer warns the film's protagonist (James Woods) in an unintentionally cringe-worthy moment. For the most part, though, they were.

4. DEEP-SEATED FEARS

The fear of Communism in the US arose almost from the publication of *Das Kapital* in the mid-nineteenth century, approximately in parallel with the country's increasing domination of Central America and Cuba. Among other things, Marx and Engels did mean to provoke. They wrote that capitalism was a phase that would pass naturally and inevitably, that the production of goods would become so efficient that cost would no longer be a concern, and that everyone would have what they needed. This was almost religious: the economic version of the immaculate conception. The threat of class conflict was clear enough, though, and as a result neither Communism nor the broader ideas of socialism ever got much political traction in the US.

Soon after World War I and the Russian Revolution, a series of bombings in the US, and fear of the spread of the strange ideas themselves,

---

11. Westad, *Global Cold War*, 185–89; Bevins, *Jakarta Method*, 124–35, 154–57.

terrified leaders in Washington. President Wilson's Attorney General Mitchell Palmer authorized a massive, mostly illegal sweep against suspected domestic Communists in 1919 and 1920. Because of the supposedly foreign source of these ideas, the Palmer Raids focused on deporting immigrants—politically safe targets in a war-weary nation. They also launched the career of J. Edgar Hoover.

It was not until World War II, and the end of US isolationism, that the government began direct support of anti-communist partisans overseas. The first effort was in China, where the Roosevelt administration had given extensive military support during World War II to the Guomindang led by Chiang Kai-Shek, and none to Mao's Communist army, though both had vowed to prioritize expelling the Japanese, their common enemy. President Truman continued to support Chiang in the civil war period following the Japanese defeat, but by 1949 Chiang's far better-armed forces were routed by Mao's far more loyal and better organized armies.

No soul-searching resulted from the collapse of this well-supported ally; almost everybody in the US was a committed Cold Warrior by then. In March 1947, Truman announced that "it must be the policy of the United States to support free peoples who are resisting attempted subjugation by armed minorities or by outside pressures."[12] This was his successful pitch for Congressional approval to support the British-allied Greek government in its fight against Greek Communists. (It was assumed in the US, incorrectly as it turned out, that the Greek Communists were fighting at Stalin's direction, that is, that the Greek conflict was a battle against Soviet expansionism.)

The Truman Doctrine laid the policy groundwork for open-ended interventions against Communism abroad, although his administration's most important actions were public rather than covert. They created and implemented the Marshall Plan to revive the Western European economies, provided financial assistance and public support to center-right coalitions against Communist parties in critical French and Italian elections, sponsored the Berlin airlift, and gave military support to Greek partisans in the Greek civil war. Combined with the Soviets' own blunders—the attempted blockade of West Berlin, the overthrow of a moderate Czech government and, most importantly, prohibiting the Soviet bloc states from participating in the Marshall Plan—the Truman administration actions helped remove Communist parties as political factors in Western Europe.[13]

12. Judge and Langdon, *Cold War*, 24–25.
13. For France, Italy, Greece, see Judt, *Postwar*, 81, 116, 127, 208; Bevins, *Jakarta*

Republicans trashed him anyway. They argued that he had lost China and claimed that his State Department and other agencies harbored Communist sympathizers. With greater plausibility, they blamed Secretary of State Acheson for inadvertently omitting Korea in a speech outlining US interests in East Asia, thus perhaps leading Stalin to acquiesce in Kim Il Sun's 1950 invasion plans.[14] (Or, in light of the Kim regime's later developments, a territorial war may have been inevitable.) From that time until at least the early 1970s and Nixon's outreach to China, US political leaders of almost every stripe found it necessary to demonstrate their hard line.

5. THE NORMS OF HUMAN CONDUCT

Anti-communist tactics changed in the 1950s. Administrations of both parties increasingly depended on semi-secret covert actions, often involving the use of force. For example: Eisenhower green-lighted coups in Iran and Guatemala, as well as direct US involvement with the Diem regime in South Vietnam following the French defeat and withdrawal; Kennedy approved the disastrous Bay of Pigs invasion and the coup against President Diem in Vietnam; Johnson supported brutal anti-communist actions in the Dominican Republic and Indonesia; Nixon took secret military actions in Cambodia and Laos and helped topple Chile's democratically elected President Allende.

To be sure, most CIA operations conformed to accepted practices (such as they were) for intelligence gathering and development of sources, and only a small fraction were military or paramilitary in nature. And these more extreme measures were not always unsuccessful in the short term, from the US perspective. The problem was that they became almost a foreign policy default rather than a last resort: a form of action that didn't require any complicated or time-consuming negotiations or political explanation. The secrecy and the need for only narrow executive branch approval created a kind of regulatory arbitrage, in which covert action ran ahead of public and private diplomacy, which required the much more cumbersome and time-consuming process of forging consensus among interested parties. These ostensibly easier and faster actions had collateral consequences in the target countries, which were nearly impossible to predict, much less control. By one count, there were over nine hundred major or sensitive

---

Method, 15–18. For Marshall Plan and Berlin airlift, see Judt, *Postwar*, 91–97, 146.

14. Halberstam, *Coldest Winter*, 48.

covert action "projects" (defined to include secret foreign political or propaganda activities as well as military aid and paramilitary actions) between 1961 and 1975 alone, along with thousands of smaller projects.[15]

Surprisingly, much of what we know about CIA history comes from government studies and reports about the organization and purview of the intelligence community. Many of these, more amazingly, focus on implementing controls over covert actions, an eternal aspiration never fully realized. One prominent example is the Doolittle report of 1954. This report is sometimes quoted out of context, but it reflects a life-or-death fear of the Soviet Union that was very common at the time.

In a bipartisan gesture barely conceivable today, President Truman had asked former Republican President Herbert Hoover to lead a review of the executive branch structure and management; President Eisenhower had liked Truman's idea and asked Hoover to lead a second commission. When it came to CIA covert activities, however, Eisenhower took the review offline. In July 1954, he asked Air Force General James Doolittle to chair a top-secret review of covert activities that would in effect be carved out of the Hoover committee's broader and more public reporting. Doolittle wasn't just any general; he was a World War II hero for flying an amazing, morale-boosting mission to drop bombs on Tokyo in 1942, in the earliest days of US involvement in the Pacific. Eisenhower appointed three prominent Republican businessmen, one of whom, William Pawley, was also an aviator and CIA veteran, to Doolittle's committee.

By September 30, 1954, the group delivered its report. Its specific recommendations seemed like routine business consulting advice: hire more high-quality personnel, improve security, coordinate with other agencies reporting up to the National Security Council (in effect, the president), and streamline operations. But in the introduction, the panel went well beyond what was needed to justify these operational recommendations, in order to emphasize the urgency and importance of the agency's mission. It was vital, first of all, that the intelligence agencies "be strengthened and coordinated to the greatest possible degree." A second consideration, "less tangible but equally important" was described as follows:

> It is now clear that we are facing an implacable enemy whose avowed objective is world domination by whatever means and at whatever cost. There are no rules in such a game. Hitherto acceptable norms of human conduct do not apply. If the United States is

15. U.S. Senate Select Committee, "Final Report," 445.

> to survive, long-standing American concepts of "fair play" must be reconsidered. We must develop espionage and counterespionage services and must learn to subvert, sabotage and destroy our enemies by more clever, more sophisticated and more effective methods than those used against us. It may become necessary that the American people be made acquainted with, understand and support this fundamentally repugnant philosophy.[16]

We should remember that this report came out only a year after the end of the Korean War, the Cold War's only hot war, in which hundreds of thousands of Chinese troops fought directly against the US army, seemingly without regard to casualties. It was also only a year since the end of Stalin's brutal rule, and considerable uncertainty remained, even in the Soviet Union, about who or what might succeed him. We should also remember that the fundamentally repugnant recommendation of abandoning prior "norms of human conduct" was the view of four hand-picked friends of Eisenhower's, and hardly a consensus view of US citizens, who at the time of course did not have access to the top-secret report. But it was the view of many in the intelligence community, and it only took a few such people, plus the president, to launch covert actions.

6. OVERSIGHT

Security was duly tightened, and the results of covert actions did not attract attention unless things went quite wrong.

The calamitous Bay of Pigs invasion in Cuba in 1961 was the most prominent example, a project so badly conceived and executed that it spawned the term *groupthink*.[17] But the post-mortems focused on avoiding future screw-ups. The policy question was little debated: Was it even a good idea to try to invade Cuba and topple the Castro regime?

Cuba was just a warm-up. Vietnam brought out a raft of skeletons. In a decidedly un-biblical chain of events, policy and military failures in Vietnam begat the Pentagon Papers (yet another internal study) which, when leaked to and published by the *New York Times* and *Washington Post*, begat President Nixon's "plumbers" unit (designed to fix leaks) which upon their inevitable mission creep begat the screwed-up political burglary at the Watergate office complex, which begat Senate and House hearings and Nixon's

---

16. President's Special Study Group, "Report," 6–7.
17. Ferrer, *Cuba*, 354–68; Westad, *Global Cold War*, 171–72.

impeachment, which, to return to our point, begat stunning disclosures about intelligence service activities at the FBI and CIA.

These disclosures led to widespread public skepticism about covert projects, perhaps for the first time since World War II. Congress, under Democratic control after Watergate, asserted the right to conduct oversight and both House and Senate committees conducted reviews. In its 1976 report, the Senate committee, chaired by Frank Church (D-ID), provided examples to support the need for greater political accountability, and asked whether extreme measures should remain exempt from public scrutiny:

> The Bay of Pigs fiasco, the secret war in Laos, the secret bombing of Cambodia, the anti-Allende activities in Chile, the Watergate affair, were all instances of the use of power, cloaked in secrecy which, when revealed, provoked widespread popular disapproval.... What can properly be concealed from ... the American people? Assassination plots? The overthrow of an elected democratic government? Drug testing on unwitting American citizens? ... Attempts by an agency of the government to blackmail a civil rights leader? These have occurred and each has been withheld from scrutiny by the public and the Congress by the label "secret intelligence."[18]

The committee absolved the US from complicity in any *successful* assassinations, but that was not because it hadn't tried. The US government initiated and participated in unsuccessful plots to assassinate Patrice Lumumba of Congo (who was later killed by domestic opponents) and Fidel Castro. In addition, the US government had encouraged coup plots that resulted, incidentally as it were, in the killings of Presidents Diem of South Vietnam (1963) and Trujillo of the Dominican Republic (1961) and General Schneider of Chile (1970). (Schneider, commander in chief of the Chilean Army, had disappointed US operatives by allowing the elected president Salvador Allende to take office.)[19]

Absent from the committee's list is any reference to the killings of ordinary citizens by US-backed regimes once in place: the half million or more in Indonesia, the disappearances of thousands of persons deemed to be political threats for decades in Brazil, Argentina, Chile, and Iran.

Instead, the history seemed to show that *some* CIA projects had worked very well. A Church Committee staff report called out two early,

---

18. U.S. Senate Select Committee, "Final Report," 12.
19. Risen, *Last Honest Man*, 247, 265–67.

"acclaimed achievements" as giving "policymakers a sense of confidence in the CIA's capacity for operational success."

> In 1953 and 1954 two of the Agency's boldest, most spectacular covert operations took place—the overthrow of Premier Mohammed Mossadegh in Iran and the coup against President Jacobo Arbenz Guzman in Guatemala. Both were quick and virtually bloodless operations that removed from power two allegedly communist-associated leaders and replaced them pro-Western officials.[20]

But that was 1975. By 1979, the shah of Iran and his brutal secret police had been chased from power and replaced with the most anti-American regime imaginable. The Islamic Republic, a great oppressor of its own people and a sponsor of regional terrorism, has now been in place for over forty years. The spectacular success of the CIA's 1953 operation was not only temporary but extremely counterproductive.[21]

Parenthetically, the same might have been said of the Guatemalan coup. Because 2 percent of landowners owned 72 percent of the land, much of which was left fallow, President Arbenz had ordered redistribution of a portion of the largest holdings, including a portion of United Fruit Company's vast fallow lands, to small farmers.[22] Although one might have thought this a capitalist measure, promoting individual ownership and initiative, the Eisenhower administration considered it Communism and green-lighted the raid.[23] However, Fidel Castro's future compatriot Che Guevara was in Guatemala when Arbenz departed; Castro himself saw in Guatemala clear evidence to the wisdom of nineteenth-century writer and revolutionary Jose Marti's warnings against US encroachment.[24] Cuba has indeed suffered for its isolation, but Castro's government and his reform measures survived, spurred in part by the Guatemalan coup. And Guatemala itself fell into a low-grade civil war that lasted over three decades.

The Church Committee stayed true to its mandate of procedural reform. It provided an invaluable basis for Congressional oversight of intelligence services. It stopped short of evaluating the long-term effects—the wisdom—of the policies that motivated covert interventions in other countries.

20. U.S. Senate Select Committee, "Final Report," book 4, 45.
21. For several historians' views on Iran, see Kinzer, *All the Shah's Men*, 212–15.
22. LaFeber, *Inevitable Revolutions*, 117.
23. Reid, *Forgotten Continent*, 84–86; Westad, *Global Cold War*, 146–49.
24. Ferrer, *Cuba*, 286, 337; Westad, *Global Cold War*, 149.

7. MISSED OPPORTUNITIES

The Cold War rivals each claimed that their system was superior in delivering prosperity and fairness, but scarcely bothered to consider the economic development of their Third World allies. What mattered more had been geographic security (for example, in Eastern Europe), access to resources (as with Iran) and denying victory to a rival while avoiding politically unpopular results at home (as in Cuba and Vietnam). Better economic development could have improved the chances of achieving and preserving all of those goals.

It wasn't as though a model didn't exist. The Marshall Plan had succeeded in cementing the Western European alliance by extending credit to, and promoting trade between, the participating countries. These included, remarkably, France and Western Germany, which had spent the previous three decades at each other's throats. It was pretty clear that the architects of the postwar economic system at Bretton Woods, including John Maynard Keynes himself, understood why such a plan would work: it induced businesses and governments to revive and invest more in their pre-war manufacturing and trade arrangements; indeed, they began to worry more about being outpaced by others.[25]

But this model was not extended to developing countries. In part, this was a legacy of imperialism, the idea that Third World peoples weren't ready to support an industrial or service-based economy. But another reason was that economists didn't yet understand what became known as "Dutch disease," a term evidently coined by *The Economist* magazine in the late 1970s.[26] When the Netherlands discovered and began exporting oil in the 1960s, the rest of its economy foundered. It turned out that exporting raw materials brings in cash, which hurts other businesses by diverting resources and by strengthening the country's currency to the disadvantage of export businesses. Further, in many cases, very few consumers have a stake in the extraction profits. This effect would help to explain the persistence of underdevelopment in the Middle East and Africa, among others, but unfortunately it was not well understood until the early 1980s.

The economies of Central America and the Caribbean suffered for an analogous reason: The dominance of export crops created vast wealth, in US dollars, for a small number of families (and US companies) that

---

25. Judt, *Postwar*, 91–97, 107–8. See chapter 1, "Cold War."
26. Reid, *Forgotten Continent*, 163n79.

owned the banana, coffee, and sugar plantations. These businesses did little for other local businesses, potential consumers or, more specifically, indigenous farmers. Local agricultural workers were paid survival wages that did not improve their own lives, much less become the source of a consumer-based economy. The dependence on exports of cash crops, and the concentration of land ownership in Guatemala, mentioned above, was repeated throughout Central America and much of the Caribbean. Worse, small subsistence farmers were often driven off their lands due to the lack of formal titles and forced to move or to become plantation workers. These were the conditions that led to rebellions in the countryside.

Several governments attempted to respond to this problem of poverty, underdevelopment, and inequality by intervening directly in the economy. These reform proposals often took the form of expropriating a portion of large estates, including those owned by wealthy families and foreign companies, which in Central America were commonly left idle. Although landowners and businesses, including US investors, had been literally fighting attempted economic reforms since the days of Smedley Butler, during the Cold War it helped to label the reformers Communists.

For example, in Iran, the Mossadegh government's frustration with its inability to renegotiate unfavorable century-long oil field leases with British companies led to threats to nationalize the oil fields; these threats significantly influenced the CIA-sponsored coup. In Guatemala, President Arbenz began to implement land reform program and met a similar fate. Remarkably few of these efforts were allowed to proceed; notably, Fidel Castro nationalized US-owned property and businesses after his 1959 revolution, although this can also be seen in part as a defensive move to keep Americans from being able to form an effective counter-revolution.

Expropriation of private interests, even with fair compensation, is certainly an extreme step, and not one that most economists would encourage except in extreme circumstances. Even the US government, however, enacted and regularly enforced antitrust laws to prevent the excessive concentration of economic power by large corporations, from the 1890s until the 1980s. For example, the breakup of AT&T in a 1982 settlement is thought to have accelerated incredible technological advances; and contemporary Americans can hardly imagine having no choice of cellular providers. (Recently, some conservative politicians have joined liberals in expressing concern about the market power wielded by tech giants such as Google and

Amazon.) We would certainly rebel if we were forced to work for a single local employer, as happened throughout Central America.

In short, the de facto US policy of opposing any redistributive economic reforms very likely perpetuated the conditions for rebellion; it was almost certainly a missed opportunity. In the southern Indian state of Kerala, Communist parties were elected to power for several decades. Their initiatives in land reform—expropriating idle estates and offering small parcels to rural families—and investments in public education transformed Kerala from a backwater to a (nearly) middle-class economy and a prime source for tech and service workers throughout India and the Middle East.[27] Some cultural sensitivity was required, certainly: in Kerala, teaching the grandmothers to read shamed parents into letting their kids go to school rather than work agricultural jobs full time. That particular innovation might not have worked in Central America. But there are transferable principles. Land redistribution, for example, can be something like the opposite of Communism, making many families into homeowners and private business operators.

To be fair, the Kennedy administration—authentic if not always competent Cold Warriors—did pay some attention to development, by launching the Peace Corps and sponsoring the Alliance for Progress aid program in Latin America. But the Peace Corps wasn't going to put universal public education in place, and none of the programs had the motivational power of land reform. The aid dollars also have a Dutch disease impact: adding money to an economy does not necessarily empower business investment, jobs, or consumer spending. In any case, the succeeding Johnson and Nixon administrations weren't much concerned with development, and most of their aid wound up being military. That didn't work in Vietnam either.

8. A WARNING LABEL FOR DESPERATION

Despite decades of quasi-colonialism, fewer than 100,000 Salvadoran immigrants lived in the United States in 1980. The migrant population more than quadrupled during the years of US-sponsored crackdowns, to about 465,000 by 1990, and has continued to increase by about 400,000 each decade since.[28] Since the entire country has a population of about 6.5 million, immigrants to the US may represent 15 to 20 percent of native Salvadorans.

27. Heller, *Labor of Development*, 6–8.
28. Menjívar and Cervantes, "El Salvador," 5.

The lack of economic opportunity is the most commonly cited reason for migration, but fear of violence continues to be a significant factor; the threat of violence hinders economic opportunities as well. Similar dynamics have motivated continued migration from Guatemala and Honduras, the other two sides of the Northern Triangle.[29]

Today's desperation is a lingering side effect of these recent civil wars. US policies and actions, taken after Vietnam, after publication of the Church report, and after the disastrous revolution in Iran, stoked violence and made local economic development nearly impossible.

While events in Iran, and a second oil crisis, occupied most of US public attention in 1979, Nicaragua's right-wing dictator Anastasio Somoza was overthrown in July by Communist-influenced Sandinista forces. The heir to a pre-CIA US intervention in the 1930s, Somoza had succeeded in eliminating most of the left-wing groups who had organized under the banner of 1930s opposition leader Augusto Sandino; Somoza probably had just not gotten around to eliminating the group led by Daniel and Humberto Ortega and the colorful guerilla leader Eden Pastora. Instead, Somoza thought it more urgent to assassinate a prominent liberal critic in Managua, and he thereby triggered a genuine popular revolt and international condemnation. The US had had enough of these excesses, and Somoza fled to Miami.[30]

Echoes of the Cuban revolution followed. The new government pursued land reform and nationalization of certain industries in an effort to improve the lives of their impoverished citizens, only to lose support among the wealthy and the (concededly very small) middle classes. The Ortegas also aligned themselves explicitly with Cuba, for much the same nationalistic reasons that Castro had denounced the US in the first place: to avoid the threat of yet another US-led restoration.[31]

This was enough to make Nicaragua and Central America a theme of the US presidential campaign in 1980. Harshly criticizing the Carter administration, Republicans put the reversal of the Nicaraguan revolt on the party platform, and Reagan himself warned that the Caribbean was "rapidly becoming a Communist lake in what should be an American pond."[32] In the wake of oil-shock economic setbacks and the far more prominent Iranian hostage crisis, Reagan swept to victory.

29. Cohn et al., "Rise in US Immigrants," 5–7.
30. Westad, *Global Cold War*, 339–41.
31. Westad, *Global Cold War*, 341–43.
32. LaFeber, *Inevitable Revolutions*, 274.

THE LONG MEMORIES... OF OTHERS

And his administration followed through. In 1981, Jeanne Kirkpatrick, Reagan's ambassador to the United Nations, proclaimed that "Central America is the most important place in the world for the United States today."[33] This was preposterous, of course, and Ms. Kirkpatrick, whose office had a global purview, surely knew it. President Reagan would fly to Reykjavik, Iceland, to negotiate nuclear arms rollbacks with Mikhail Gorbachev; he would stand on an outdoor platform in Berlin and call for Gorbachev to "open this gate" and "tear down this wall."[34] His administration risked tremendous political capital to complete the unpopular sale of AWACs advance aircraft to Saudi Arabia, as part of a thaw (if not a backroom deal) to keep oil exports flowing after two OPEC-led embargoes had torpedoed the US economy in the 1970s. But no one in the administration was going to tell Margaret Thatcher or other leaders in Western Europe, or in East Asia or in Israel, that they should reschedule their meetings with President Reagan because of an urgent phone call from, for example, Salvadoran President Jose Napoleon Duarte.

Ms. Kirkpatrick's hyperbole really made a different point: The US was no longer concerned with negotiations or human rights, and certainly not with land reform, only with winning the Cold War. As Undersecretary of State Fred Iklé put it, "We do not seek a military defeat for our friends. We do not seek a military stalemate. We seek victory for the forces of democracy."[35] Presumably those democratic "forces" knew which way to vote.

The White House had, however, learned at least one lesson from Vietnam: don't send US troops—at least not in uniform. Instead, working around serious opposition from a Vietnam-wary Congress, the CIA armed, trained and supplied about fifteen thousand Contras in Nicaragua, with bases in neighboring Honduras. Despite being lucratively supplied, the Contras were notoriously inept soldiers, and their brutality did not win them significant political support in the country either, despite the clear limitations of the Ortegas' government.[36] Disruption, not victory, was the real objective in the eyes of some Contra supporters. But the disruption came at a heavy price: The civil conflict led to the deaths of about thirty thousand citizens, perhaps one hundred thousand displaced persons, and

33. Kamen, "Reagan-Era Zeal," 1; LaFeber, *Inevitable Revolutions*, 5.
34. Judge and Langdon, *Cold War*, 230.
35. Westad, *Global Cold War*, 345.
36. LaFeber, *Inevitable Revolutions*, 304, 307, 339; Westad, *Global Cold War*, 346.

a corresponding crisis of inflation and unemployment.[37] And even Republican support would be undermined in 1986, when it emerged that the Reagan White House had sold arms to its ostensible arch-enemies in Iran, of all places, in order to provide Congressionally forbidden funding to the Contras.[38]

The situation grew even worse in El Salvador. As the US poured military aid into the country, Duarte's ostensibly center-right government was forced to stand aside for vicious paramilitary actions led by Duarte's political rival, Roberto D'Aubuisson.[39] Their aim was to suppress the FMLN, Marti National Liberation Front, a somewhat fractious alliance among rebellious rural groups seeking land and wage reform in a country noted for its sharp concentration of wealth in a few families.[40] The hostilities left some seventy thousand dead, around 1 percent of the entire population, and displaced many times that number.[41] Asylum claims from Salvadorans fearing violent retribution from the government or paramilitaries were routinely rejected by the US Immigration and Naturalization Service, in stark contrast to the INS view of those fleeing the Ortegas' Nicaragua.

Despite the forces arrayed against them, both the Nicaraguan government and the Salvadoran FMLN rebels held out to the end of the Cold War and participated in the regional peace process led by Costa Rican president Oscar Arias in 1987. Although the right-wing government remained in power in El Salvador, the FMLN gained recognition as a political party. Westad quotes a former FMLN member as reflecting, "What was the war for? For the solution to the land problem. We feel something already, and we're sure that we'll be free . . . [T]hat we not be seen as slaves, that we've won."[42]

In neighboring Guatemala, the largest country in Central America, the military had controlled the government more or less continuously since the 1954 coup. The US continued to supply extensive military aid but had lost its ability to influence behavior. The government had attempted to suppress insurgency campaigns since the early 1960s, but these had only grown in

---

37. Westad, *Global Cold War* 347; Kamen, "Reagan-Era Zeal," 1.

38. LaFeber, *Inevitable Revolutions*, 333–39; Westad, *Global Cold War*, 347–48; Brown University, "Understanding the Iran-Contra Affair."

39. LaFeber, *Inevitable Revolutions* 353–54; White, "Problem," paras. 1–4.

40. LaFeber, *Inevitable Revolutions*, 72–73.

41. Westad, *Global Cold War* 347; Kamen, "Reagan-Era Zeal," 1.

42. Westad, *Global Cold War*, 395.

size, especially in rural Indian regions from the late 1970s. What amounted to a civil war continued past the end of the Cold War and the Arias peace process until peace accords were reached in 1996. It has been estimated that two hundred thousand civilians were killed during the decades-long struggle, 93 percent by government or government-allied forces. Some 83 percent of the dead were Maya.[43]

Daniel Ortega, ironically, lost the first Nicaraguan election after the formal end of hostilities, although he would soon make a political comeback. He now runs one of the most corrupt autocracies in the world, an embattled survivor in the mold of the Castros and the Iranian ayatollahs, whose regimes continue to hold power. Meanwhile, as noted above, violence and underdevelopment in the Northern Triangle countries have continued to drive migration to the US, in numbers that trail only Mexico.

We should remember and try to learn something from these terrible outcomes: Things were bad before and bad today, but the US has had a heavy hand in the region since the late nineteenth century. And by 1980, after Vietnam and Iran, among others, the risk of blowback should have been widely understood. Sending weapons to one faction is going to make enemies (and refugees) of the others, and enemies can have long memories. Ms. Kirkpatrick and her colleagues either ignored recent history or, more likely, understood the risks and counted on armies to keep the peace. As the US had so often done.

---

43. Canby, "Death Squad Dossier," 10.

Two views of Shanghai illustrate China's economic transformation. Top: A 2015 image of the Huangpu riverfront with the well-preserved European banking houses built before the 1948 revolution. Bottom: Directly across the river, the ultramodern skyscrapers of the Pudong district in 2012.

Credits: (Top) Soramimi, Wikipedia Commons.
(Bottom) Gerd Eichmann, Wikimedia Commons.

7

The Paradox of China's Rise and the Veneration of Mao

THE FILMS OF ZHANG Yimou gave many Westerners our first and most vivid impressions of life in twentieth-century China. The Frances Ford Coppola *and* Steven Spielberg of Chinese filmmaking, Zhang started as a cinematographer in the early 1980s, and his love of the saturated colors of Kodachrome, then newly available in China, carried through his career. Red, especially. *Red Sorghum* (1987) and *Raise the Red Lantern* (1991) were novelistic works focusing on the difficult lives of peasants, especially women and children. *Raise the Red Lantern*, which is on every critic's list of all-time classics, made a star of Gong Li, in the role of a young woman sold by her family to become the third wife of a rich merchant in pre-Communist times.

Zhang's multigenerational epic *To Live* (1994) carried on his themes of the powerlessness and resiliency of ordinary Chinese people, but in a very different political context: from the Chinese Communist Party (CCP) victory over the nationalist Guomindang in the Civil War of the 1940s, through the Great Leap Forward in the late fifties and the Cultural Revolution of the sixties and early seventies. In these dangerous and disorienting times, the characters declare, almost like an incantation, that they want "to live," "to live a quiet life," "to make it back alive," to "live a good life." Despite the modesty of this goal, the family is literally disfigured, collateral damage of wartime and government incompetence. They understand that they are "lucky to be alive."

Fugui (played by Ge You), son of a wealthy landowner, gambles away the family's beautiful home in the years before the revolution, and his wife Jiazhen (Gong Li) walks out. Yet the loss, perversely, saves Fugui: the Communists publicly execute the man who won the house at the dice tables as a landlord. During the civil war, the Guomindang (nationalist) army conscripts Fugui, but the Communist army captures him. He is again fortunate that his talent with traditional shadow puppets (an otherwise frivolous hobby) boosts the Communist soldiers' spirits, and later entitles him to claim that he participated on the Communist side in the revolution. But these lucky breaks quickly come to an end. During the Civil War, the couple's first child, a daughter, becomes mute due to an untreated fever; in the Great Leap Forward, their young son, exhausted by overwork in the CCP's wild industrialization drive, is killed in an accident involving the local party chief's car; the mute daughter later marries an improbably nice, young Red Guard during the Cultural Revolution, but she hemorrhages and dies in childbirth because all the experienced doctors have been purged. The terrified young doctors even permit her husband to bring back the senior doctor, a class enemy who has been humiliated, beaten, and starved by other Red Guards. Attempting to revive the doctor, Fugui gives him too many pork buns and water, and he collapses due to bloating—that is, improbably, due to overindulgence rather than the punishments of the Cultural Revolution.

The film helped raised the curtain on the precarity of Chinese life under Communist rule, but it also it dealt very gently with terrible events. The family must surrender its pots and pans under the Great Leap's absurd mandate to match British steel production, but they eat at a seemingly well-supplied communal kitchen. In reality, millions starved. (And for no purpose: Even if it had met the targets, the country had no way to put that much steel to use.) The film ends after the Cultural Revolution, with Fugui and Jiazhen visiting their children's graves and, despite the tragedies, promising their grandson an ever-improving future: rather than oxen, he "will ride trains and planes."

With its light touch, *To Live* might have passed the CCP censors if it had come out before the 1989 military crackdown on Tiananmen Square protesters, but authorities prohibited domestic release of the film in 1994. The hospital scene surely didn't help.

THE PARADOX OF CHINA'S RISE AND THE VENERATION OF MAO

1. THE INDISPENSABLE LEGACY

Besides the sudden collapse of the Soviet bloc, the size and speed of China's post-Mao, or post-Tiananmen Square, rise may be the greatest surprise ending of the Cold War era. Especially considering its impoverished starting point, how can China already be challenging the US? Why has its path been so different from those of the former Soviet Union or other very populous countries like India or Brazil? There may be "a hundred schools of thought" on these questions, in the words Mao used to encourage free expression and open-mindedness for a few short weeks in 1957.[1] China's complexities stretch the capacity of history—at least of Western history—to describe it.

To appreciate China's recent achievements, remember how profoundly its people suffered during the reign of Mao, "one of the bloodiest leaders of the twentieth century, very much in a league with Hitler and Stalin."[2] The brilliant revolutionary strategist failed abysmally at governing, quashed dissent in a manner eerily like that of his mentor, Josef Stalin, and left the country traumatized, divided, and economically and educationally impoverished at his death in 1976. Many Chinese families, especially those accused of having privileged or intellectual backgrounds, had been ostracized, imprisoned, or exiled. Economic incentives were abolished in favor of frequently changing political priorities. And it is not the case that the Chinese people have forgotten, or become nostalgic for, the Cultural Revolution: a Chinese high school student, born long after, once told me that the period was like living in North Korea today, and not in a good way.

A few Westerners got a glimpse of how bad things got, even in the most carefully managed settings. Jan Wong of Montreal, granddaughter of Chinese emigrants and, like many ill-informed liberals, a self-described Maoist, became one of two Western exchange students at Beijing University in 1972. The huge university, China's Harvard, had only just reopened to a few hundred politically safe undergraduates, having been closed in the self-destructive frenzy of the Cultural Revolution. Quite aside from the constant surveillance from classmates and the strictures of CCP-approved political education, Wong remembered that "as the daughter of a restaurateur, I never dreamed Chinese food could be so bad." At this flagship institution, "my classmates were so undernourished that they usually ate

---

1. Spence, *Search*, 570.
2. French, "Mao's Shadow," 18.

every scrap" of the unchanging offerings of "tasteless cornmeal mush with a teaspoonful of inedible salted vegetables" or "a sliver of pork fat mixed with stale cabbage." When one of these meals was left half-eaten, the canteen workers angrily objected that "the students are losing touch with their class backgrounds."[3] To paraphrase a common saying of the time, it's no wonder they couldn't send up the satellites.

Yet Mao's legacy abides. Writing in *The New Yorker*, Pankaj Mishra recently suggested that the Cultural Revolution—from which Mao's successors swiftly distanced themselves—provided a necessary demolition of Mao-era bureaucracy from which the current, capitalism- (and corruption-) friendly bureaucracy could emerge. "China's unique 'model'—a market economy supervised by a technocratic party-state—could only have been erected on ground brutally levelled by Mao's Cultural Revolution."[4] This brush-clearing is even said to help explain the different outcome in post–Cold War Russia, where the former Communist bureaucrats themselves became capitalism-speaking bigwigs in a seriously corrupt and monopolistic system, and have failed to free the country from dependence on mineral exports and cyberpiracy.

But others see Mao as the source of the CCP's power. Its legitimacy—entitlement to govern—arose from the 1949 revolution and, unlike the Soviet Union, it had only one founding military and political leader. Even though many contemporary Chinese consider the Mao era somewhat of an embarrassment, according to Howard French, "Maoism—built on the style and rhetoric of a paternalistic and all-powerful leader, whose personality cult keeps his benign visage in view at all times, with slogans that all citizens should be able to recite—remains such a potent tactic and resource that [current President Xi] cannot afford to dispense with it."[5] A quarter century earlier, Yale professor Jonathan Spence had written, in a similar vein, that by the early 1990s the revolutionary CCP had stepped into a dynastic role similar to that of the late Ming and Qing and even of their Nationalist arch-enemies, the Guomindang.[6] The CCP's power certainly hasn't abated since then.

---

3. Wong, *Red China Blues*, 46, 49–50. Many Chinese memoirists have recounted Mao era struggles, for example Jung Chang's *Wild Swans*. Additional sources are discussed in Mishra, "Struggle Sessions"; and French, "Mao's Shadow."

4. Mishra, "Struggle Sessions," 65.

5. French, "Mao's Shadow," 20.

6. Spence, *Search*, 746–47.

THE PARADOX OF CHINA'S RISE AND THE VENERATION OF MAO

2. HERO

Zhang Yimou went on to make the historical action blockbusters *Hero* (2002) and *House of Flying Daggers* (2004). *Hero* is a magnificently photographed and multilayered story of a political assassin whose target is a brutal warlord. In order to get close to his target, the assassin, Nameless (played by the heartthrob Jet Li), constructs an elaborate tale of his loyal efforts to eliminate other equally talented (and attractive) would-be assassins of the warlord. But in the end, Nameless is persuaded that the warlord's brutality is in service of the greater goal of ending the wars by unifying China—indeed we learn that the warlord would become China's first emperor. Nameless abandons his quest in order to serve the greater good of unification, and for the same reason the warlord, the story's real hero, has him killed anyway.

Zhang could hardly have been unaware that Mao had long compared himself to that first Chinese emperor of the Qin dynasty, who had unified seven separate fiefdoms of the Warring States period in 221 BCE. The Qin emperor also spent ruinously: on an early version of the Great Wall and on his famous tomb of thousands of terra-cotta warriors near modern Xi'an. Though his dynasty crumbled after his death—he had failed to plan for succession—history has generally credited him for the enduring identity of a unified China. The parallel with Mao's reign would not have been lost on a Chinese audience.

When I visited China in the comparatively open period before the 2008 Olympics—its no-expense-spared opening ceremony staged by none other than director Zhang—the country's public narrative was distinctly proud and competitive, though tinged with some humility. At the Shanghai Museum, a long wall paralleled the historical achievements and advances of the West, broadly defined to include Egypt, Greece, Rome, Constantinople, Western Europe, and America (almost an afterthought), with those of China alone. A few of the entries struck me as a little odd or exaggerated, but there was no arguing with the brilliance of the antiquities. Its dynasties have come and gone, and sometimes fragmented, but in time a new identifiably Chinese empire has always emerged.

Chairman Mao was 70 percent good, our Chinese hosts and guides would observe, with amazing consistency, mainly because he ended one hundred years of Chinese subservience to foreigners (*waiguoren*). The Cultural Revolution was a mistake. We must do more to combat pollution (and no kidding about that). The forced displacement of residents from inner cities has caused some problems. We have to catch up with Western technology, maybe in fifty years. The menu of a self-consciously retro restaurant in Beijing winked at Mao-era slogans; paintings in a Shanghai art gallery parodied heroic images of the Great Leader.

But there was no masking the underlying ambition. The scale of city building and the wild creativity of the architecture in Beijing and Shanghai made America look staid, even fifteen years ago. The government had preserved the elegant, turn-of-the-century European trading houses on the Bund in Shanghai, four-to-six story stone and mortar buildings on prime harbor real estate from the era when foreign powers held and governed the port on humiliating treaty terms. Across the Huangpu River in Pudong, one-hundred-story skyscrapers cast morning shadows on the Bund. My family twice hosted high school students from Xi'an for a semester. Our guests took the most challenging physics course in the local high school, while also surviving regular literature and history classes taught entirely in English and marveling at the amount of free time American teens—my kids—enjoyed.

Also, when socializing with our Chinese friends and their families, I found it impossible to pick up a check at a restaurant. In either country.

3. A RISING MIDDLE CLASS

People can remember, and still move on.

It is possible that the primary explanation for China's phoenix-like rise is simply that, after Mao's death, the CCP under Deng Xiaoping simply did a better job finding a way out of the failure of Communist economic planning. Capable leadership is a rare enough thing. That leadership, however, was also capable of ordering the Tiananmen crackdown in 1989, which greatly discouraged uncomfortable questions and solidified hard-liner support. "Let's not bring up the past," declares a character in *To Live*, perhaps echoing Deng's admonition to "unite and look forward." Such unity rules out much Western-style entrepreneurship as well. For better or worse, figures like Jeff Bezos, Elon Musk, or Mark Zuckerberg, whose companies are largely financed with public stock offerings, are impossible to imagine in China. In November 2020, the government scotched the planned IPO of Jack Ma's Ant Group, which would have been one of the biggest ever worldwide, just days in advance.[7] Now it has turned to silencing popular

---

7. Zhong and Li, "China Halts Ant Group's," para. 2.

celebrities, including the actresses Zhao Wei and Zheng Shuang,[8] possibly to chill the emergence of politically active media figures along the lines of Bono, Brad Pitt, Ariana Grande, and even, I feel obliged to add, Donald Trump.

Yet limitations on freedoms have not thus far crippled the Chinese economy. Deng and his successors have by all accounts delivered several hundred million people—perhaps twice the population of the United States—into a rising middle class,[9] an achievement that must have earned a significant measure of gratitude and toleration of a few doctrinal inconsistencies.

It's also quite possible that China's economic rise is due to structural factors having little to do with Deng's policies or any political narrative. Despite its vast size and population, China is extremely homogeneous: according to its government reports, over 90 percent of the population is Han.[10] Serious ethnic conflict has been limited to far western provinces, including Tibet and Xinjiang, where the government does still face serious problems. The absence of ethnic tensions in China's largest and richest cities is a huge advantage for the CCP as compared to the diversity of the US, Europe, Brazil, and even Russia.

China's terribly low starting point at the end of Mao's reign also contributed to its later success. As in post–World War II Western Europe and Japan, China's vast, impoverished population and decimated infrastructure left huge economic demand. Everything from food to construction to basic services needed improvement, and from there a second wave of demand for consumer goods arose: the Eight Bigs including a color television, refrigerator, washing machine, motorcycle, stereo, camera, electric fan, and furniture set. And so on, into the internet age.[11] Economic aspirations also fueled demand for employment and cash wages, and millions relocated to cities designated for development, despite low wages, isolation, and difficult working conditions. When it became permissible to "look for money" (an ironic paraphrase of a Deng slogan), business leaders could be confident that domestic consumers and world markets would respond.

---

8. Stevenson et al., "Chinese Culture Is Raucous," paras. 4–5.

9. Piazza, "Poverty and Living Standards," abstract; Gill, "Deep Sixing Poverty," paras. 5–6; Tompkins, "Extreme Poverty," paras. 7–11.

10. University of North Carolina Library, "Chinese Ethnic Groups" (2010 Chinese government census).

11. For Eight Bigs, see Spence, *Search*, 733. In the Mao era, the Four Musts had been more modest: a bicycle, radio, watch, and sewing machine.

China also benefited, economically though not environmentally, from a gigantic demographic dividend. The CCP-inspired baby boom of the early 1960s became a huge cohort of young adults by the mid to late 1980s, who are only now nearing the end of their productive working lives. Later population control measures—the semi-official one child policy—changed the ratio of workers to dependents (children and retirees) in a way that has thus far been extremely favorable to China. The one-child policy, together with impact of education and wealth on urban childbearing, have kept the birth rate below replacement level. These demographic advantages may turn into headwinds as the population ages—the population is only now nearing its projected peak, and China can hardly count on immigration.

Finally, Chinese economic growth rates roughly parallel the earlier paths of its export-driven neighbors, the so-called Asian Tigers. (The Tigers followed Japan on this course, and have been followed by Tiger Cubs, such as Vietnam.) The growth of regional trading partners is a huge boon in itself, of course, but the larger point is that China's productivity gains from industrial and technological advances may also begin to level off. The tree does not grow to the sky.

Average Annual GDP Growth[12]

	Hong Kong	Singapore	South Korea	Taiwan	China
1960–70	11.15%	10.54%	8.56%	10.27%	4.48%
1970–80	22.47%	20.00%	21.93%	10.45%	12.70%
1980–90	10.30%	11.75%	15.79%	8.20%	2.57%
1990–2000	8.36%	10.27%	7.35%	6.69%	11.87%
2000–10	2.91%	9.58%	7.10%	4.20%	17.52%
2010–20	4.18%	3.81%	3.70%	2.54%	9.21%

While this growth has not come without problems, it is mostly very good news for China's people. It's mostly good news for the rest of the world as well. To the extent that China has been able to improve its citizens' lives domestically, rather than exporting its problems (though some such exports are certainly occurring), China's neighbors and others should be relieved.

---

12. Growth rates derived by the author from GDP data maintained by Federal Reserve Bank of St. Louis, "International Data."

Yet if we credit any combination of post-Mao policy, pent-up demand, demographics, and trade, Mao's regime was little more than an impediment to the country's prosperity. Like the Qin emperor in *Hero*, his place in the contemporary Chinese pantheon, the "70 percent good," must come from something else.

4. OUTSIDE THE WALLS

Father Matteo Ricci dreamed of converting the Ming emperor Wanli to Christianity. The Italian Jesuit priest devoted his career, from 1583 to his death in 1610, to establishing Christianity in China, then the richest and, arguably, most powerful nation in the world. Chinese authorities, suspicious of even small-scale activities of Portuguese traders and Japanese pirates, gradually allowed Ricci to move his mission from Macao to the ancient capital of Nanjing and finally to Beijing. Both fluent and literate in Chinese, he contributed important scholarship by translating Western works in astronomy, mathematics, and religion. Chinese scholars admired Ricci's book on Western notions of friendship, which they found harmonious with Confucian ideas. He even converted some prominent individuals to Christianity. But he never met Wanli, shielded behind layers of walls, guards, and eunuchs in the Forbidden City.[13]

Europeans and Americans would continue to go to China with their own agendas. The British surely believed they were doing the Chinese a favor in offering to introduce their "ingenious articles" of manufacture, of which the Qing emperor Qianlong famously saw no need.[14] Instead, from the Opium War of 1839–42 to the Qing dynasty's fall in 1911, the British and other powers forced China forced to concede to foreign occupation of treaty ports like Shanghai, the open preaching of Christianity, and the application of foreign law to foreigners, even if they committed murder.[15] These intrusions spurred unrest in China. The anti-foreign Boxer Rebellion (1898–1901) was suppressed only by a large, coordinated expeditionary force from Japan, Russia, Britain, France, and the US, resulting in yet another indemnity obligation for the weakening Qing dynasty.[16]

---

13. Spence, *Memory Palace*, xiii–xiv, 137–54, 214.
14. Spence, *Search*, 122–23.
15. Spence, *Search*, 158–61, 179–81.
16. Spence, *Search*, 231–35.

The West lost any chance for a post-Qing reset on May 4, 1919. Despite President Wilson's rhetoric of self-determination, World War I peace negotiators in Paris awarded Germany's Asian interests to Japan, delivering China's Shandong province into the hands of an aggressive regional rival. This was both terrifying, as Japan had already reduced neighboring Korea to a colony, and politically toxic within China. It was a huge missed opportunity as well. The nationalist Guomindang Party had advocated a Western-style republican form of government, and its founder Sun Yat-Sen had received a Christian missionary education in Hawaii in the 1880s.[17] But after May 4, the Guomindang could not afford to align with Western powers; it joined the newly formed CCP in working with Soviet advisers and in promoting deeply anti-imperialist policies.[18]

Americans overwhelmingly supported an isolationist foreign policy, believing they could stay out of another World War. Most thought of China, if at all, as mired in poverty and in need of aid. Pearl Buck, daughter of missionaries, wrote the Pulitzer Prize–winning international bestseller *The Good Earth* (1931) about a peasant family's stoic endurance of hardship and political turmoil—themes that later resonated in Zhang Yimou's films. Despite their good works, Western missionaries and expats posted to China, including Buck, still occupied privileged positions and therefore endured anti-foreign violence.

US government policy toward China was shaped by the China Lobby, led by former Christian missionaries or their children. Henry Luce, publisher of *Time* and *Life* magazines, was the Hearst or Murdoch of his generation; Representative Walter Judd of Minnesota was the intellectual leader of an important bloc in Congress. To their credit, the China Lobby advocated against anti-Asian racism in the US and an overly Eurocentric foreign policy. But they used their power toward a single political outcome. They lavished praise and attention on nominally Christian Guomindang leader Chiang Kai-shek and his elegant Wellesley-educated wife Madame Chiang (Soong Mei-ling), without regard to the weakness, corruption, and brutality of Chiang's coalition.[19] Chiang or his wife appeared on the cover of Luce's *Time* magazine at least a dozen times from 1927 through 1955.

US leaders followed this line for years. The Guomindang and CCP both pledged to fight the Japanese invaders during World War II, but the

---

17. Spence, *Search*, 227–28.
18. Spence, *Search*, 336–38.
19. Halberstam, *Coldest Winter*, 239–47.

US poured military and financial aid solely to Chiang's government, despite almost constant frustration with Chiang's preference to avoid conflict. The US continued to support the Guomindang in its civil war with the CCP after 1945. But the Truman administration could see no end to it, and a year of mediation led by the universally respected envoy General George Marshall led to nothing. One episode encapsulates American frustration with the ineffectiveness of Chiang's armies. In late 1948, Wellington Koo, Chiang's ambassador to Washington, asked President Truman for more aid, without knowing that thirty-two Guomindang divisions with American-supplied equipment had just surrendered to Communist forces near Xuzhou. Truman, who did know, declined the invitation.

When Chiang's government fell to CCP forces in 1949, disbelief in the US was followed by domestic retribution against the Truman administration. "Who lost China?" Republican leaders demanded, as though it were an overseas possession. This episode only served to feed the era's feverish suspicions of Communist infiltration. Senator Joseph McCarthy made his infamous (and baseless) claim that he had the names of 205 Communists in the US State Department, on February 9, 1950, barely four months after Mao's triumphant entry in Beijing.

The effect of the Republicans' political attack lasted a generation. US leaders could not afford to lose face domestically by backing away from Chiang's rump Republic of China on the island of Taiwan, and to this day the US devotes enormous economic and military resources to the island's defense. (The ROC's economic success and transition to democracy has raised the stakes: Evan Osnos of the *New Yorker* recently called Taiwan "the landmine at the center of the [US-China] relationship."[20]) Perhaps worse, the US would not recognize the government that actually ruled China. For decades, "Red China" was not a place Americans could travel, was not admitted to the United Nations, did not participate in the Olympics. Finally, the fear that Mao's China might dominate smaller neighbors helped justify America's intervention in Vietnam.[21]

If missionaries and Republicans clung unrealistically to the dream of a Christian China, many Western leftists of the late 1960s venerated Maoism. Some, like Black Panthers Huey Newton and Bobby Seale, really did mean to foment something like a revolution. Others, like the Rolling Stones and the actor Shirley MacLaine, had less to complain about, and little idea what

---

20. Osnos, "Fight Fight, Talk Talk," 44.
21. Lawrence, *Vietnam War*, 48.

Mao was really doing.[22] Instead their attitude was largely a piece of their anti-Vietnam War activism: if Mao was okay, a Communist victory might not be so bad for the Vietnamese. (It would in fact be very bad for the Vietnamese; so too was the war.) In the end, Mao veneration showed that the left, too, had a huge blind spot about China. After the truth emerged, there would be no defenders of the Cultural Revolution.

In a nesting series of ironies, Republican President Richard Nixon, another Luce favorite who had hurled the supposed American loss of China in the face of Democratic opponents for twenty years, eventually "played the China card" with his 1972 diplomatic visit. His intent was to worry the Soviet leadership and to facilitate an "honorable" peace in Vietnam. The opening of this new relationship, beginning with an enormously appealing match between the national table tennis teams, proved to be the most popular achievement of his presidency. But no lasting peace was reached in Vietnam, and few, if any, in the US fully understood that Nixon was elevating Mao's regime while the horrors of the Cultural Revolution were still going on.

Then again, Father Ricci spent almost his entire career in China and never gained more than a partial picture.

5. OUTLASTING THE USSR

In China's 2,500-year history, Mao's harsh reign could be seen as a short chapter, his domestic misrule perhaps outweighed by his resetting troubled relationships with foreign powers, including Russia. Moreover, China played many roles during that time: as a counterexample to Marxist-Leninist theory; as the leader and inspiration for the anti-colonial movement in the Third World; as a direct participant in the Korean War; as an imagined Lost Cause that drove American politicians, almost reflexively, to make grave mistakes; as an exporter of labor and culture throughout Asia and the Americas; and as the most populous nation on the planet, ever.

Indeed, contemporary Chinese may view the Cold War as a US-Soviet sideshow—frequent standoffs, few casualties—or a laughable misnomer given the nonstop shooting in East Asia. China or one of its immediate neighbors were involved in hot wars almost continuously from the late 1920s through the early 1980s. After the end of World War II and the long

---

22. Mishra, "Struggle Sessions," 61 (Bobby Seale, John Lennon, and the Rolling Stones); French, "Mao's Shadow," 19 (Shirley MacLaine, Eldridge Cleaver).

Chinese civil war, the US and other Western powers actively participated in wars causing millions of deaths in Korea (1950–53), Vietnam (1946–54 and 1960–75) and Cambodia (1972–78), and intervened in a counterrevolution in Indonesia (1965). The Americans' domestic angst over having lost China may have been unmoored from reality, but it had real effects: it gave Mao real reason to remain isolated, and that isolation allowed Mao's disastrous policies to persist.

Mao also viewed the Soviet Union with suspicion, despite their long strategic alliance dating back to the May Fourth movement. The CCP's resiliency when the Soviet Union itself collapsed can in part be traced to Mao's stubborn independence, further legitimizing the CCP's hold on power.

After the CCP's 1949 victory, Mao occupied the roles of both Lenin, founder and theorist, and Stalin, war leader and state builder. He was also like a younger sibling trying to emulate his brothers' achievements while striving for recognition of his own success. Of necessity, Mao had created a new path to Communism based on the rural peasantry rather than industrial workers, an example of great interest to other pre-industrialized countries colonized by Western powers. This made Soviet leaders uneasy, because Mao had stretched Marxist/Leninist dialectical theory, which held that economies had to reap the benefits of industrialization before advancing to socialism, nearly to the breaking point. If Communism was the solution in these wildly different cases, was it anything more than a justification for revolution? As the Soviet leaders realized, when given a real choice, voters in industrialized countries had never *chosen* Communism. Mao's rural path to Communism might wind up being more important than Lenin's.

An initial period of close cooperation with the USSR, when China desperately needed recognition and economic aid it could not get anywhere else, lasted only into the mid-1950s: through the Korean War, the French War in Vietnam, and the conference of non-aligned or Third World countries at Bandung, Indonesia, in 1955. The Soviet Union allowed China to send a top-level delegation to Bandung, but nervously: the conferees organized around the idea of opposing colonialism, including alignment with either the US or the USSR. Most of the resentment was directed to America's Western European allies, with the US as a lesser offender. But due to the Soviet domination of Eastern Europe and incorporation of Muslim-majority "republics" from Azerbaijan to Kazakhstan, the USSR came in for its share of criticism.[23]

23. Westad, *Global Cold War*, 99, 101, 103.

Mao felt betrayed when Khrushchev denounced the excesses of the Stalin era in a Politburo speech in early 1956. Khrushchev was soon forced to back away from this glimmer of reform, sending the Red Army to put down the Hungarian independence movement in October of the same year. But his speech created problems for Mao because he had so closely and loyally sought to follow Stalin's example. Now Mao had a job keeping his own party under control and out of the hands of those free-thinking Soviets, and he broke with them sharply in 1960.[24] His renewed fear of political threats led to two more terrible decades for the Chinese people.

Yet it was the more advanced, more internationally engaged Soviets who fell. The Soviet Union was burdened by an ethnically diverse empire it could not afford to maintain; an unsustainably expensive arms race with the US; an economy hampered, like that of Saudi Arabia, by its dependency on volatile petroleum exports; and an aging and declining population. China, in contrast, had no empire and few natural resource exports; a huge, young, and ethnically homogeneous population; and an inherited history of pre-industrial capitalism. Rather than colonial possessions to manage, it had expatriate populations to keep up with.

6. COSMOPOLITANS

If Mao's positive legacy consists mainly in nationalism, the eviction of imperialists, and revival of traditional suspicion of outsiders—all of which is understandably valuable to the autocratic Xi regime—the inspiration for future reforms may need to come from Chinese sources.

China does not, to its current leaders' regret, have a monopoly on Chinese culture, high or popular, because it has long been an exporter of Chinese people. In the recent Hollywood blockbuster *Crazy Rich Asians*, a beautiful and brilliant second-generation Chinese American, a tenured professor of economics at NYU at the apparent age of about twenty-seven, does not know, despite her field of study, that her fiancé is the scion of the richest of Asia's nouveau-riche families. Swept many time zones away from the "salmonella and despair" of JFK airport to his family's glitzy enclave in Singapore, our heroine encounters and, at the last minute, draws her fiancé back from his glamorous and icy mother. In a China-meets-Jane-Austen kind of way, we learn that his mom had never been fully accepted in her

---

24. For China's alliance with and later break with the Soviet Union, see Westad, *Global Cold War*, 65, 69–70; Spence, *Search*, 544, 552, 583–90.

own husband's family and was determined to assure that the movie's heroine didn't get a better deal. In a very American twist, however, the couple, with the help of her up-by-her-bootstraps single mom and some wacky American pals, goes back to New York, breaking free of the traditional Chinese expectation that brides take care of their husbands' families. Whew!

Ironically, the groom's mother is played by the elegant Michelle Yeoh, who has a migration story of her own. Born in Malaysia to Chinese parents, Yeoh is fluent in Malay and English. She reportedly had to learn her Cantonese lines phonetically for her international breakout role in Ang Lee's gorgeous, indeed Zhang-worthy, martial arts film *Crouching Tiger, Hidden Dragon* (2000).

Chinese Americans have long worked in Hollywood, of course. Tyrus Wong arrived with his father at Angel Island in San Francisco Bay, in 1916 at the age of nine. (The US was not admitting Chinese women, lest they start families.) As told in the documentary *Tyrus* (2016), he found a way to attend art school in Los Angeles and got a job as a junior illustrator at Disney. There, a senior executive somewhat surreptitiously advanced his Asian-inspired design concepts for the thematic backgrounds of *Bambi* (1942). Look past the big-eyed animal characters: the layered colors and sweeping brushstrokes of forest and sky backgrounds set the emotional tone of each scene.

A wave of ethnic Chinese auteurs, contemporaries of Zhang Yimou working outside China, later brought Chinese stories to the international scene. Wayne Wang (b. Hong Kong, 1949) made his first film *Chan Is Missing* (1982) on a shoestring budget in San Francisco's Chinatown. One of *Chan*'s themes is the discord between families of earlier immigrants, almost all from southern China, who identified with the nationalist Republic of China, and more recent arrivals from the gradually opening People's Republic. Wang later became famous for *The Joy Luck Club* (1993), his adaptation of Amy Tan's multigenerational novel about a Chinese immigrant family.

Cosmopolitan communities in Asia have contributed even more. Wong Kar-Wai (b. Shanghai, 1958) was at the vanguard of the Hong Kong New Wave, from *As Tears Go By* (1988) through his most beloved film, the noirish romance *In the Mood for Love* (2000). Before the international blockbuster *Crouching Tiger, Hidden Dragon*, Ang Lee (b. Taiwan, 1954), broke through with the contemporary comedy *Eat, Drink, Man, Woman* (1994); Lee has also worked well beyond Chinese stories, and made, for example *Life of Pi* (2012), *Brokeback Mountain* (2005), and the Emma Thompson version of *Sense and Sensibility* (1995). Steven Chow (b. Hong Kong, 1962) has made over-the-top martial arts comedies like *Shaolin Soccer* (2001) and *Kung Fu Hustle* (2005)—the kinds of movies where the winning soccer goal tunnels under the length of the field.

This is not simply to tell a feel-good story about Chinese emigrants: they have long been treated badly in their adopted countries; their presence has, on the other hand, sometimes sharply disadvantaged others, for example in Singapore and Indonesia. The point is that Chinese culture thrives in many places outside China. Mainland Chinese can learn of the achievements of their overseas contemporaries, through the internet and family connections, as East Berliners surreptitiously learned what was happening on the west side of the wall. But the difference is that prominent expatriate Chinese communities are so widely dispersed: Hong Kong, Singapore, Taiwan, Malaysia, California, New York, Vancouver. The CCP is smart enough to pay attention to the competition, but right now it seems to be betting that economic success and heavy censorship will forestall the need for more political or expressive openness. Ironically, the CCP's recent move to suppress popular celebrities in China may only highlight the freedom enjoyed by artists of the diaspora.

As a corollary, perhaps the most effective way for the US and others to encourage Chinese government reform would be to continue to welcome the overseas Chinese and foster their successes. Recent attacks and harassment of Asian-Americans in the US are not just illegal but idiotic, pointlessly feeding the CCP's xenophobia and providing excuses for its oppression at home.

President Truman with officials of the Federal Deposit Insurance Corporation. The photo is undated but probably from 1946. The FDIC was formed in the wake of Depression-era bank failures, to guarantee the safety of deposits at participating banks. The US did not suffer another financial liquidity crisis until 2008. Rather than simply provoking revolution as Marxist theory predicted, Western countries took steps to reform the hard edges of capitalism.

Credit: Department of Interior, National Park Service, White House Photographs, U.S. National Archives.

8

Marx's Crafty Nemesis
The Evolutions of Capitalism

For the first time among great power rivalries, the Cold War featured an important, spirited, and sometimes sophisticated public debate about the comparatively new social science of economics. Lenin had founded the Soviet Union with his spin on Marxist doctrine. He expressly aimed to replace capital-c Capitalism all over the world with an egalitarian, worker-led paradise, though a few harsh measures might be needed for the transition. The leaders of countries with more traditional hierarchies, including those rooted in religious beliefs as well as the prosperous nations of Europe and North America, took the threat seriously. As a result, if you listened to the dire rhetoric of each system's true believers, you could be forgiven for thinking that a binary choice of economic systems dictated everything else. Capitalism meant mass poverty. Communism meant totalitarianism, and a godless one at that. To compromise would be to court disaster.

This debate had a Potemkin quality: like the village facades supposedly erected by an ambitious Russian minister to impress Catherine the Great (the story has been embellished in service of the metaphor), the rhetoric about economic theory seemed hollow before the raw struggles for power over territory and alliances. The differences between the political systems were also stark and substantial. The US and its European allies allowed real voter choice and changes of government, with their flaws and limitations; they were far more open and more concerned with opportunity or fairness of process than with equality or fairness of outcomes. The Soviet Union leaders mostly did care about fairness of outcomes but, unfortunately, they cared much more about remaining in office. This does not mean that capitalism and socialism are mutually exclusive. In practice, the economic systems were more like the results of the political models rather than the other way around.

The different economic systems did produce big differences in the prosperity of each country's citizens and the relative burdens of military buildup, but these outcomes only became clear with time. The Soviet Union managed real economic growth in the decade or more after World War II.[1] Western economies hit a lot of headwinds as late as the 1970s, when no one thought the Cold War was in its last phases. Although the Soviet bloc collapse came as a surprise, with hindsight, its economic failures can be explained.[2] The Soviet Union's central economic planning required it to dictate production levels, assign jobs, and repress personal or private initiatives; harsh measures that turned out not to work. Its finances became dependent on exports of its oil and other commodities, the prices of which fluctuated unpredictably. Over time, their leaders found that they couldn't afford the newest military technology or even smaller foreign interventions, resulting in a vacuum of power that contributed directly to the empire's collapse. There was plenty of military buildup and political oppression on the Western side as well, especially when we think of colonialism and dictatorships in the developing world, but it was something the US and its allies managed to sustain without ruinous cost.

So, we have a pretty good idea of what didn't work for the Soviets. What this leaves out is capitalism, Marx's nemesis. At least as practiced by the US and its Western European allies, capitalism evolved from a much longer history and was greatly affected by the world wars and the Cold War. With the benefit of hindsight, we can see that in some ways the Marxist critique of capitalism, in particular of extreme inequalities of wealth, was less compelling during the Cold War than it was before or since.

1. CLUES FROM THRIVING CIVILIZATIONS

Capitalism does not actually have a set of first principles, though you might not know it from critics or cheerleaders. Karl Marx and Ayn Rand both wrote speculative fiction. The most advanced market economies of the

1. Spufford, *Red Plenty*, 87–90, 377–78.
2. See chapter 1, above.

Cold War period, and today, resulted from advances—or at least evolving practices—in science, technology, education, and government, as well as business, over many centuries. Clearly there is a lot of variation among the end results, not what one would expect if every capitalist country followed the same playbook.

This essay will provide several examples of this co-evolution of government and business and will discuss how countries deemed capitalist—mostly democracies—have reacted to criticisms by Marxists and others. But first I want to explain why I think all of these things are so connected.

It's not about money. Money is a medium of exchange, a means to measure value, a remarkable invention of seminal importance, but not an end in itself. With money, we don't need to barter goods or services directly with a person who has what we need. A specialized network of symbiotic exchange can develop. Money can be borrowed and invested. Trade can take place without the king's approval, although probably at his sufferance. Adam Smith, the first modern economist, was right about all of that. Yet, at bottom, the value is in the goods and services, and the goods and services are the fruit of human effort. Marx was right about that.

The urbanologist Jane Jacobs had what I think is a crucial insight in her book *Cities and the Wealth of Nations*. Wealth, she said, results from the labor specialization and innovation fostered by cities, and from trade between cities. She gave two examples. One was an impoverished mountain region in France that has the remains of remarkably durable Roman roads. It was an iron mining area, from which ore was exported for refinement and manufacturing, and therefore depended utterly on demand from elsewhere in the empire. When the Roman trade dried up, the place had nothing. At the other extreme was the astonishing success of the modern Tokyo-Osaka corridor on the east coast of Japan. The region's success was neither inherently Japanese (rural rice farmers there depend heavily on subsidies and import protections) nor the result of natural advantages or colonization. Rather the cities had developed the skills and internal markets necessary to replace and then to export goods and services they formerly had to buy from elsewhere, leading to the growth of a dense network of specialized industries, creating jobs, attracting new residents, and thereby expanding internal markets for all manner of goods and services. This pattern is not unique to Japan, of course, but the closeness of the major cities and excellent transportation helped.[3]

---

3. Jacobs, *Cities*, 32–35, 38–42, 45–46. Japan also had the advantage of minimal

Jacobs's insight probably does not have quite the generality she ascribed to it, but it reveals the connection between the successes of such different places as ancient Rome and medieval Venice, or the modern US and Singapore. It helps to explain why Britain's little Atlantic colonies did so much better than Spain's hemispheric New World empire and the plantation colonies like those of the Caribbean and the American Deep South. Nations that depended on extractive or supply industries like oil exports (Saudi Arabia and, indeed, Russia) are at risk of fluctuating commodity prices and ultimately of substitution; worse, their rulers are often tempted to underinvest in their people, since retaining political and military control is the key to securing the benefits of commodity sales. It's not economically bad for a country to control a large patch of land, but it's not necessary and, often enough, a distraction from the critical goal of developing their people and enabling them to specialize, innovate, and trade.

This is nothing new: Humans have always prized specialization and invention. The remarkable cave paintings in France and Spain date from twenty and thirty thousand years ago. We may not know much about those societies or tribes, or about the use and meaning of their art. But it seems clear that these were not the works of novices, and they were not made by solo artists. Valuable resources of time for teaching and practice, and of material for painting and light, had to be devoted to these vast installations. The end results had to be esteemed or valued, envied or worshiped, for this expenditure to have been worthwhile.

Over and over again, in places too far apart to have communicated meaningfully with each other, empires in ancient Egypt, China, India, and the Americas evolved elaborate religious, funerary, and artistic traditions evidenced by artifacts that could only have been produced by communities of trained specialists. These artisans obviously weren't living hand to mouth, they weren't working alone, and they weren't producing tools for hunting or farming or military conquest. It's true those ancient societies had become rich by other means, usually from the development of large-scale agriculture, but that is further evidence of a high degree of specialization in crop and herd management.

But these advances depend on the sufferance of the king. There is no separating economics from politics. The king, like the modern state, needs to maintain a monopoly on military power and influence, lest the

---

defense spending, because its postwar constitution had abolished the military; it had little choice but to rely on the US defense umbrella. Bass, *Judgment at Tokyo*, 162, 496.

country fall back into the hands of warring clans (or modern gangs). The anthropologist Jared Diamond, writing about Hatfield-versus-McCoy-like clan warfare in Papua New Guinea, has explained that "nearly all human societies today have given up the personal pursuit of justice in favor of impersonal systems operated by state governments."

> Without state government, war between local groups is chronic; cooperation between local groups on projects bringing benefits to everyone—such as large-scale irrigation systems, free rights of travel, and long-distance trade—becomes much more difficult; and even the frequency of murder within a local group is higher.[4]

Besides security, if there is to be a medium of exchange, the king's blessing—or the "full faith and credit" of the taxing authority—may be needed to back it up. The government provides internal security and civil authority through police and military forces and the legal or regulatory systems for enforcing obligations and ensuring fair play. These services are critical to ordinary, Adam Smith-ian economic life. At the same time, even with a monopoly on power, the king and state are vulnerable. They need their subjects to prosper, in order to keep up with rivals, to pay for external defense and a suitable lifestyle. If they repress, overtax, or otherwise inhibit economic activity, they too will be poorer for it. A successful balance is hard to find and to maintain; over and over again, empires have collapsed or been overtaken.

On the subject of balance, Jacobs also wrote that military expenditures were inherent drags on the economy but, in my view, she undervalued the benefits of internal and external security. Security is first of all a human right, and secondly a near necessity for successful economic development. It's not a do-it-yourself proposition, and if it's not provided by the government, it's unstable, dangerous, and cripplingly expensive. In other words, security needs to be reliable and available at a reasonable price. Jacobs was half right in her assessment of the defense spending of the Cold War powers, writing in 1984 that "today the Soviet Union and the United States each predicts and anticipates the decline of the other. Neither will be disappointed."[5] She turned out to be wrong only about the US, not because her theory was wrong but because the measurement was wrong: the US has been able to field a world-leading military with a remarkably small fraction of its GDP. Even so, the surprisingly high additional costs of what were

---

4. Diamond, "Vengeance Is Ours," para. 5.
5. Jacobs, *Cities*, 200.

expected to be small wars in Iraq and Afghanistan demonstrated how close the US might be to shackling its broader economy.

2. THE ENGLISH ROOTS OF AMERICAN CAPITALISM

I don't agree with strong assertions of American exceptionalism, but we Americans really are unique in the shortness of our national history. Our histories too often give less than full credit to the fact that the new United States were starting from a highly evolved, and wealthy, British system. The modest-sized island was the richest place on earth by then, and it certainly wasn't because of natural resources. What had they figured out?

Nationhood was one thing. England was just a regional power, one of many, when everyone's favorite tyrant Henry VIII came to power. Not only did he fall scandalously short as a husband and father, he mostly ignored the Magna Carta's principles of representative government, rebelled against papal authority, and did not greatly advance England's immediate economic or military prospects either.

But Henry did obsess about leaving a legitimate male heir, for without clear succession he would have lost influence like a lame duck president after a lost election. In the process, he broke with the Roman church, which was dependent upon England's French and Spanish rivals, seized power over English churches and their vast properties, and established that the English government would set its own standards for legitimacy as well. Like the Qin emperor who first unified China, his seizure of power over church and state, and the divorce that ruptured ties with Spanish nobility, clearly marked out England as a political state separate from the interlocking royalties of continental Europe.

Henry did not, however, eliminate succession struggles. Six dramatic and bloody power shifts took place over the next 150 years, culminating in the Glorious Revolution of 1688. (For all the books and films about Henry and his daughter Queen Elizabeth, you'd think we'd have more about the lives of King James, sponsor of everyone's favorite English language Bible, the ill-fated Charles I, or the revolutionary Oliver Cromwell.) Eventually, the turmoil led to the establishment of a more stable and effective parliamentary system. The leading strategist for the new regime, John Locke, articulated ideas of individual rights and separation of powers that we sometimes ascribe to the Magna Carta; his writings formed the intellectual framework for the American demands for representative government a century later.

In fact, 1688 might have been a better starting point for this pocket history, or 1776 (the year that Adam Smith published *The Wealth of Nations*, of course), if the English hadn't already accomplished so many of the things that led them to bestride the earth. Often, like Japanese automakers of the 1960s and 1970s, they copied and improved upon practices of others: surpassing the imperialistic naval prowess of the Spanish and Portuguese; building on the trade and manufacturing model of Amsterdam. They defeated the Spanish Armada in 1588, obtained the *asiento* (or monopoly contract) for the sale of slaves to Spanish colonies following the War of the Spanish Succession in the Treaty of Utrecht (1713), gained dominance over the Indian subcontinent in the eighteenth century, and forced the French out of Quebec by 1763.[6] They established more successful colonies in North America than their European rivals, stumbling upon the unprecedented model of middle-class farms and villages founded by religious self-exiles in New England. The British government also innovated in the use of private incentives for overseas development, by establishing trade monopolies like the East India Company, granting American estates to prominent noblemen as in New Jersey, and endorsing the practices of British privateers. Capitalist ideas were thus used in service of colonialism, but just as important, the government learned that it could enhance its own wealth and power by ceding authority to private interests.

To be clear, English energy and innovations were mostly in service to exploitive and extractive colonial enterprises. The East India Company dominated South Asia through bald military force, and British ships had the largest share of the Atlantic slave trade in the 1700s.[7] Even as the British government, to its eternal credit, was the first to abolish slavery and the slave trade and acted as the world's police in interdicting slave ships in the first part of the nineteenth century,[8] it simultaneously "opened" a highly resistant Chinese empire to trade via the sale of opium and a series of humiliating military interventions.[9] American economic development, at least through the nineteenth century, similarly combined manufacturing and trade with oppression in the form of slave-based agriculture and riflepoint Indian evacuations. The Americans even copied the British in "opening" Japan with Admiral Matthew Perry's black warships in 1853–54,

---

6. Thomas, *Slave Trade*, 231, 272.
7. Thomas, *Slave Trade*, 246–84.
8. Thomas, *Slave Trade*, 551–52, 556.
9. See chapter 7, above.

but the Japanese—no great friends of the Chinese—quickly saw the need to keep up with the Europeans and avoided the Chinese experience.

In short, it is impossible to separate the history of Anglo-American economic successes from colonizing practices. Our predecessors succeeded in part by displacing people, enslaving others, and stealing a lot of stuff. That is shameful, but to that time great empires had often prospered through conquest and extraction. Genghis Khan, Tamurlaine, and the Ottoman and Russian empires did not achieve power without violating modern human rights standards. And the Soviet critique of colonialism was especially hypocritical: no one in the twentieth century exercised tighter control over nations in its sphere or forcibly moved more people than Stalin did from Eastern Europe to Siberia and Kazakhstan.[10] It was only during and immediately after World War II that explicit colonialism by the US and European allies began its rapid decline, including for example the US withdrawal from the Philippines, Britain from India, the Netherlands from Indonesia, France from Vietnam.

Nationalism and colonialism were part of capitalism as it evolved, alongside increasingly democratic governments in both England and the US. What changed over time was that this jerry-rigged system had its critics and reformers.

3. A MISUNDERSTANDING OF BRITISH SUCCESS

Napoleon probably never called Britain a "nation of shopkeepers," but there is a long history of misreading the visible signs of capitalism as end results rather than an ongoing process. As we have seen, the Chinese emperor Qianlong did reject the British offer to trade in latest English manufactured products, simply because he didn't see the need for them. Stalin, Khrushchev, and Mao would all be preoccupied with matching the quantity of production from their capitalist rivals, sometimes by fiat, failing to see those quantities as the results of customer demand. Those extra tons of steel aren't worth anything without end product manufacturers which have their own customer orders to fill.[11] Quarterly reports on GDP growth or shrinkage are oversimplified for the same reason: they don't measure how well the activity reflects or meets customer needs. These were, ironically, exactly the wrong measure to illustrate the differences between the Soviet and US economies.

10. Applebaum, *Iron Curtain*, xxix, 117, 127; Judt, *Postwar*, 30–31; Stone, *Atlantic*, 105.
11. Spufford, *Red Plenty*, 206–10, 393–95, 324–25, 411–12; Judt, *Postwar*, 578.

Marx was a much more subtle critic. He characterized the capitalism or industrialism of his time as an advanced stage *en route* to universal socialism, which would ultimately play into the Russians' historical sensitivity about lagging behind Europe. Following Hegel's mysterious dialectic, Marx even thought of the stage as inevitable, which in a way took the industrialists off the hook for their companies' excesses. He was not clear, however, on how this might happen.[12]

His lasting insight, though, was that workers' lives were wasted in the mills. In the Industrial Revolution period of one hundred years or more, the growth of factory production coincided with fantastic advances in transportation (railroads and shipbuilding), materials (concrete and steel), and energy (coal and oil). The opportunities were so great that management did not need—and certainly did not bother—to worry about maximizing the value of their human resources. They could treat factory and railroad workers and miners as though they were pieces on an assembly line, and often went out of their way to do so. The exploitation of employees in remote company towns inspired the famous refrain "you work so hard and what do you get / another day older and deeper in debt." In the cities, workers and their families at least had some chance to change jobs, to seek schooling or training, and some chance that the next generation could find other work.

Marx was obviously wrong, however, in seeing this era as an end state of capitalism. Amazing as it may seem, the industrialists of the nineteenth century almost certainly sacrificed opportunities and slowed progress by treating workers so poorly. The labor movement saw the situation as profoundly unfair; Henry Ford saw it as an opportunity to get the best workers (and a new class of customers) by treating them decently. In the late twentieth century, Toyota would go on to demonstrate that the workers' ideas were critical to efficiency, quality control, and product improvement. The democratic/capitalist model turned out to be a moving target.

4. FINANCIAL CRISES AND THE EVOLUTION OF MONEY

Memories of the worldwide Great Depression of the 1930s strongly influenced Cold War leaders, on one hand by prompting an expanded role of government in the US economy, and on the other by helping to persuade the Soviet leadership that Marx was right—capitalism was doomed

---

12. See chapter 1, above.

and would self-destruct in time.[13] It was crucial that the advanced market economies did not experience another financial crisis until 2008, when the Cold War was long over.

Financial crises are crises of trust and confidence, and the government has regularly played a critical role in restoring both. At the foundation is money, a credible medium of exchange that can be widely used for transactions and as a measure for valuing other assets like securities and real estate. Long before the 2008 financial crisis, governments learned to respond to recurring panics with reforms to the financial systems and, eventually, with fiscal stimulus, that helped to restore a sense of trust and opportunity.

All money is symbolic. Its physical substance may have no intrinsic value, in the case of paper or cowrie shells, or some modest value as a commodity, like coins. In any case, it represents something else which is understood and accepted as having far greater value. Usually this is a payment obligation, an IOU, from a government or another party that is viewed as wealthy and reliable. The US government issues its promises in many ways, including one hundred dollar bills and book entries crediting the balance sheets of regional Federal Reserve banks, which in turn do the same for commercial banks in their respective regions. Banks and merchants and consumers accept these promises because the US government has vast assets, for example in land, gold bullion, and money on deposit at commercial banks, plus great power to obtain more through its taxing authority. Although dollars can lose real value through inflation and in relation to the value of other currencies, no one seriously doubts the ability of the US to meet its dollar-denominated obligations. The fact that dollars are symbolic does not mean the obligations they symbolize are not real.

People must have understood this better in the early days of the US republic. Central banks like the Federal Reserve, which do literally print money (though this is a very small part of the money supply), are fairly recent developments. In the early US, central banking was a sharply partisan issue. In a dramatic policy change for the Jeffersonian Democratic Party, President Madison's administration proposed the Second Bank of the United States in 1816, in part to provide a uniform national currency.[14] But President Jackson famously allowed the bank's charter to expire in 1836. The day-to-day effect, unimaginable to us, was that people used dollar-denominated bank notes issued by hundreds of different institutions. Bank

13. Judt, *Postwar*, 119–20.
14. Howe, *What Hath God Wrought*, 81.

notes were IOUs of the bank, not the government, backed simply by the ability of issuing banks to make good on the stated obligations. This did not just mean that depositors had to worry about the health of their banks—that would be true until the advent of federal deposit insurance in the 1930s. Until after the Civil War, bankers, merchants, farmers, manufacturers, and consumers alike also had to worry about their media of exchange: whether others would accept as payment the particular type of cash they held, and whether they should in turn accept payment in the notes of a potentially questionable bank. Accordingly, bank failures impacted not only deposits but the value of the cash in people's hands.

When they are not simply boring on financial history, history textbooks often jump from crisis to crisis—from the anti-Federalist President Jackson shuttering the Second National Bank, to railroad industry scandals, to William Jennings Bryan and the "Cross of Gold," to the Great Depression—without mentioning that the central banking advocates actually won the battle, decisively and repeatedly. The reasons were the Civil War and Panics. The Panic of 1837, for example, in the immediate aftermath of the dissolution of the Second National Bank, cost Jackson's hand-picked successor, Martin van Buren, his reelection in 1840. The Whigs, slightly less snooty pro-business successors to the Federalists, fumbled their only electoral victory when William Henry Harrison died shortly after taking office and his poorly vetted vice president, John Tyler, basically defaulted back to the Democratic line. (Harrison's survival is a great counterfactual for the entire pre-war period.)

Lincoln's Republicans were the Whigs' political descendants. When they finally gained power, in 1861, they did not hesitate to act in the absence of southern Democrats during the Civil War. Not only did they enact legislation to build the transcontinental railroads, they passed the National Banking Act of 1863 in part to create a standard national currency: dollar-denominated banknotes issued by federally chartered banks meeting minimum regulatory standards.[15] These policies aimed both to strengthen the federal government for the post-war era and to knit the divided country back together through common transportation and widely acceptable currency. The NBA's requirement that national banks hold gold as security for their banknotes may have stabilized the currency but also contributed to a long period of deflation in the late 1800s. Residents of rural states in the South, Midwest, and West, disadvantaged in their access to credit by a tight

---

15. McPherson, *Battle Cry of Freedom*, 593–94.

money policy (the "Cross of Gold"), lobbied in effect for inflationary policies to ease credit. To little political avail: the Republicans held the presidency for all but eight years between 1861 and 1912. But state-chartered banks, with more flexible lending standards, grew vastly in number to address the credit gap.

Tight money did not prove to be the answer to Panics, however. In 1907, a massive liquidity crisis required a bailout, not from the US government, which was too small, but from a group of the biggest New York banks organized—if not press-ganged—by the biggest name of all, J. P. Morgan. The resulting reform was the 1913 Federal Reserve Act, strongly influenced by Morgan as a result of his 1907 rescue, which finally created a single US currency, backed by gold, in the form of the familiar Federal Reserve notes we carry in our pockets today. This wonderful reform facilitated economic growth by simplifying the unnecessarily complex swirl of banknotes, and with postwar economic growth it also led to the dollar's becoming the world's reserve currency, a significant advantage to the US government in transaction costs and policy flexibility. But it didn't prevent the Depression. It was just a better medium of exchange.

Far from fulfilling Marx's predictions, the Depression prompted, or demanded, further evolution of capitalism. The federal government expanded its regulation of banks and introduced federal deposit insurance, which not only gave individuals faith that they could again trust banks with their money but also required FDIC regulation of any bank, including state-chartered banks, that had the benefit of the insurance. New federal securities laws went well beyond anti-fraud measures, comprehensively regulating the public offering of securities, broker-dealer firms, public securities markets, and mutual funds.[16] These reforms succeeded for decades in averting financial panics. Tellingly, most subsequent brushes with systemic failure occurred in less regulated corners. These included: the collapse of the US savings and loan industry in the late 1980s following a deregulatory push, the crash in the developing high-yield (or "junk") bond sector in the early 1990s, and crises in the largely unregulated and highly nontransparent financial derivatives markets due to the failure of the obscure hedge fund Long-Term Capital in the late 1990s, and the near-collapse of

---

16. For New Deal banking and securities law reforms, see Kennedy, *Freedom from Fear*, 366–67; for Securities Act of 1933, the Securities Exchange Act of 1934, and the Investment Company and Investment Advisers Acts of 1940, see 15 U.S.C. sections 77a et seq., 78a et seq., 80a-1 et seq., and 80b-1 et seq.

insurance conglomerate AIG during the 2008 financial crisis (averted only through creative and dramatic federal intervention).

Probably more important, the Depression would validate the ideas of British economist John Maynard Keynes. Keynes had written that, in a recession where demand has collapsed—that is, when consumers and businesses are simultaneously tightening their belts and unemployment is rising—the government could and should stimulate the economy by its own procurement (e.g., infrastructure projects) and/or by putting dollars in the hands of people and businesses to spend.[17] The Roosevelt-era programs of the 1930s, significantly delayed by the Supreme Court, were probably too small to restore full employment, but the vast stimulus of the war effort completely changed that. The acceptance of Keynes's theory, however, was never clearer than in the US government's remarkably rapid response to the COVID crisis, which included both backstops for financial services and very large stimulus measures to maintain employment.

Keynes would also be instrumental in the post-war international economic framework adopted by the US and Western Europe.[18] This coordinated effort would prove critical to the outcome of the Cold War.

5. THE PARALLEL EVOLUTION OF BUSINESS ORGANIZATIONS

As with money, capitalism has evolved with business structures, technology advances and governmental and political priorities. An example is my own field of corporate and securities law. These laws arose from the eternal need of entrepreneurs to raise money to start or expand their ventures.

Before there were corporations, a prospective business owner would make a promise to investors: to repay a loan with interest over time or to share the business profits. These transactions could, and historically were, made among individuals as a matter of contract, through a loan agreement or a partnership agreement. No need for an abstract entity like a corporation. One problem with individual or family ownership, and general partnerships, though, is that of potential personal liability for debts or unexpected losses. The owners could get insurance, which is really another source of capital, but only for risks that can be anticipated and accurately estimated. The risk assessment can easily go wrong. Business owners might

17. Kennedy, *Freedom from Fear*, 354.
18. See chapter 1, above.

get too little insurance or the wrong kind; they could encounter unanticipated risks, like the toxicity of asbestos.

In short, a corporate structure has never been necessary to the financing of business operations, and unincorporated business operations were just as capable of imposing externalities as corporations—violating human rights or otherwise harming the public or the environment (as did the whaling industry). Tremendous profits flowed to English investors from the slave trade and its related ecosystem: shipbuilding, cotton mills, rum, and other products for trade.[19] Financial backing, such as marine insurance, was centered in London, and it too facilitated the trade.[20]

Instead, corporations offer more mundane advantages over simple partnerships, especially for financing businesses with ongoing operations. These advantages include limited liability, transferability of shares, and governance laws designed to ensure the loyal and capable service of management.

Government action has always been required to create corporations and to give effect to those advantages. Originally corporations were chartered one at a time by the British parliament or US federal or state legislatures. Modern corporation law arose in the nineteenth century, as the technological advances of the industrial revolution, such as railroads, required far larger initial capital investments in plant and equipment.[21] US state corporation laws evolved to allow formation by private sponsors as a matter of right, now simply by registering and filing certain forms with a state agency (often a Secretary of State office). To attract a larger pool of investors, including people who did not know the management or lead investors, rules were needed to protect outside investors. The first and most important is limited liability, the rule that, with rare exceptions, shareholders can't be sued individually for the contract or tort liability of the corporation. In other words, once a shareholder has fully paid for her shares, the company's creditors cannot look to her for any additional money. The second I would characterize as a set of accounting and conflict of interest

---

19. Thomas, *Slave Trade*, 239–49.

20. For the record, the insurers did *not* in the end pay the claims of the sponsors of the infamous slave ship *Zong*, whose captain had ordered hundreds of slaves thrown overboard when supplies ran low. He evidently thought that insurance would cover a distressed ship's abandonment of its human cargo, though it would not cover the routine loss of life. Thomas, *Slave Trade*, 489–90. The insurance term for such perverse incentives was never more apt: "moral hazard."

21. Howe, *What Hath God Wrought*, 558–59, 566–67.

rules, including shareholder ownership and voting control, designed to ensure that directors and officers are capable, report honestly, and don't act against the interests of the company or shareholders.[22] (The notion that shareholder voting is a form of democracy misapprehends its original purpose.) Third is a constantly evolving set of antifraud statutes, of which the US federal securities laws, enacted as New Deal reforms in 1933–34, are now the most important. These provide for standardized public financial disclosures and legal remedies for misleading investors in the purchase and sale of shares.

The purpose of these laws is benign—fair treatment for small investors—and their content is procedural and, to many, boring. It is accurate to say that they are one sided, protecting investors and business owners and doing nothing for employees or anyone else, either, including customers, neighbors, or the environment. But it is also a little unfair. These laws were never intended as vehicles to regulate all economic activity. Rather, the failure of corporate and securities laws to treat such externalities is a default, the effect of regulating to protect investors, and thereby to encourage capital formation and new business. Critics have pointed out that, by insulating shareholders from liability, corporate laws have the effect of encouraging corporations to maximize externalities, or at least to act with indifference toward risks being imposed on everyone else. But that too is a little unfair. As we have seen, people did not need corporations or securities laws in order to abuse—indeed to buy and sell—laborers, or to strip forests, level mountains, or pollute the environment.

Perhaps more to the point here, in its drive to catch up with its Cold War rivals, Soviet economic development caused many of the very same externalities (a term that sounds odd in the context of a fully planned economy). Far from a worker's paradise, Soviet industry was violently intolerant of worker protests for greater wages or better working conditions.[23] Its poorly managed mines and factories caused much more pollution (at least on a per capita basis) than was tolerated in Western democracies.[24] The roots of these problems are in conflicting priorities, not merely in the structure of business organizations.

22. Cox and Hazen, *Treatise*, sections 2.1, 2.5; Armour et al., "Essential Elements," 9, 12–15.

23. Applebaum, *Iron Curtain*, 238 (suppression of strikes in Poland and Hungary, 1946–47), 438–43 (Berlin, 1953); Spufford, *Red Plenty*, 205, 391 (Novocherkassk, 1962).

24. Judt, *Postwar*, 491n2, 492, 570–71.

That said, the regulation of corporate rights and responsibilities remains a very hot area in its own right. Since 2010, the Supreme Court decisions in *Citizens United*[25] and *Hobby Lobby*[26] have given astonishingly broad readings of the privileges attached to a corporate charter. But there is tension here, too. Recent court decisions have called into question the ability of large companies to cabin their liabilities for mass torts by splitting off the responsible business units. The bankruptcy of Purdue Pharma and, specifically, the accompanying efforts to limit the financial responsibility of the individual Sackler family members for the company's part in the opioid crisis, are now being challenged in the Supreme Court. The Securities and Exchange Commission recently adopted rules requiring climate change disclosures by large companies, and a suit to block the measure was filed the next day. Similarly, some shareholder groups are challenging the authority of corporate officers and fund managers to consider environmental, social, and governance (ESG) factors in their business plans.

These are all symptoms of the lack of a political consensus on these issues. In the absence of a common enemy like the Soviet Union, we must hope that our political system still works well enough to reform itself in response to very real problems.

6. EXTERNALITIES AND INEQUALITIES ON A PENDULUM

Writing at a time when Hitler and Mussolini had risen to power through more or less popular means, the Anglo-Irish writer Rebecca West wrote that "there is a special whimsicality about modern democracies."[27] Though she acknowledged that monarchies were also lucky when they got capable rulers, her observation captures the built-in difficulties that rich, modern states have experienced when trying to address the (mostly unintended) harms that result from business activities, as well as the many issues that come under the umbrella of inequality.

---

25. Citizens United v. Federal Election Commission, 558 U.S. 310 (2010), holding that corporations' First Amendment rights trump laws limiting political campaign contributions.

26. Burwell v. Hobby Lobby Stores, Inc., 573 U.S. 682 (2014), holding that privately owned corporations have First Amendment religious freedoms that sometimes entitle them to opt out of facially neutral regulations that offend their religious beliefs.

27. West, *Black Lamb*, 49.

This may seem obvious, but it's almost always better—more effective, more comprehensive, and fairer—when the government can regulate harm-causing conduct directly. The harms may result from business activity regardless of the type of organization or, indeed, the type of government. To reduce the harms from alcohol use, state and federal governments raised the drinking age, lowered speed limits, and increased penalties for drunk driving. Smoking has been reduced with a combination of advertising bans, higher taxes, public service programming, and direct bans on indoor use. To achieve clean air, Congress passed the Clean Air Act. Many separate laws—such as the Sherman Antitrust Act, Fair Labor Standards Act, Clean Water Act, Foreign Corrupt Practices Act, CERCLA (the Superfund law)—as well as court decisions (especially in the product liability and toxic tort areas) have helped to reduce and remediate harm and assign responsibility. The most recent example is Dodd-Frank, legislation enacted in response to the 2008 financial crisis, when overleveraged investment banks collectively took on so much risk that the default of a relatively small corner of the mortgage market nearly toppled the entire financial system.

But it takes time, usually many years, to gain anything like a political consensus in a large democracy, and there is no assurance against backsliding toward older attitudes. The most prominent current example in the US is environmental policy. A divided Congress has had practically no success advancing legislation to regulate carbon emissions—the one exception, the Build Back Better Act, passed at a rare moment of narrow Democratic control, and even that was limited to providing financial incentives toward future clean energy, rather than regulating current harm-causing conduct. At the same time, Congress's prior delegations of regulatory authority to the Environmental Protection Agency and other agencies, previously given substantial deference by the courts, have been successfully challenged and limited in the Supreme Court.

The nature and degree of inequalities since Marx's time has also swung back and forth, though for different reasons. I pluralize inequalities because there are several different types, and most are not about anything like mathematical equality. For example, the term encompasses the concerns about poor living standards of those with low incomes and few assets, who may make up as much as 50 percent of the population. It also reflects the increasingly extreme concentration of wealth and political power in the upper 1 percent, or 0.1 percent or even 0.01 percent of the population. It probably also refers to fairness of opportunity in education and career, with clear advantages available to the children of families with high education and/or of the "mass affluent"—some portion of the top 50 percent in income or assets. These different types of problems have different constituencies and would need to be addressed in different ways.

In 2013, the French economist Thomas Piketty published the results of his study of very long-term changes in the allocation of income and wealth in Western Europe and North America. The data shed light on all three aspects of inequality described above, but Piketty's passion is the issue of concentration. He invokes the early nineteenth-century novels of Balzac and Jane Austen, which describe the family and financial dynamics of the upper class. Balzac's character Vautrin, for example, advises a young friend that there is no point attending law school: even the most successful lawyers and judges earn only a fraction of the income that he could expect from marrying a certain young, but unattractive, heiress. In Austen's *Sense and Sensibility*, an heir and his wife run the numbers and quickly decide that sharing any of his inheritance with his two half-sisters would unacceptably reduce their social standing, in part by reducing the number of servants they could afford. The figures cited in these novels correspond with Piketty's statistics about the allocation of wealth and income at the time. In that era of low inflation, both real estate and financial assets yielded about 5 percent, so wealth could be expressed equally well in terms of expected income.[28] The incomes of the two very rich families in these two stories correspond to something like thirty to fifty times the average income of the time, by definition enough to support a staff of a couple of dozen servants.

High concentrations and vast inequalities of wealth in the early nineteenth century may no longer shock us, because we live in such a different world today. But this history is still relevant, according to Piketty, because it helps reveal principles that apply across all ages and drives conclusions about how they can be addressed. Using over two hundred years of data mainly from England, France, and the US, including French property tax filings dating back almost to the French Revolution, Piketty reached several conclusions that would have been difficult or impossible for earlier observers to see, even during the Cold War.

Capital tends to become concentrated over long periods of time, provided that the return on capital (r) remains significantly greater than the growth (g) of national income. Piketty describes this as a general law of economics: if people who have real estate or financial assets can get returns

---

28. Piketty, *Capital*, 206.

that exceed the income growth available to the working population, the additional return compounds over decades and makes the owners or heirs even richer. That is, the wealthier you are, the more your wealth is likely to grow, while r exceeds g (r > g). Piketty found that r > g during the low growth environment of England and France throughout the nineteenth century, and in the US in the last decades of the nineteenth century, up until World War I.[29] Edith Wharton was writing society novels about early twentieth-century New York society with the same sharp wealth dynamics that Jane Austen employed a century earlier. It also helps us understand the difficulty of effecting change. He notes that r > g held true for a century before World War I and seems to have returned in the twenty-first century. It has held true, in other words, unless something interrupted.

The concentration of wealth in western Europe and the US dropped precipitously in the period 1914–45 and remained at lower levels for several decades. The drop was obviously due to the shock of two world wars and the Great Depression, which destroyed wealth rather than redistributing it.[30] Naturally one can't rent out a bombed-out building, but the more widespread causes seem to have been the warring governments' needs for resources to fight the war, requiring heavy taxation and commandeering labor and factory output. The Depression also resulted in heavier government intervention in the respective economies: the concentration of wealth was not helpful when unemployment reached 25 percent at times in the 1930s. The wars and interwar period were brutal and destructive, hopefully never to be repeated; they had the side effect of reducing inequalities and stimulating demand for just about everything, due to long deprivation.

As a result, when the Cold War began, wealth inequalities in the West were at a low ebb, viewed even as a thing of the past. Inequalities likely increased, but only slowly, during the high-growth period from roughly 1945–75; that is, r exceeded g, but not by much, because g was relatively high. And Piketty finds evidence that the post–Cold-War wealth distribution has remained broader in two respects. One is the emergence of a "patrimonial middle class," roughly the households from the tenth to fiftieth percentile by assets, which hold assets (a house, a mature 401(k) plan) that are not life-changing but provide a significant reserve against falling into poverty.[31] (The lowest 50 percent, he noted, still own very little in the

---

29. Piketty, *Capital*, 356.
30. Piketty, *Capital*, 146–48.
31. Piketty, *Capital*, 260–61.

way of such assets and many even have a negative net worth due to debt.) The second is that the top 10 percent of incomes are now mostly earned by high-ranking corporate officers and other highly paid individuals who earn incomes mainly from their labor rather than their investments.[32] At the extreme end, this includes CEOs and other star professionals (such as well-known investment managers, lawyers, or doctors), plus a relatively few celebrity athletes and performing artists. This is a big change from the era of Balzac and Austen when, as described, one could only reach such income strata via marriage or inheritance.

But those changes have not solved the problems of poverty or of concentration of wealth and income, especially in the top 1 percent or 0.1 percent levels. Piketty looks at this in many different ways, but one example should suffice. Before World War I, US wealth was almost as concentrated as in Europe: the top 10 percent owned 80 percent of assets; the top 1 percent held 65 percent. In the postwar period through about 1970s, these figures dropped to 65 percent for the top 10 percent and 30 percent for the top 1 percent. But by 2010, these figures were back to 70 percent (top 10 percent) and 35 percent (top 1 percent).[33] The concentration of incomes has also reached very high levels.

To look at this in a more personal way, he describes the role of inheritances. We intuitively understand that significant inheritances are the privilege of a very few. So it is startling to learn that, in nineteenth-century France up until 1914, around 25 percent of all lifetime resources available to the entire population of individuals born in any given year consisted of inheritances and family gifts. This meant that the vast majority, who inherited nothing, had only their labor to live on, and could hardly dream of catching up to those who inherited substantial sums. That situation turned dramatically around by mid-century: for the group born between 1910 and 1920, who would have begun inheriting in 1940–60, inheritances and gifts represented only 8 percent of their generation's lifetime resources. Nearly everybody had to work, and most children of wealthy families could not count solely on inheritances. This changed gradually, so that nearly everyone who came of age during the Cold War expected to support themselves through work. But the most comparable figure rose almost back to the Balzac-era 25 percent by 2010, changing expectations again for those born after 1970.[34]

32. Piketty, *Capital*, 277–78.
33. Piketty, *Capital*, 349.
34. Piketty, *Capital*, 406.

As a result, those who became adults during the Cold War perceived that almost everyone needed to work for a living, so that the Marxist critique of Western inequalities actually resonated much less than it would have in earlier periods. Historical problems of poverty and wealth concentration seemed at least reasonably manageable. In Western Europe, this was partly due to competition with local Communist parties: major industries were owned by the state and the manufacturing unions were very powerful. Government-supported social services expanded to include welfare, healthcare, and retirement benefits, including in the US with Social Security (a New Deal program), and the adoption of Medicare/Medicaid and federal antipoverty programs in the 1960s.

7. DEREGULATION: REFORM AND EXCESS

By most accounts, and in my recollection, the West's era of economic growth ended not with Vietnam or Watergate but with the first OPEC oil embargo—a sudden assertion of power mainly by Middle Eastern oil exporters in response to Western countries' support of Israel in the 1973 Yom Kippur War. A similar crisis occurred in 1979 after the Iranian revolution. The energy shortages jacked up prices in the extremely petroleum-dependent US, Western Europe, and Japan, throwing economies into recession and exposing (like all recessions) many other problems that had been hidden by steady growth. "You don't find out who's swimming naked until the tide goes out," as the sage investor Warren Buffett has said of the reinsurance business.[35]

In the US, these recessions had dramatic effects on politics and policies as well as the structure of the economy. Over time, higher energy prices and the risk of future oil shocks led to dramatic efforts to reduce dependency on oil and natural gas. For example, many more consumers now wanted fuel-efficient cars, most of which were then made in Europe or Japan; construction firms were quick to adopt new reflective glass and new HVAC systems in commercial buildings to keep energy costs down.

Other economic policy changes had the effect of removing barriers to many kinds of externalities. But it's not a simple story: the recession had exposed real problems. The push for deregulation, or the removal of inefficient regulations, actually began in the late 1970s under President Carter. For example, his administration began the deregulation of the airline industry,

---

35. Buffett, "You Don't Find Out," 1994.

which like the Post Office had been required to maintain many unprofitable routes and was rewarded by limited competition on popular routes. This sharply reduced costs of travel, opening travel opportunities to millions who couldn't afford the regulated fares. Of course, we also now know that unfettered competition has come at a huge price to the atmosphere and customer service. (In a recent *New Yorker* cartoon, a grandfather offered consolation: "As you go through life, son, you'll find that you'll be angry at *all* the major airlines.")

Even so, the 1980 election was the real watershed. Ronald Reagan made it okay to campaign against government itself, a theme that Republicans could run on for decades to come and that centrist Democrats would come to accommodate in many ways. Again, many of these changes addressed real problems; the problem has been that it's politically easier to run against the idea of regulation rather than the degree (and the same is true of running in favor of regulation). For example, it made sense to reduce the top federal tax bracket of 70 percent (over 80 percent counting some states' taxes).[36] By the late 1970s, doctors and other high earners were happily investing in economically ludicrous tax shelters, like oil and gas wells that might pay off like a lottery ticket, but were guaranteed to create tax write-offs if the hole was dry; at those rates the real cost was barely 10 percent of the list price. Those extreme rates were detrimental, but it did not follow that zero percent would be better. Low rates too can be an obstacle if we are concerned with extreme concentrations of wealth.

If he had just sponsored his two major tax reform acts, in 1981 and 1986, both requiring heavy negotiations with the Democratically led Congress, Reagan's presidency would have been just as important—and a lot less complicated. But that was certainly not all:

- In 1982 and 1984 the Justice Department rewrote the standards it would use for reviewing large corporate mergers and for bringing enforcement actions under antitrust laws. The basic idea was to focus on quantitative measures of market power that could increase consumer prices, with a much-reduced focus on other forms of corporate power. A Justice Department official explained that "the Department currently interprets and enforces antitrust laws to condemn only those practices that threaten to raise prices or reduce output to US

---

36. U.S. Internal Revenue Service, "SOI Tax Stats" (historical US federal income tax brackets).

consumers."[37] Coming as it did after nearly a decade of high inflation, the prioritization of prices and efficiency was understandable at the time. However, the exclusive focus notably left no room for concerns about corporate power over other externalities, such as domination of certain labor markets, which is known as monopsony, or local markets, such as the effect of Walmart on small town retailers. In any case, it is well understood that merger activity soared during the 1980s.[38]

- The Reagan administration also continued the deregulation that began under Carter, which came to include broadcasting, communications, ground transportation, and oil and gas industries, as well as airlines.[39] The loosening of restrictions on lending by banks and savings and loans did fuel borrowing and pumped money into the economy, but weaker oversight enabled the S&Ls to take lending risks that they didn't necessarily understand, leading to a mini financial crisis (and bailout) under the first President Bush in 1989.

- The US Securities and Exchange Commission (SEC) adopted Regulation D in 1982 to establish clear rules about when limited offerings of corporate stock and investment funds needed to be federally registered.[40] Clear standards were certainly preferable to case-by-case negotiations with SEC staff. However, over time private investment offerings—early-stage start-ups, hedge funds, and private equity—have become a much larger share of the capital markets than originally imagined. Specifically, the amount invested in private funds was close to zero in the early 1980s; by 2019, Regulation D offerings actually exceeded the value of registered (public) offerings by about 25 percent, $1.5 trillion to $1.2 trillion. Similarly, the number of hedge fund and private equity managers has soared from a few hundred in the early 1990s to over ten thousand by 2020.[41] Certainly this reflects Reg D's success in reducing the cost of raising capital, but it has also drawn criticism because, among other things, there is less information about the funds or their investments available to investors or for regulatory

37. Rule, "Justice Department's Antitrust Enforcement," 3.
38. Ravenscraft, "1980s Merger Wave," 19, 31.
39. Ravenscraft, "1980s Merger Wave," 32–33.
40. Regulation D. 17 C.F.R. 230.501 et seq.; see SEC Release No 33-6389, March 8, 1982.
41. Mauboussin and Callahan, "Public to Private Equity," 6; SEC Staff, "Report on Regulation A/Regulation D," 3–4; McKinsey and Company, "Year Of Disruption," 8.

oversight.[42] To mention a very few high-profile examples: In 1998, the ironically named hedge fund Long-Term Capital Management required a federally facilitated 3.6 billion dollar capital injection to avert a financial crisis, due to its huge and highly leveraged currency derivative bets. Similarly, and long after the 2008 financial crisis, the hedge-fund-like family office Archegos closed its doors in 2021 when its derivatives bets failed, forcing the liquidation of 10 billion dollars in previously undisclosed stock holdings.[43] Facebook (now Meta) grew so large with private financing that its Wall Street investment bankers had great difficulty pricing its stock when shares were finally offered to the public in 2012. The shares fell by nearly 50 percent in the first months of trading (about 40 billion dollars in market capitalization), causing a lot of harm to the first public investors. Much of that harm was unnecessary: FB shares proved to be an excellent long-term investment for those who had the stomach for those early price swings.[44]

- President Reagan almost single-handedly broke the federal air traffic controllers' union in August 1981, by firing everyone who stayed out on strike and hiring replacement workers.[45] This was an outrage to labor leaders, but no planes crashed, and the public relations blowback was limited enough that corporate leaders felt much safer taking a hard line with unions. The number of strikes plummeted.

- President Reagan sent a similar all-clear on energy use by removing President Carter's solar panels from the White House roof. He also demanded severe budget cuts at the relatively young EPA and proposed opening vast stretches of wilderness and offshore areas for energy development. The new Superfund cleanup program got off to a halting start when the EPA official in charge was fired due to conflicts of interest in the award of contracts for the famous Stringfellow site in Southern California.[46] Although political pushback, especially from the Democratic-led Congress he needed to enact tax reforms, led him to replace the tin-eared Interior Secretary James Watt and the relatively inexperienced EPA Administrator Anne Gorsuch (Supreme

42. Lee, "Going Dark," 2–3.
43. Kelly et al., "Banks Face Billions in Losses," para. 4.
44. Fidelity Investments, "Meta Platforms Class A Stock Price Chart"
45. Ronald Reagan Presidential Library, "Remarks and a Question-and-Answer," para. 5.
46. Ronald Reagan Presidential Library, "Superfund/EPA."

Court Justice Neil Gorsuch's mother) with more moderate managers, Reagan politicized what had been bipartisan issues. To be sure, the Reagan administration did include some pro-environmental achievements in the areas of wilderness designations and participation in the international agreements to eliminate ozone-depleting emissions; there were Republicans in support of cost-effective pollution control measures in those days.[47]

The Cold War ended in a period of deregulation in the US, in which efficiency, productivity, and low prices came before the regulation of problems like pollution and inequality. And there is no doubt that the reduction in oil prices, specifically, helped push the Soviet Union, then as now a major oil exporter, toward the brink. The point is that this set of priorities reflected policy choices made primarily by the Reagan administration, and majorities of voters supported them in 1980, 1984, and 1988, and perhaps during the Clinton and George W. Bush administrations as well. As circumstances change, we are always free to make other choices.

8. THE TRUE BELIEVERS WERE WRONG

Besides their initial disadvantages in wealth and sophistication as of 1917, the Soviets misunderstood the source of strength of the Western economies in a tragically ironic way. Focusing so intently on the incredible growth of factory production and poor labor conditions of mid-nineteenth-century Britain, Germany, and the US, they almost copied the system despite their stated desire for fairer treatment of workers. What they ignored was the specialization of labor and industry that evolved in the West due to competition, labor shortages, and the absence of central planning. In other words, the Soviets didn't give their own workers and managers, or their family farmers or consumers, enough credit, quite the opposite of what Marx's critique would have implied. Instead, they tried to dictate supply and demand, aiming to catch up with a moving target.

On the other hand, it should be clear from the above that the greatest promoters of capital-C Capitalism had no better grip on the subject. Effective government is a pre-condition of a market economy, not its enemy. Ayn Rand's great heroes, with cinematic names like John Galt, Howard Roark, and Dagne Taggart, were individual geniuses and builders who dreamed of

---

47. Shabecoff, "Reagan and Environment," 1; Little, "Look Back," paras. 8–13.

escaping the mediocrity and bureaucracy of ordinary mortals and establishing their own exclusive paradise. In Colorado, as I recall. What a disaster that would have been! I suppose they could have brought people with them to make food and clean their houses but—who would have been the suppliers and customers for their great businesses? Would they bother with annoyances like middle managers and accountants? Would their citizens have needed health care, schools, public safety? A form of currency other than bitcoin, which has proven to be awkward for daily use and dangerous for speculation? And these heroes were leaders of huge, capital-intensive businesses like mining, railroads, and auto manufacturing, as if drawn, with unintended irony, from Soviet misperceptions about the sources of Western success. It seems not to have occurred to Rand that dedicated geniuses might inhabit other fields, like medicine, education, law, or civil rights. Think of the tragedies avoided by the work of Florence Nightingale and Jonas Salk, the talent and resources unlocked by Martin Luther King and Thurgood Marshall.

Instead, contrary to Rand's escapism and Marx's prophesy of post-capitalist equality, we are cohabiting with various incarnations of John Galt, founders of mass-market technology companies, though some of them really do seem eager to visit other planets. Clearly these technological advances bring great benefits, but like other businesses they impose externalities that may require reform. Regardless of the issue—from poverty to the concentration of wealth, from healthcare to the environment—new circumstances should lead to adaptive responses. Just as in the Cold War, evolution is capitalism's secret weapon.

GHAZAL OF A MATHEMATICIAN'S LAMENT

I don't want you to think I'm obsessed with the infinite.
But I hate that its sign has to mess with the infinite.

The sideways eight is enclosed, like that labyrinth we walked.
Could they not have paired something boundless with the infinite?

The rune may be clean and stylish, known universally—
but too cool to call out the darkness with the infinite.

A twisted band of any size has no inside or out,
an engagement ring to fit Alice, with the infinite.

David Foster Wallace came closer, I think you'd agree
in the way he recounted his jest with the infinite.

I know, I know, we're too late to begin such a journey;
new lovers alone make promises with the infinite.

Now Freud might infer, or Jung see the precedent: my fear
that our lives leave no mark once we rest, with the infinite.

Mark C. Jensen

Bibliography

Alexander, Michelle. *The New Jim Crow: Mass Incarceration in the Age of Colorblindness*. New York: New Press, 2010.
Applebaum, Anne. *Iron Curtain: The Crushing of Eastern Europe, 1944–1956*. New York: Doubleday, 2012.
Armour, John, et al. "The Essential Elements of Corporate Law: What Is Corporate Law?" The Harvard John M. Olin Discussion Paper series, 2009. http://www.law.harvard.edu/programs/olin_center/papers/643_Kraakman.php.
Bass, Gary J. *Judgment at Tokyo*. New York: Knopf, 2023.
Bevins, Vincent. *The Jakarta Method*. New York: Public Affairs, 2020.
Borstelmann, Thomas. *The 1970s: A New Global History from Civil Rights to Economic Inequality*. Princeton, NJ: Princeton University Press, 2012.
———. *The Cold War and the Color Line*. Cambridge, MA: Harvard University Press, 2001.
Boyle, Kevin. *The Shattering: America in the 1960s*. New York: Norton, 2021.
Braden, Tom. "What's Wrong with the CIA?" *Saturday Review*, Apr 5, 1975.
Branch, Taylor. *Pillar of Fire: America in the King Years, 1963–1965*. New York: Simon & Schuster, 1998.
Brown, Archie. *The Rise and Fall of Communism*. New York: HarperCollins, 2009.
Brown, Dee. *Bury My Heart at Wounded Knee*. New York: Picador, 2007.
Brown University. "Understanding the Iran-Contra Affair." https://www.brown.edu/Research/Understanding_the_Iran_Contra_Affair/index.php.
Buffett, Warren. "You Don't Find Out Who's Been Swimming Naked until the Tide Goes Out." Warren Buffet Archive, Apr 25, 1994. https://buffett.cnbc.com/video/1994/04/25/buffett-you-dont-find-out-whos-been-swimming-naked-until-the-tide-goes-out.html.
Canby, Peter. "The Death Squad Dossier." *New York Review of Books*, Dec 8, 2022, 10.
Carter, Jimmy. "Crisis of Confidence." Presidential address, July 15, 1979. https://www.pbs.org/wgbh/americanexperience/features/carter-crisis/.
Chang, Jung. *Wild Swans*. New York: HarperCollins, 1991.
Cima, Ronald, ed. *Vietnam: A Country Study*. Washington, DC: U.S. Library of Congress, Federal Research Division, 1987.
Clines, Francis X. "Gorbachev, Last Soviet Leader, Resigns." *New York Times*, Dec 26, 1991, 1.

BIBLIOGRAPHY

Cohn, D'Vera, et al. "Rise in US Immigrants from El Salvador, Guatemala and Honduras Outpaces Growth from Elsewhere." Pew Research Center, Dec 7, 2017. https://www.pewresearch.org/hispanic/2017/12/07/rise-in-u-s-immigrants-from-el-salvador-guatemala-and-honduras-outpaces-growth-from-elsewhere/.

Cox, James D., and Thomas Lee Hazen. *Treatise on the Law of Corporations (3d)*. November 2023 update. New York: Thompson Reuters, 2023.

Dawisha, Karen. *Putin's Kleptocracy*. New York: Simon & Schuster, 2014.

Diamond, Jared. "Vengeance Is Ours." *New Yorker*, Apr 14, 2008. https://www.newyorker.com/magazine/2008/04/21/vengeance-is-ours.

Didion, Joan. *The White Album*. New York: FSG, 1990.

Duberman, Martin. *Andrea Dworkin: The Feminist as Revolutionary*. New York: New Press, 2020.

Dudziak, Mary. *Cold War Civil Rights: Race and the Image of American Democracy*. Princeton, NJ: Princeton University Press, 2000.

Eisenberg, Carolyn. *Drawing the Line: The American Decision to Divide Germany, 1944–1949*. Cambridge: Cambridge University Press, 1996.

Faulkner, William. *Absalom, Absalom!* New York: Random House, 1936.

Federal Reserve Bank of St. Louis. "International Data." Accessed Feb 13, 2024. https://fred.stlouisfed.org/categories/32264.

Ferrer, Ada. *Cuba: An American History*. New York: Scribner, 2021.

Fidelity Investments. "Meta Platforms Class A Stock Price Chart" Accessed Feb 3, 2024. https://digital.fidelity.com/prgw/digital/research/quote/dashboard/summary?symbol=META.

Figes, Orlando. *Revolutionary Russia, 1891–1991*. New York: Henry Holt, 2014.

FitzGerald, Frances. *Fire in the Lake*. New York: Back Bay, 2002 ed.

Flanner, Janet. *Paris Journal 1944–1965*. New York: Atheneum, 1965.

Foner, Eric. *Reconstruction: America's Unfinished Revolution, 1863–1977*. New York: Harper Perennial, 2014 ed.

French, Howard W. "Mao's Shadow." Review of *Maoism: A Global History* by Julia Lovell and *China's New Red Guards* by Jude Blanchette. *New York Review of Books*, Mar 12, 2020, 18.

Gaddis, John Lewis. *The Cold War: A New History*. New York: Penguin, 2005.

Geyelin, Philip. "When Reagan Was Being Reagan." *Washington Post*, Apr 21, 1984. https://www.washingtonpost.com/archive/opinions/1984/04/22/when-reagan-was-being-reagan/f6b2531c-9348-4761-aaa4-1d086afd1039/.

Gill, Indermit. "Deep Sixing Poverty in China." Brookings Institution, Jan 25, 2021. https://www.brookings.edu/articles/deep-sixing-poverty-in-china/.

Goodwin, Doris Kearns. *No Ordinary Time: Franklin and Eleanor Roosevelt: The Home Front in World War II*. New York: Simon & Schuster, 1994.

Gordon-Reed, Annette. *The Hemingses of Monticello: An American Family*. New York: Norton, 2008.

Goscha, Christopher. *Vietnam: A New History*. New York: Basic, 2016.

Greenfield, James L., et al., eds. *The Pentagon Papers*. New York: Racehorse, 2017 ed.

Gross, Samantha. "What Iran's 1979 Revolution Meant for US and Global Oil Markets." Brookings Institution, Mar 5, 2019.

Halberstam, David. *The Coldest Winter*. New York: Hyperion, 2007.

Harris, Aisha, and Dan Kois. "The Black Film Canon—The 50 Greatest Movies by Black Directors." *Slate*, May 30, 2016. https://slate.com/culture/2016/05/black-film-canon-greatest-movies-black-directors.html.

Harris, Gardiner. "In Hiroshima, Summoning Better Angels." *New York Times*, May 27, 2016, 1.

Heller, Patrick. *The Labor of Development: Workers and the Transformation of Capitalism in Kerala, India*. Ithaca, NY: Cornell University Press, 1999.

Herman, Arthur. *Douglas MacArthur: American Warrior*. New York: Random House, 2016.

Herring, George C. *From Colony to Superpower: U.S. Foreign Relations Since 1776*. Oxford: Oxford University Press, 2008.

Howe, Daniel Walker. *What Hath God Wrought: The Transformation of America, 1815–1848*. New York: Oxford University Press, 2007.

Jacobs, Jane. *Cities and the Wealth of Nations*. New York: Random House, 1984.

Judge, Edward H., and John W. Langdon, eds. *The Cold War: A History through Documents*. New Jersey: Prentiss Hall, 1999.

Judt, Tony. *Postwar: A History of Europe since 1945*. New York: Penguin, 2005.

———. *Reappraisals: Reflections on the Forgotten Twentieth Century*. New York: Penguin, 2008.

Kamen, Al. "Reagan-Era Zeal for Central America Fades." *Washington Post*, Oct 16, 1990. https://www.washingtonpost.com/archive/politics/1990/10/16/reagan-era-zeal-for-central-america-fades/5da147ad-d112-4369-a098-34780ac62468/.

Karnow, Stanley. *Vietnam: A History*. New York: Penguin, 1997 ed.

Kelly, Cynthia. ed. *The Manhattan Project: The Birth of the Atomic Bomb in the Words of Its Creators, Eyewitnesses, and Historians*. New York: Black Dog and Leventhal, 2007.

Kelly, Kate, et al. "Banks Face Billions in Losses as a Bet on ViacomCBS and Other Stocks Goes Awry." *New York Times*, Mar 29, 2021. https://www.nytimes.com/2021/03/29/business/archegos-hwang-viacomcbs-discovery.html?searchResultPosition=9.

Kempe, Frederick. *Berlin 1961*. New York: Putnam, 2011.

Kennan, George. "February 22, 1946: George Kennan's 'Long Telegram.'" Wilson Center Digital Archive. https://digitalarchive.wilsoncenter.org/document/92093/download.

Kennedy, David M. *Freedom from Fear: The American People in Depression and War*. Oxford: Oxford University Press, 2005.

Kinzer, Stephen. *All the Shah's Men*. Hoboken, NJ: Wiley, 2005.

LaFeber, Walter. *Inevitable Revolutions: The United States in Central America*. New York: Norton, 1993.

Lawrence, Mark Atwood. *The Vietnam War*. New York: Oxford University Press, 2008.

Lee, Allison Herren. "Going Dark: The Growth of Private Markets and the Impact on Investors and the Economy." U.S. Securities and Exchange Commission, Oct 12, 2021. https://www.sec.gov/news/speech/lee-sec-speaks-2021-10-12.

Levine, Bruce. *The Fall of the House of Dixie*. New York: Random House, 2013.

Lifton, Robert Jay, and Greg Mitchell. *Hiroshima in America*. New York: Avon, 1995.

Little, Amanda. "A Look Back at Reagan's Environmental Record." *Grist*, Jun 11, 2004. https://grist.org/politics/griscom-reagan/.

Lyons, Richard. "Psychiatrists, in a Shift, Declare Homosexuality No Mental Illness." *New York Times*, Dec 16, 1974, 1.

MacMillan, Margaret. *Peacemakers*. London: John Murray, 2001.

Mauboussin, Michael J., and Dan Callahan. "Public to Private Equity in the United States: A Long-Term Look." Morgan Stanley Investment Management, Aug 4,

2020. https://www.morganstanley.com/im/publication/insights/articles/articles_publictoprivateequityintheusalongtermlook_us.pdf.

McKinsey and Company. "A Year of Disruption in the Private Markets." April 2021. https://www.mckinsey.com/~/media/mckinsey/industries/private%20equity%20and%20principal%20investors/our%20insights/mckinseys%20private%20markets%20annual%20review/2021/mckinsey-global-private-markets-review-2021-v3.pdf.

McMahon, Tim. "Historical US Inflation Rates and Inflation Calculator." https://inflationdata.com/Inflation/Inflation_Rate/HistoricalInflation.aspx.

McPherson, James. *Battle Cry of Freedom.* Oxford: Oxford University Press, 1988.

Menand, Louis. *The Free World: Art and Thought in the Cold War.* New York: FSG, 2021.

Menjivar, Cecilia, and Andrea Gomez Cervantes. "El Salvador: Civil War, Natural Disasters, and Gang Violence Drive Migration." *Migration Information Source,* Aug 29, 2018.

Mishra, Pankaj. "Struggle Sessions." *New Yorker,* Feb 1, 2021, 61.

Moyar, Mark. *Triumph Forsaken: The Vietnam War, 1954–1965.* Cambridge, UK: Cambridge University Press, 2006.

Newton, Jim. *Eisenhower: The White House Years.* New York: Anchor, 2012.

Nguyen, Viet Thanh. *The Sympathizer.* New York: Grove, 2015.

Ogunwole, Stella. "The American Indian and Alaska Native Population: 2000." U.S. Census Bureau, Feb 2002. https://www.census.gov/history/pdf/c2kbr01-15.pdf.

Osnos, Evan. "Fight Fight, Talk Talk." *New Yorker,* Jan 13, 2020, 32.

Ouimet, Matthew. *The Rise and Fall of the Brezhnev Doctrine in Soviet Foreign Policy.* Chapel Hill: University of North Carolina Press, 2003.

Patterson, James T. *Grand Expectations: The United States, 1945–1974.* New York: Oxford University Press, 1996.

Piazza, Alan. "Poverty and Living Standards since 1949." May 2014. https://www.researchgate.net/publication/346960323_Poverty_and_Living_Standards_since_1949.

Piketty, Thomas. *Capital in the Twenty-First Century.* Cambridge, MA: Harvard Belknap, 2014.

The Planetary Society. "How Much Did the Apollo Program Cost?" Accessed Mar 5, 2024. https://www.planetary.org/space-policy/cost-of-apollo#:~:text=The%20United%20States%20spent%20%2425.8,billion%20(%24280%20billion%20adjusted).

The President's Commission on the Accident at Three Mile Island. "Report of the President's Commission on the Accident at Three Mile Island." Oct 30, 1979. http://large.stanford.edu/courses/2012/ph241/tran1/docs/188.pdf.

President's Special Study Group. "Report on the Covert Activities of the Central Intelligence Agency" (Doolittle Report). Sept 30, 1954. https://www.cia.gov/readingroom/docs/CIA-RDP86B00269R000100040001-5.pdf.

Ravenscraft, David J. "The 1980s Merger Wave: An Industrial Organization Perspective." Federal Reserve Bank of Boston, 1987.

Reich, David. *Who We Are and How We Got Here.* New York: Pantheon, 2018.

Reid, Michael. *Forgotten Continent: A History of the New Latin America.* New Haven: Yale University Press, 2017 ed.

Resendez, Andres. *The Other Slavery: The Uncovered Story of Indian Enslavement in America.* New York: Mariner, 2017.

Risen, James. *The Last Honest Man.* New York: Little Brown, 2023.

Ronald Reagan Presidential Library. "Remarks and a Question-and-Answer Session with Reporters on the Air Traffic Controllers Strike." Aug 3, 1981. https://www.

reaganlibrary.gov/archives/speech/remarks-and-question-and-answer-session-reporters-air-traffic-controllers-strike.

———. "Superfund/EPA: Historical Note." Last updated Feb 21, 2023. https://www.reaganlibrary.gov/archives/topic-guide/superfundepa.

Rothstein, Richard. *The Color of Law: A Forgotten History of How Our Government Segregated America*. New York: Norton, 2017.

Rousso, Henry. *The Vichy Syndrome: History and Memory in France since 1944*. Cambridge, MA: Harvard University Press, 1991.

Rule, Charles. "The Justice Department's Antitrust Enforcement Guidelines for International Operations—A Competition Policy for the 1990s." Speech, Nov 29, 1988. https://www.justice.gov/atr/speech/file/1237351/dl?inline.

Sarotte, Mary Elise. *The Collapse: The Accidental Opening of the Berlin Wall*. New York: Basic, 2014.

Schneider, Steven Jay, ed. *1001 Movies to See before You Die*. Hauppauge, NY: Barron's, 2011.

Schwartz, Stephen I. *Atomic Audit: The Costs and Consequences of U.S. Nuclear Weapons since 1940*. Washington, DC: Brookings Institution, 1998. https://www.brookings.edu/books/atomic-audit/.

Schweber, Silvan. *Einstein and Oppenheimer*. Cambridge, MA: Harvard University Press, 2008.

Scigliano, Robert. *South Vietnam: Nation under Stress*. New York: Houghton Mifflin, 1964.

Shabecoff, Philip. "Reagan and Environment: To Many, a Stalemate." *New York Times*, Jan 2, 1989, 1.

Sheehan, Neil. *A Bright Shining Lie*. New York: Modern Library, 1988.

Sidel, Mark. *Old Hanoi*. Oxford: Oxford University Press, 1998.

Sorley, Lewis. *A Better War: The Unexamined Victories and Final Tragedy of America's Last Years in Vietnam*. New York: Harcourt, 1999.

Spence, Jonathan. *The Memory Palace of Matteo Ricci*. New York: Penguin, 1984.

———. *The Search for Modern China*. New York: Norton, 1990.

Spufford, Francis. *Red Plenty*. Minneapolis: Graywolf, 2012.

Stevenson, Alexandra, et al. "Chinese Celebrity Culture Is Raucous. The Authorities Want to Change That." *New York Times*, Aug 27, 2021. https://www.nytimes.com/2021/08/27/business/media/china-celebrity-culture.html?searchResultPosition=2.

Stone, Norman. *The Atlantic and Its Enemies: A History of the Cold War*. New York: Basic, 2010.

Thomas, Hugh. *The Slave Trade*. New York: Touchstone, 1997.

Thompson, Hunter. *Fear and Loathing on the Campaign Trail '72*. New York: Grand Central, 1973.

Tompkins, Lucy. "Extreme Poverty Has Been Sharply Cut. What Has Changed?" *New York Times*, Dec 2, 2021. https://www.nytimes.com/2021/12/02/world/global-poverty-united-nations.html.

Tye, Larry. *Bobby Kennedy*. New York: Random House, 2016.

University of North Carolina Library. "Chinese Ethnic Groups: Overview Statistics." https://guides.lib.unc.edu/china_ethnic/statistics.

U.S. Census Bureau. "1900 Census, Part 1, cxxiv (Indian population)." https://www2.census.gov/library/publications/decennial/1900/volume-1/volume-1-p3.pdf.

U.S. Department of Labor, Bureau of Labor Statistics. "Household Data, 1953–2023." Accessed Feb 4, 2024. https://www.bls.gov/cps/tables.htm#monthly.

BIBLIOGRAPHY

———. "Work Stoppages 1947–Present." Accessed Feb 3, 2024 https://www.bls.gov/web/wkstp/annual-listing.htm.

U.S. District Court, Western District of Washington. *United States v. Washington*, 384 F. Supp. 312 (W.D. Wash. 1974), *aff'd*, 520 F.2d 676 (9th Cir. 1975).

U.S. Inflation Calculator. "Historical Inflation Rates 1914–2024." Accessed Feb 4, 2024. https://www.usinflationcalculator.com/inflation/historical-inflation-rates/.

U.S. Internal Revenue Service. "SOI Tax Stats—Historical Table 23." Accessed Feb 3, 2024 https://www.irs.gov/statistics/soi-tax-stats-historical-table-23.

U.S. Securities and Exchange Commission Staff. "Report to Congress on Regulation A/Regulation D Performance." Aug 2020. https://www.sec.gov/files/report-congress-regulation.pdf.

U.S. Securities Laws. Securities Act of 1933, 15 U.S.C. sections 77a et seq.

———. Securities Exchange Act of 1934, 15 U.S.C. sections 78a et seq.

———. Investment Company Act of 1940, 15 U.S.C. sections 80a-1 et seq.

———. Investment Advisers Act of 1940, 15 U.S.C. sections 80b-1 et seq.

U.S. Senate Select Committee to Study Governmental Operations with respect to Intelligence Activities. "Final Report" (Church Committee Report). Apr 26, 1976.

U.S. Supreme Court. *Burwell v. Hobby Lobby Stores, Inc.*, 573 U.S. 682 (2014).

———. *Citizens United v. Federal Election Commission*, 558 U.S. 310 (2010).

———. *Meritor Savings Bank v. Vinson*, 477 U.S. 57 (1986).

Vanderbilt, Tom. *Survival City*. Chicago: University of Chicago Press, 2002.

Vietnam Veterans Memorial Fund. "About the Wall." https://www.vvmf.org/About-The-Wall/.

Wakeman, Rosemary. *The Heroic City: Paris 1945–1958*. Chicago: University of Chicago Press, 2009.

West, Rebecca. *Black Lamb and Gray Falcon*. New York: Penguin, 2007 ed.

Westad, Odd Arne. *The Global Cold War*. New York: Cambridge University Press, 2007.

White, Robert E. "The Problem That Won't Go Away." *New York Times Magazine*, Jul 18, 1982, 25.

Wills, Garry. *Under God*. New York: Simon & Schuster, 1990.

Wilkerson, Isabel. *The Warmth of Other Suns*. New York: Vintage, 2010.

Wilkinson, Charles. *Blood Struggle: The Rise of Modern Indian Nations*. New York: Norton, 2005.

Wong, Jan. *Red China Blues*. New York: Anchor, 1996.

Zhong, Raymond, and Cao Li. "China Halts Ant Group's Blockbuster I.P.O." *New York Times*, Nov 3, 2020. https://www.nytimes.com/2020/11/03/technology/ant-ipo-jack-ma-summoned.html?searchResultPosition=5.

Zubok, Vladislav M. *A Failed Empire: The Soviet Union in the Cold War from Stalin to Gorbachev*. Chapel Hill: University of North Carolina Press, 2007.

Index

2001, A Space Odyssey, 57
A Clockwork Orange, 29, 96
Aaron, Hank, 68
Abrams, Creighton, 30, 46
Absalom, Absalom!, 70
Acheson, Dean, 62, 118
Act of Killing, The, 116
Adams, Abigail, 70
Adams, John Quincy, 112
Afghanistan, xiii, 4, 5, 7, 47, 99, 111, 153
Africa, xv, 37, 69–71, 76, 79, 123
    See also country names
Aganbegyan, Abel, 24
Agee, James, 56
Agnew, Spiro, 87
Aiken, George, 45
Alabama, 68, 72, 84, 85
Alcatraz, 102
Alexander, Michelle, 69
Ali, Muhammad, 86
Allen, Paul, 107
Allende, Salvador, 91, 118, 121
Altman, Robert, 27
Amsterdam, 154
Andropov, Yuri, 4
Angola, xv
anti–communism (US), 22, 43, 44, 64, 76–79, 86, 88, 89, 98, 109, 114–22, 126–29, 141
apartheid, 76, 79
Apocalypse Now, xiv, 26, 28, 29
Apollo. *See* space program (US)

Arbenz, Jacobo, 122, 124
Argentina, xv, 121
Asia, xv, 7, 30, 32, 34, 37–39, 92, 118, 127, 138, 140, 142, 144, 145, 154
    See also country names
Atlee, Clement, 98
atomic bomb. *See* nuclear weapons
Attica (prison), 95
attrition, war of, 45, 46
Austen, Jane, 144, 165–67
Austria, 5, 16
Australia, 6, 34, 115
auto industry (US), 93, 173

Baby Boom generation (US), 81, 89, 100
Baker, Josephine, 78
Baldwin, James, 83
Baltic states, 6, 15
Balzac, Honore de, 165, 167
Bandung, Indonesia, 143
banking, 114, 130, 147, 157–59, 164, 170–71
    Federal Deposit Insurance Company (FDIC), 147, 158, 159
    gold (as security), 74, 92, 157–59
    Second Bank of the United States, 157–58
Baruch, Bernard, 62
Baryshnikov, Mikhail, 97
baseball, 67–69, 99, 101
Batista, Fulgencio, 113
Bay of Pigs, 84, 118, 120, 121

INDEX

Beauvoir, Simone, 103, 105
Beijing, 32, 133, 136, 139, 141
    Forbidden City, 139
Berkeley, California, 82, 94
Berlin, 9, 127
    Airlift, 24, 117
    East, xiii, 3, 5, 146
    Wall, xiii, 3, 5, 24, 60, 84
    West, xiii, 24, 105
Bevel, James, 83, 85
Bidault, Georges, xvi, 22, 23
Birmingham, Alabama, 83, 84
Black Panthers (organization), 83, 95, 141
Blade Runner, 57
Blob, The, 57
Boldt, George, 102
Boxer Rebellion, 34, 139
Brando, Marlon, 28, 29, 102
Brazil, xv, 121, 133, 137
Bretton Woods agreements, 10, 11, 13, 18, 19, 92, 123
Brezhnev, Leonid, 4, 5, 62
Britain. *See* Great Britain
Brock, Lou, 68
Brodsky, Joseph, 97
Brotherhood of Sleeping Car Porters, 66, 77
Brown, Dee, 101–2
Brown v. Board of Education (US Supreme Court), 77, 82, 83
Brownmiller, Susan, 105
Bryan, William Jennings, 74, 158
Buck, Pearl, 115
Budapest, 20, 24
Bulgaria, 8
Bundy, McGeorge, 41
Bury My Heart at Wounded Knee, 101
Bush, George H. W., 5, 170
Bush, George W., 89, 172
Butler, Smedley, 109, 114, 124,

Caffery, Jefferson, 113
California, 77, 82, 94, 146, 171
Calley, William, 90
Cambodia, xv, 30, 31, 35, 49, 118, 121, 143

capitalism, xiv, 11–14, 19, 24, 116, 122, 134, 144, 147–73 (Chapter 8)
Caribbean, 37, 109, 111, 113, 123, 124, 126, 151
    See also country names
Carson, Rachel, 87
Carter, Jimmy, 92, 96, 99, 100, 107, 108, 126, 168, 170, 171
Castro, Fidel, 61, 78, 120–22, 124, 126, 129
Catholic. *See* Christianity
Central America, 37, 73, 109–16, 123–28
    See also country names
Central Intelligence Agency, US ("CIA"). *See* United States, Executive Branch
Cepeda, Orlando, 68
Chan Is Missing, 145
chemical weapons, 47, 52, 56, 63
Chernobyl, 5
Chesnut, Mary, 71
Chiang Kai-Shek, 117, 140
Chiang, Madame (Soong Mei-ling), 140
Chicago, 68, 76, 84, 94, 95, 101
Chile, xv, 91, 118, 121
China, xiv, xv, 6–8, 20, 25, 32–36, 38, 39, 43, 44, 49, 51, 59, 77, 88, 96, 97, 117, 118, 120, 130–46 (Chapter 7), 151, 153–55
    Cultural Revolution, 131–35, 142
    Guomindang (Chinese Nationalist Party), 34, 36, 117, 131, 132, 134, 140, 141
    See also China, Republic of (Taiwan)
China Lobby (US), 140
China, Republic of (Taiwan), 138, 141, 145, 146
China Syndrome, The, 57, 98
Chinese Communist Party (CCP), 34, 131–34, 136–38, 140, 141, 143, 146
Chow, Steven, 146
Christianity
    Catholics (Vietnamese), 33, 36, 39
    English, 153
    Ephesian Church of God, 82
    evangelical, 106, 107

in civil rights movement (US), 82, 84
missionaries in China, 139–41
Protestant, 106
Church, Frank, 121
Church committee. *See* US Congress, Church committee
Churchill, Winston, 8, 15, 16, 53, 54, 59, 76, 98
Citizens United (Citizens United v. Federal Trade Commission), 163
civil rights (US), xiv, 66–86 (Chapter 4), 89, 95, 101–7, 121, 146, 173
Civil War (US), 31, 71, 72, 75, 102, 111, 158
civil wars
   China, 117, 131, 132, 141, 143
   Greece, 117
   Guatemala, 122, 129
   See also El Salvador; Nicaragua; Vietnam, war in; Korean war
Clinton, Bill, 89, 172
Coates, Ta-Nahesi, 69
Colombia, 113
colonialism, xv, 22, 25, 32–38, 42, 79, 86, 104, 111, 125, 140, 142–44, 149, 151 154, 155
   imperialism, 19, 35, 123, 140, 144, 154
Cominform, 20
Coming Home, 27, 29, 96
common law. *See* government functions
communism, xiii, 6, 13, 18, 148
   China, 7, 20, 34, 77, 117, 131, 132, 134, 136, 143
   Eastern Europe, 16, 19, 20
   Indonesia, 115
   Kerala (India), 125
   Latin America, 116, 122, 126
   Long Telegram analysis, 11–13
   Marxism/Leninism, 13–15, 18–20, 116, 148, 149, 156, 157
   planned economy, 13, 15, 24
   Vietnam, 25, 35, 36, 89
   Western Europe, 22, 117, 168
   See also anticommunism (US)
competition (economic), 93, 169, 172
Confederacy (US) and pre-war South, 69–73, 78

Congo, xv, 121
Congress, US, *see* US Congress
Connor, Bull, 83, 84
Contras. *See* Nicaragua
Coppola, Francis Ford, 26, 31, 131
corporations, 15, 100, 107, 109, 124, 160–63, 167, 169–71
corruption, 41–44, 129, 134, 140
covert actions. *See* United States, Executive Branch, Central Intelligence Agency
Crazy Rich Asians, 144
Crip Camp, 103
Crosby, Stills and Nash ("CSN"), 94, 101
"Cross of Gold" speech. *See* Bryan, William Jennings
Cuba, xv, 5, 7, 60, 61, 73, 78, 110–14, 116, 120, 122, 123, 126
Cuban missile crisis, 50–62, 64, 84, 97
Cultural Revolution. *See* China
currency. *See* money
Czechoslovakia, 4, 7–9, 19, 97, 114, 117

D'Aubuisson, Roberto, 128
Daley, Richard, 68, 84, 94
Declaration on Liberated Europe, *see* Europe
Deer Hunter, The, 27, 29, 96
Defense Department, US, *see* United States, Executive Branch
DeGaulle, Charles, 21
democracy, 8, 9, 16, 40, 46, 76, 91, 116, 118, 121, 127, 141, 150, 155, 156, 162–64
Democratic Party (US), 43, 68, 72, 74–78, 83, 86, 88, 90, 94, 96, 100, 107, 121, 142, 157, 158, 164, 169, 171
Deng Xiaoping, 20, 136, 137
deregulation, 100, 159, 168, 170, 172
Detroit, Michigan. 67, 68, 85, 91, 93
Diamond, Jared, 152
Didion, Joan, 94, 95
Diem, Ngo Dinh, 30, 33, 39–42, 46, 84, 118, 121
Dien Bien Phu (Vietnam), 38
Dominican Republic, 113, 118, 121

INDEX

domino principle, 44
Doolittle, James, 119
Dr. Strangelove, 57, 60
Dresden, 57
DRV (Democratic Republic of Vietnam).
    See North Vietnam
Duarte, Jose Napoleon, 127, 128
Dulles, Allen and John Foster, 98
"Dutch disease," 42, 123, 125
Dworkin, Andrea, 105

East Berlin. See Berlin, East
East Germany. See Germany, Eastern
East India Company (British), 154
economics, xiv, xvi, 10, 12–20, 24, 148–73 (Chapter 8)
    inflation, 6, 42, 92, 93, 99, 108, 128, 157, 159, 165, 170
    Marxism. See Marx, Karl and Marxism
    unemployment, 6, 92, 99, 128, 160, 166
economy,
    British, 19, 153, 155
    Chinese, 6, 7, 20, 130, 133, 134, 136–39, 143, 146
    European, xvi, 16–22, 117, 123, 149, 160, 166, 168
    market, 13, 15, 149, 157, 172
    planned, 5, 13, 15, 17, 36, 48, 149, 162
    rest of world, 11, 52, 65, 98, 111, 113, 116, 123–26, 141, 168
    Soviet, 5–7, 12, 13, 15, 19, 20, 24, 91, 144, 149, 155, 162
    US, 6, 10, 17, 19, 66, 72–75, 90–93, 99, 100, 103, 108, 112–14, 126, 127, 149, 153–56, 159, 160, 168, 170
    Vietnamese, 41–43, 48, 49
Edo. See Tokyo
education, 13, 32, 33, 36, 39, 74, 103–5, 115, 125, 133, 138, 140, 150, 164, 165, 173
Egypt, 90, 135, 151
Einstein, Albert, 53, 62, 63, 107
Eisenhower, Dwight David, 37, 39, 44, 59–61, 64, 76, 78, 98, 118–20, 122

El Salvador, xv, 111, 113, 116, 125, 127, 128
Ellington, Duke, 76
Ellsberg, Daniel, 90
energy (supplies), 62, 93, 100, 108, 156, 164, 168, 171
England. See Great Britain
English (language), 34, 36, 102, 103, 136, 145, 153
environment (ecology), 15, 39, 51, 87, 100, 138, 161–64, 172, 173
    pollution, 135, 162, 172
Equal Rights Amendment, 105, 107
equality, 14, 34, 59, 73, 75, 77, 104, 148, 164, 173
Erdrich, Louise, 104
Eugenics, 70, 72
Europe, 7–10, 23, 32–34, 112, 130, 136, 137, 153, 155, 156
    colonialism, xv, 32, 111, 136, 139, 143, 154, 155
    Conference on Security and Cooperation (Helsinki Final Act), 96, 97
    Declaration on Liberated Europe, 8, 9, 16
    Eastern, xiv, 5–7, 9, 18–20, 76, 114, 123, 143, 155
    European Union, 18, 24
    Marshall Plan in, 17–22
    postwar shortages in, 16, 17,
    Western, 9, 24, 38, 79, 91–94, 117, 123, 127, 135, 137, 148, 149, 160, 165–68
    See also country names
export. See trade
expropriation (nationalization), 48, 97, 124–26
externalities, 15, 161–63, 168, 170, 173

Faubus, Orville, 78
Faulkner, William, 70, 71
FDR. See Roosevelt, Franklin Delano (FDR)
Federal Deposit Insurance Corporation, see banking
Feliciano, José, 67

184

INDEX

feminism, 103–6
Ferrer, Ada, 112
Filipino. See Philippines
films, discussion of, 1, 2, 26–30, 57, 58, 79–82, 95, 96, 98, 103, 114–16, 131, 132, 135, 144–46
Finland, 8,
Finland Station (Petrograd), 14
Fitzgerald, Ella, 76
FitzGerald, Francis, 42, 43
Flanner, Janet, 17, 22, 23
Flood, Curt, 68, 101
Florida, 101, 112
FMLN (Marti National Liberation Front), 116, 128
Foner, Eric, 73
Forbidden City, see China
Ford, Gerald, 92, 95, 96, 100
Ford, Henry, 156
foreign exchange. See trade
Fourteen Points. See Wilson, Woodrow
France, 9, 70, 97, 139, 150, 151
    and Vietnam, 25, 31, 33–38, 42, 79, 118, 143, 155
    historic inequality, 165–67
    in postwar period, xvi, 1, 17–19, 21–24, 58, 91, 92, 117, 123
freedom, 70, 75, 76, 78, 106, 146
Freedom Rides, 83, 84
French, Howard, 134
Friedan, Betty, 103
Full Metal Jacket, 28
Fulton, Missouri, 15

Gaddis, John Lewis, 52, 60
Gagarin, Yuri, 2
Gates, Bill, 107, 108
gay rights, 95, 103, 107
General Agreement on Tariffs and Trade, 10
Geneva, 38, 39
Georgia (state), 74
Germany, 34, 39, 53, 62, 63, 70, 113, 140, 172
    Eastern, and German Democratic Republic ("DDR"), xiii, 3–5, 7, 9, 13, 16, 20, 24, 97, 114
    postwar period, xv, 3–24 (Chapter 1), 38
    Western, and Federal Republic of Germany ("BRD"), xvi, 5, 9, 13, 16, 17, 22, 24, 38, 60, 91, 123
Gibson, Bob, 67, 68
Glorious Revolution. See Great Britain
Godzilla, 57
Goldwater, Barry, 43, 44, 82, 85, 91
Gorbachev, Mikhail, 4–7, 24, 49, 127
Gordon-Reed, Annette, 70, 71, 82, 104
Gore, Al, 89
Gorsuch, Anne, 171
Goscha, Christopher, 35
government functions, 15, 151–53, 157–64, 168–73
    See also communism; democracy; money; regulation; security (governmental)
Grady, Henry, 49
Grant, Oscar III, 86
Grant, Ulysses S., 74
Grave of the Fireflies, 57
Great Britain (England), 13, 53, 54, 57, 132, 153–55, 160, 161, 165, 166, 172
    as colonial power, 32, 33, 37, 97, 98, 115, 124, 139, 154, 155
    Glorious Revolution, 153
    interwar period, 34, 46, 63
    postwar period, xvi, 8–11, 15–17, 19, 21, 22, 24, 38, 53, 117
Great Depression, 10, 90, 113, 147, 156, 158–60, 166
Great Leap Forward, 131, 132
Great Migration (US), 75, 76
Great War. See World War I
Greece, 8, 117, 135
Greensboro, 83, 84
Groves, Leslie, 54, 62
Guam, 112
Guardia Nacional (Nicaragua), 113
Guatemala, xv, 111, 118, 122, 124, 126, 128
Guomindang (Chinese Nationalist Party). See China

INDEX

Haiphong, Vietnam, 35, 47
Haiti, 113
Haley, Alex, 101
Hampton, Fred, 95
Hanford, Washington, 54
Hanoi, 35, 36, 47, 49
Harlem, 76, 77, 81, 85
Harrison, William Henry, 158
Havana, 113
Hawaii, 37, 140
Hay, John, 34
Hearst, Patricia, 95
Hearst, William Randolph, 140
Hegel, G.W.F., 14, 156
Helsinki Final Act. *See* Europe, Conference on Security
Hemings (family), 70, 71
Hemings, Sally, 70
Henry VIII, King of England, 153
Hero, 135, 139
Hersey, John, 56
Hersh, Seymour, 90
Hiroshima, Japan, 10, 48, 51–58, 63
Hiroshima, Mon Amour, 57, 58
Hitler, Adolph, 8–10, 17, 70, 133, 163
Hobby Lobby (Burwell v. Hobby Lobby Stores), 163
Ho Chi Minh (Nguyen Ai Quoc), 25, 33, 35–39, 48, 79
Ho Chi Minh City (Saigon), Vietnam, 26, 35, 41–43, 46, 48, 49, 91
Hollywood, 26, 27, 79, 80, 102, 144, 145
Honduras, 109, 114, 126, 127
Hong Kong, 32, 138, 145, 146
Hoover, J. Edgar, 78, 117
Hoover, Herbert, 119
Horton, Willie (baseball star), 68
Hue, Vietnam, 35
Hue, Treaty of, 33
human rights, 72, 89, 96, 127, 152, 155, 161
Humphrey, Hubert, 68, 94
Hungary, 4, 5, 7, 8, 16, 97, 114, 144

Iceland, 127
Iklé, Fred, 127
Imperialism. *See* colonialism
Import. *See* trade
In the Heat of the Night, 80
Independence. See country entries
India, xv, 32, 33, 35, 125, 133, 151, 154, 155
Indians (American), 101–4, 111, 112, 114, 116, 129, 154
    Indian Self-Determination and Education Assistance Act (US), 103
Individuals with Disabilities Education Act (1975), 103
Indonesia, xv, 33, 115, 118, 121, 143, 146, 155
industrial, 6, 14, 19, 21, 33, 42, 47, 75, 123, 132, 138, 143
    Industrial Revolution, 13, 15, 156, 161
inequality, 124, 149, 163–66, 168, 172
innovation, 15, 81, 94, 101, 125, 150, 151, 154
insurance, 160, 161, 168
    deposit. *See* banking
insurgency, 30, 34, 46, 113, 116, 128
International Monetary Fund. *See* money
Iran, xiii, 6, 65, 97–99, 111, 118, 121–24, 126, 128, 129, 168
    Shah of, 87, 91, 97
Iran-Contra scandal, 111
Iron Curtain, 15, 16, 18, 76, 97
Israel, 90, 127, 168
Italy, 8, 34, 117, 139

Jackson, Andrew, 157, 158
Jackson State University, 90
Jacobs, Jane, 150–52
Japan, 92, 139
    "opening" of, and Meiji restoration, 32–34, 139, 154, 155
    Postwar economic development, 93, 137, 138, 150, 154, 168
    Versailles negotiations, 34, 140
    World War II and atomic bombing, 8, 10, 35, 48, 51–59, 62, 63, 117, 140
Javier, Julian, 68
jazz, 80, 81, 101

INDEX

Jefferson, Martha (Wayles), 70
Jefferson, Thomas, 70, 71
Jim Crow. *See* segregation
Jobs, Steve, 107
Johnson, Andrew, 74
Johnson, Lyndon Baines, 40, 41, 43–45, 47, 61, 68, 82, 85, 86, 88–90, 100, 118, 125
Jonestown, Guyana, 95
Judd, Walter, 140
Judt, Tony, 8, 9, 23
Jurassic Park, 57

Kaysen, Carl, 60
Kemeny, John, 98, 104, 107, 108
Kennan, George, 11–13, 17
Kennedy, John Fitzgerald, 40, 41, 44, 60, 61, 78, 82, 84, 85, 88, 104, 118, 125
Kennedy, Robert, 68, 78, 82, 84, 89
Kent State University, 90
Kenya, xv
Kerala (Indian state), 125
Kerry, John, 89
Keynes, John Maynard, 10, 123, 160
Khmers Rouges, 30, 31, 48, 49
Khomeini, Ruhollah, Ayatollah, 97
Khrushchev, Nikita, 24, 39, 60–62, 84, 91, 144, 155
Killing Fields, The, 30
Kim Il Sun, 118
King, Martin Luther, 68, 78, 82–86, 89, 173
Kirkpatrick, Jeanne, 127, 129
Kissinger, Henry, 39
Koo, Wellington, 141
Korea, 33, 43, 140
    North, 2, 13, 38, 59, 133
    South, 13, 38, 51, 138
Korean war, xv, 7, 27, 38, 39, 59, 77, 79, 95, 118, 120, 142, 143
Kremlin. *See* Soviet Union.
Ku Klux Klan, 74, 75
Kubrick, Stanley, 28, 29

labor, 14, 21, 72, 73, 93, 112, 114, 142, 150, 166, 167, 170, 172

unions, 93, 101, 156, 171
    Fair Labor Standards Act, 164
land reform, 36, 48, 74, 122, 124–28
Laos, xv, 35, 91, 118, 121
Last Man on the Moon (film), 1, 2
Latin America, xv, 110, 113, 125
    See also Caribbean; Central America
    See also country names
Lawrence, David, 56
Learning Tree, The, xiv, 80
Lee, Ang, 145
LeMay, Curtis, 46
Lenin, Vladimir Ilyich, 13, 14, 20, 36, 143, 148
Leninism, 20, 142, 143
    See also Marx, Karl and Marxism
liability, 15, 160–64
Lilienthal, David, 62
Little Rock, Arkansas, 78, 84
Littlefeather, Sacheen, 102
Lindsay, John, 81
Locke, John, 153
Lodge, Henry Cabot, 40, 41
Lolich, Mickey, 67
London, 22, 23, 36, 57, 70, 161
Long Telegram. *See* Kennan, George
Lord Palmerston, 32
Los Alamos, New Mexico, 54
Los Angeles, California, 76, 85, 94, 145
Louisiana, 72
Louisiana Purchase, 112
Luce, Henry, 140, 142
Lumumba, Patrice, 121

M*A*S*H, 27, 29, 96
Ma, Jack, 136
MacArthur, Douglas, 37, 59
MacKinnon, Catherine, 104
MacLaine, Shirley, 141
Madison, James, 157
Magna Carta, 153
Malaysia, 145, 146
Malcolm X, 82, 83
Manhattan Project, 53, 54, 59, 62
Manson, Charles, 94
Mao Zedong, xiv, 7, 32, 36, 38, 117, 131–46 (Chapter 7), 155

INDEX

Maoism, 30, 133, 134, 141, 143
Marshall, George, 17–20, 141
Marshall Plan, 5, 17–20, 22, 74, 117, 123
Marshall, Thurgood, 82, 83, 173
Marti, Jose, 122, 128
Marx, Karl and Marxism, 11–15, 19, 20, 116, 142, 143, 147–50, 156, 159, 164, 168, 172, 173
Masaryk, Jan, 19, 20
May Fourth Movement, 34, 140, 143
Mays, Willie, 68
McCain, John, 89
McCarthy, Eugene, 94
McCarthy, Joseph, 77, 79, 141
McNamara, Robert, 61
McPherson, James, 72, 73
Menand, Louis, 82, 83
Menominee reservation, 103
Meredith, James, 84
Mexican War, 72, 73, 112
Mexico, 111, 129
Middle East, xv, 65, 123, 125, 168
Milk, Harvey, 95
Mishra, Pankaj, 134
Mississippi, 70, 72, 75, 76, 80, 84, 90
Missouri, 15,
Missouri Compromise, 73
money (currency) 10, 15, 24, 92, 93, 123, 125, 150, 156–60, 171, 173
    gold standard, 92
    International Monetary Fund, 10
money (wealth), 5, 7, 16, 19, 41–43, 71, 73, 74, 91–93, 123, 124, 126, 128, 131, 132, 137–39, 148–73 (Chapter 8)
Monroe Doctrine, 110, 112
Monroe, James, 112
montagnards (ethnic group), 28, 35
Montgomery, Alabama, 82–84
Moral Majority, 100, 106, 107
Morse, Wayne, 44
Moscone, George, 95
Moscow, 16, 19, 36, 62
Mossadegh, Mohammed, 97, 122, 124
movies. *See* films
Moyar, Mark, 40, 41, 46
Munich, 8, 9

Mussolini, Benito, 163
My Lai, Vietnam, 30, 90

NAACP (National Association for the Advancement of Colored People), 77, 82
Nader, Ralph, 93
Nagasaki, Japan, 51
Nanjing, China 32, 139
Napoleon Bonaparte, 155
national defense. *See* security (governmental)
nationalization. *See* expropriation
Nazi (National Socialist German Workers' Party), 8, 9, 22, 35, 53, 72
negligence, 15
Netherlands, 33, 42, 123, 155,
neutrality (foreign relations), 9, 38
Nevers, France, 58
New Deal (US government programs), 76, 85, 159, 160, 162, 168
New England, 91, 154
New Hampshire, 10
New Jersey, 154
New York, 36, 60, 76, 95, 100, 145, 146, 159, 166
New York Post, The, 100
New York Times, The, 42, 90, 120
New Yorker, The, 17, 56, 134, 141, 169
New Zealand, 34
Newton, Jim, 59
Newton, Huey, 141
Nguyen (Southeast Asian dynasty), 33
Nguyen Ai Quoc. *See* Ho Chi Minh
Nguyen Cao Ky, 41
Nguyen Van Thieu, 41
Nguyen, Viet Thanh, 31
Nicaragua, xv, 109, 113, 114, 116, 126–29
    Contras, 111, 127, 128
Nicholas (Tsar of Russia), 14
Nigeria, xv
Nixon, Richard, 39, 44, 48, 68, 86, 87, 89–92, 94, 96, 100, 103, 118, 120, 125, 142
North America, 70, 148, 154, 165

INDEX

See also country names
North Korea. *See* Korea, North
North Vietnam. *See* Vietnam, North
nuclear power, 5, 57, 62, 98, 99
nuclear weapons, xiv, 3, 7, 48, 50–65
    (Chapter 3), 77, 79, 92, 97, 111
    arms control efforts, 52, 127, 62–65
    radiation from, 51, 52, 56, 57
    Super (nuclear fusion bomb), 59

Oak Ridge, Tennessee, 54
Oakland, California, 86
Obama, Barack, 51
Ohio, 75, 90
oil, xiii, 5, 6, 42, 64, 97–100, 123–27,
    149, 151, 156, 168–70, 172
    OPEC (Organization of Petroleum
    Exporting Countries), 5, 90, 92,
    93, 108, 127, 168
opium, 32, 139, 154
Oppenheimer, Josh, 116
Oregon, 44, 68, 75, 104
OPEC (Organization of Petroleum
    Exporting Countries), *see* oil
Ortega, Daniel and Humberto, 126–29
Orwell, George, 20, 78, 96, 97
Osaka, Japan, 150
Osnos, Evan, 141
Ouimet, Matthew, 4
Our Bodies, Ourselves, 106
oversight. *See* regulation
Owens, Jesse, 76

Packwood, Robert, 44
Paige, Satchel, 68
Palmer, Mitchell, and Palmer Raids, 117
Panama, 113
panic (economic), 74, 157–59
    See also Great Depression
Paris, 17, 19–23, 34, 36, 70, 94, 140
Parks, Gordon, xiv, 80
Parks, Rosa, 82
Peace Corps, 125
Pearl Harbor, 55, 57, 63
Penn Central Railroad, 93, 100
Pennsylvania, 27, 28, 72, 98
Pentagon Papers, 40, 46, 47, 90, 120

See also, United States, Executive
    Branch, Defense Department
Perry, Matthew (Admiral), 32, 34, 154
Peru, 111
Petain, Philippe (Marshall), 21
Petrograd (Leningrad), 14
Philippines, 33, 34, 37, 112, 155
Phnom Penh, 30, 48
Piketty, Thomas, 165–67
Pine Ridge Reservation (South Dakota),
    102
Pittsburgh, Pennsylvania, 91
Platoon, 28, 29
Platt, Orville, and Platt amendment,
    112, 113
Plessy v. Ferguson, 75, 77
Poitier, Sidney, 79, 80
Poland, 4, 5, 16, 20, 96, 97
    Solidarity movement, 4, 5
pollution. *See* environment
pornography, 105
Portugal, 79, 139, 154
Potsdam, Germany summit conference,
    8, 54
Prague, 19, 24
public safety. *See* security
    (governmental)
Puerto Rico, 101, 112
Putin, Vladimir, 12

Qianlong (Chinese Emperor), 32, 139, 155
Quayle, Dan, 89
Quebec, 154
Questlove, 81

racism. *See* civil rights (US); colonialism
radiation. *See* nuclear weapons
Raise the Red Lantern, 131
Rand, Ayn, 107, 149, 172, 173
Randolph, A. Philip, 66
Rankine, Claudia, 69
Reagan, Ronald, xiii, 99, 106, 108, 127
    Central America, 116, 126–28
    economic program, 5, 169–72
    on nuclear weapons, 46, 52
    Strategic Defense Initiative ("Star
    Wars"), 5, 64

INDEX

Reconstruction (US), 72–75
Red Army. *See* Soviet Union (USSR)
Red Guards. *See* China, Cultural Revolution
Red Sorghum, 131
Redeemers (US movement), 72, 73, 75
regulation, 62, 93, 103, 118, 120–22, 152, 158, 159, 161–64, 168–72
Republican Party (US)
    Nineteenth century, 73, 74, 158, 159
    Twentieth century, 37, 38, 40, 43, 44, 77, 78, 81, 85, 88, 89, 91, 92, 100, 118, 119, 126, 128, 141, 142, 169, 172
revolution. See country names
Reykjavik, Iceland, 127
Ricci, Matteo, 139, 142
Robeson, Paul, 78
Robinson, Jackie, 68
Rocky Horror Picture Show, The, 103
Rolling Stone, 94
Rolling Stones, 81, 141
Romania, 8
Rome, 135, 150, 151
Roosevelt, Franklin Delano (FDR), 53, 54, 62, 76, 113, 117, 160
Roosevelt, Theodore, 34
Rostow, Walt, 47
Rothstein, Richard, 69
Ruckelshaus, William, 87
Russell, Bertrand, 63
Russia (pre-Soviet Union), 9, 12, 21, 33, 35, 116, 139, 142, 148, 155, 156
Russia (post-Soviet Union), 5, 6, 64, 134, 137, 151
Sacramento, California, 95
Saigon. *See* Ho Chi Minh City
Sakharov, Andrei, 97
Salazar, Antonio, 79
Salvador, 116
San Francisco, California, 95, 102, 103, 145
San Martin, Ramon Grau, 113
Sandinistas (Nicaraguan movement), 126
Sandino, Augusto, 113, 126

Santo Domingo. *See* Dominican Republic
Sarotte, Mary Elise, 4
Saudi Arabia, 5, 90, 99, 127, 144, 151
Schlafly, Phyllis, 105
Schneider, Rene (Chilean General), 121
Scigliano, Robert, 41
Sculley, John, 107
Seale, Bobby, 82, 141
securities (financial) and US regulation, 157, 159–63, 170
security (governmental), 9, 21, 22, 40, 41, 45, 75, 92, 96, 113, 119, 120, 123, 152, 173
security (collateral). *See* banking
segregation, 75–78, 83, 86, 103
    Jim Crow system, 68, 72, 76, 85
self-determination (national), 25, 34, 113, 140
Selma, Alabama, 83, 84
Shah of Iran, 87, 91, 97–99, 122
Shanghai, 130, 135, 136, 139, 145
shareholders (corporate), 15, 161–63
Sheehan, Neil, 42, 43, 45
Sherman Antitrust Act, 164
Sherman, William Tecumseh, 74
Silicon Valley, California, 107
Simone, Nina, 67, 80–82
Singapore, 138, 144, 146, 151
Slaugherhouse Five, 57
slavery, 70–73, 101, 104, 111, 112, 128, 154, 161
Smith, Adam, 150, 152, 154
Smoot-Hawley Tariff Act, 10
Social Security (US program), 108, 168
socialism, 4, 11, 12, 15, 19, 22, 23, 91, 111, 116, 143, 149, 156
Solidarity. *See,* Poland.
Solzhenitsyn, Aleksandr, 97
Somoza, Anastasio, 113, 126
Sorley, Lewis, 46,
soul (music), 67, 68, 81
South Africa, xv, 79
South America, 112
    See also country names
South Dakota, 102
South Vietnam, *see* Vietnam

INDEX

Southern US states, 68, 69, 71–78, 83, 84, 111, 151, 158
  See also state names
Soviet Union (USSR), xiii–xv, 1–24 (Chapter 1)
  Afghanistan, xiii, 4, 5, 7, 99, 111
  Brezhnev doctrine, 4, 5
  China, 140, 143, 144
  Cominform, 20
  criticism of US, 76, 155
  Cuban missile crisis, *see* Cuban missile crisis
  defense spending, 5, 144
  division of Europe, 7–10, 16–20, 24, 38
  economy and economic planning, 5–7, 13, 15, 24, 36, 91, 149, 155, 162, 172
  See also communism, Marxism/Leninism
  emigres, 97
  fall of xiii, xiv, 3–6, 24, 144
  Helsinki accords, 96, 97
  nuclear treaty negotiations, 63, 64
  nuclear weapons, 2, 43, 59, 60, 77
  oil revenues, 5, 144, 172
  opening of Berlin Wall, 3, 4
  reputation in West, 96, 97
  response to Bretton Woods and Marshall Plan, 10–15, 18–20, 117
  response to Polish Solidarity movement, 4, 5
  space program (Soviet), 2, 87
  Third World involvement, 5, 98, 111
  US fear of, 120
  See also anticommunism (US)
  Vietnam, 36, 38, 39, 48, 49
  Warsaw Pact and interventions, 4, 5, 7, 24, 96, 97, 114, 117, 144
  See also leaders' names
space program (US), 1–3
Spain, 33, 34, 111, 112, 151, 153, 154
Spence, Jonathan, 134
Springfield, Illinois, 105
Sputnik. *See* space program (Soviet)
St. Louis, Missouri, 67, 68, 101

Stalin, Josef, 8–15, 18–20, 22, 24, 36, 38, 39, 53, 54, 62, 63, 96, 117, 118, 120, 133, 143, 144, 155
states' rights (US), 72, 73
Stettin (now Szczecin, Poland), 15
Stimson, Henry, 54, 56
Stone, Norman, 23
Stone, Oliver, 28, 116
strategic bombing (in Vietnam), 46–48
Suharto, 115
Sukarno, 115
Summer of Soul, 81
Sun Yat-Sen, 140
Super (nuclear fusion bomb). *See* nuclear weapons
Superfund (CERCLA), 164, 171
Symbionese Liberation Army, 95
Syria, 5
Szilard, Leo, 62

Taiwan. *See* China, Republic of
Tan Son Nhut airfield, 43
tariffs, 10
technology, 2, 15, 45, 55, 56, 62, 124, 136, 138, 149, 150, 160, 161, 173
  See also nuclear weapons, nuclear power
Tennessee, 54
Texas, 73, 85
Thailand, 35
Thatcher, Margaret, 127
thermonuclear. *See* nuclear weapons
Third World, 37, 38, 97, 111, 123, 142, 143
Thompson, Hunter S., 94
Three Mile Island, Pennsylvania, 57, 98
Tiananmen Square, 132, 133, 136
Time (US magazine), 56, 106, 140
Tito, Josip Broz, 20, 38
To Live, 131, 132, 136
Tokyo, 32, 57, 119, 150
Tonkin, 32, 57, 119, 150
Tonkin (region of Southeast Asia), 33, 35
Tonkin Gulf Resolution (US), 43, 44, 85
totalitarian, 20, 76, 148

191

INDEX

trade (international), 7, 10, 11, 19, 21, 24, 32, 38, 74, 96, 123, 139, 150–55, 161
    export, 6, 111, 113, 114, 123, 124, 127, 134, 138, 142, 144, 149–51, 168, 172
    import, 16, 32, 42, 92, 108, 150
Trans Pacific Partnership, 49
Trieste, Italy, 15, 16
Trujillo, Rafael, 121
Truman, Harry S, 15, 48, 52–55, 59, 62–66, 77, 88, 90, 98, 117, 119, 141, 147
Trump, Donald, 65, 89, 137
Twenty Feet from Stardom, 81
Tyler, John, 158

Ukraine, 65
Ulbricht, Walter, 16
Union (US civil war), 72, 73, 102
    See also state names
Union, European, *see* Europe
union, labor, *see* labor unions
United Fruit Company, 113, 114, 122
United Nations, 39, 62, 63, 77, 127, 141
United States (US).
    Congress (US), 44, 55, 72–74, 78, 85, 90, 91, 100, 102, 103, 107, 117, 121, 122, 127, 128, 140, 164, 169, 171
    Church committee (US Senate), 91, 98, 121, 122, 126
    Compromise of 1850, 73
    House of Representatives, 44, 112, 120, 121
    Missouri Compromise, 73
    Senate, 76, 85, 91, 120, 121
    Executive Branch (US)
    Central Intelligence Agency, US ("CIA"), xiii–xv, 6, 47, 91, 97, 98, 100, 110–29 (Chapter 6)
    covert actions, xiv, 6, 84, 91, 98, 109, 117–22
    Defense Department (Pentagon), 47, 60, 90, 95, 107
    Department of Health, Education and Welfare, 103
    Justice Department, 169
    State Department, 11, 77, 78, 95, 118, 141
    Treasury Department, 10, 11
    White House, 54, 59, 75, 107, 127, 128, 171
    See also presidents' names
    Supreme Court (US), 75, 77, 82, 83, 104, 105, 160, 163, 164, 171–72
    See also state names
    See also anticommunism (US); civil rights (US); Civil War (US); Confederacy (US) and prewar south; economy, US; nuclear weapons; southern US states (post civil war);Union (US); Vietnam, US war policy; Vietnam, US antiwar views
Utrecht, Treaty of, 154

van Buren, Martin, 158
Vanderbilt, Tom, 3
Vann, John Paul, 45
Vel d'Hiv, 22
Venice, 151
Versailles (treaty), 10, 63
Vietcong, 40, 45, 46, 89
Vietnam, 25–49 (Chapter 2)
    movies, 26–30
    North (Democratic Republic of), 30, 35, 38, 39, 43, 44, 46–48, 52, 85, 91
    South (Republic of, or "DRV"), 30, 37–43, 45–48, 84, 89, 90, 118, 121
    Post-1975, 5, 48–49, 138
    Pre-1945, 25, 32–37
    US war policy, 37–48, 59, 84, 89, 92, 114, 118, 120, 121, 123, 125–27, 129, 141, 142
    US antiwar views, 26, 27, 29, 44, 46, 68, 86, 88–90, 95–96, 142
    See also Diem, Ngo Dinh; economy, Vietnam; Ho Chi Minh; France, and Vietnam
Vietnam, war in, xiii–xv, 1, 3, 6, 7, 24, 26–31, 37–48, 64, 142, 143

INDEX

Virginia, 69, 71
voting rights (suffrage), 15, 73, 74, 84, 85

Wallace, George, 82
Wallace, Henry, 77
Wang, Wayne, 145
Warsaw Pact. *See* Soviet Union
Washington (state), 54, 102
Washington, D.C. (US Capital), 31, 60, 115, 117, 141
  March on, 66, 84
Washington Naval Treaty, 63
Washington Post, The, 90, 120
Watergate (US political scandal), xiii, 90, 91, 94, 95, 100, 120, 121, 168
Watts (Los Angeles), 85
Wayles, John, 70
Wealth. *See* money (wealth)
weapons. *See* chemical weapons; nuclear weapons
Weather Underground, 95
Wehrmacht. *See* Germany
Weir, Peter, 115
West, Rebecca, 163
West Berlin. *See* Berlin, West
West Germany. *See* Germany, Western
Westad, Odd Arne, 111, 128
Westmoreland, William, 45, 46
Wharton, Edith, 166
Whig (US political party), 158
White, Dan, 95
White House. *See* United States, Executive Branch
Wilkerson, Isabel, 75

Wilkinson, Charles, 102, 103
Wills, Garry, 106
Wilmot, David, 72
Wilson, Woodrow, 25, 34, 35, 75, 113, 117, 140
  Fourteen Points, 34
Wisconsin, 103
Wong Kar-Wai, 145
Wong, Jan, 133
Wong, Tyrus, 145
Woodstock (music festival), 81, 101
Woolworth, 84
World Trade Organization, 10, 24
World War I (Great War), 25, 34, 46, 56, 63, 109, 116, 140, 166, 167
World War II, xiii, 8, 18, 31, 32, 35, 37, 47, 48, 51, 57, 74, 76, 88, 91, 117, 119, 121, 137, 140, 142, 149, 155
Wounded Knee, South Dakota 102
Wozniak, Steve, 107
Wright, Richard, 76

Xi Jinping (Chinese president), 134, 144
Xi'an, China, 135, 136

Yalta, Crimea (Soviet Union) summit conference, 8, 17, 53
Year of Living Dangerously, The, 115
Yeltsin, Boris, 6
Yeoh, Michelle, 145
Yom Kippur War, 90, 168

Zhang Yimou, 131, 135, 140, 145
Zubok, Vladislav, 4, 5

www.ingramcontent.com/pod-product-compliance
Lightning Source LLC
Chambersburg PA
CBHW070742160426
43192CB00009B/1548